Learn Sprite Kit for iOS Game Development

Leland Long

Apress®

Learn Sprite Kit for iOS Game Development

ISBN-13 (pbk): 978-1-4302-6439-2

ISBN-13 (electronic): 978-1-4302-6440-8

Publisher: Heinz Weinheimer
Acquisitions Editor: Michelle Lowman
Development Editor: Gary Schwartz
Technical Reviewer: Matthew Knott
Editorial Board: Steve Anglin, Mark Beckner, Ewan Buckingham, Gary Cornell, Louise Corrigan, Jim DeWolf, Jonathan Gennick, Jonathan Hassell, Robert Hutchinson, Michelle Lowman, James Markham, Matthew Moodie, Jeff Olson, Jeffrey Pepper, Douglas Pundick, Ben Renow-Clarke, Dominic Shakeshaft, Gwenan Spearing, Matt Wade, Steve Weiss
Coordinating Editor: Mark Powers
Copy Editor: Kezia Endsley
Compositor: SPi Global
Indexer: SPi Global
Artist: SPi Global
Cover Designer: Anna Ishchenko

Distributed to the book trade worldwide by Springer Science+Business Media New York, 233 Spring Street, 6th Floor, New York, NY 10013. Phone 1-800-SPRINGER, fax (201) 348-4505, e-mail orders-ny@springer-sbm.com, or visit www.springeronline.com. Apress Media, LLC is a California LLC and the sole member (owner) is Springer Science + Business Media Finance Inc (SSBM Finance Inc). SSBM Finance Inc is a Delaware corporation.

For information on translations, please e-mail rights@apress.com, or visit www.apress.com.

Apress and friends of ED books may be purchased in bulk for academic, corporate, or promotional use. eBook versions and licenses are also available for most titles. For more information, reference our Special Bulk Sales–eBook Licensing web page at www.apress.com/bulk-sales.

Any source code or other supplementary material referenced by the author in this text is available to readers at www.apress.com/9781430264392. For detailed information about how to locate your book's source code, go to www.apress.com/source-code/.

To William "Bill" VanBelle

For guiding a young computer science student toward all-things Apple

Contents at a Glance

Contents

About the Author

Leland Long's programming career began on a VIC-20 computer. He moved up to the Apple IIe and then on to the Mac 512, where he began using Lightspeed Pascal to write fancier and more complex games. As a hobbyist, Leland has written a few programs over the years in BASIC and Pascal, but he never pursued learning the more common languages (like C) or learning object-oriented concepts. The release of the iPhone SDK changed that! Based on that event, Leland dove headfirst into learning all that he could about Objective-C and iOS programming. He is currently an IT Director for a flooring installation company in South Carolina, where he lives with his youngest daughter. His oldest daughter and four grandchildren live close enough to keep life entertaining.

About the Technical Reviewer

Matthew Knott has been writing code for as long as he can remember—from marveling at moving pixels on a BBC Micro to writing ridiculous text adventures for his mother on an overheating ZX Spectrum 48k. Matthew has been a professional software developer for the past 12 years, six of which have been spent in the educational sector where he has now entered the sometimes-scary world of management (although when they see the mess he made of the budget, that won't last long). Matthew's work and hobbies are basically the same things, but when he's not working, he loves life in a beautiful part of Wales with his wife, Lisa, and two kids, Mikey and Charlotte.

Acknowledgments

This book could not have been written without the hard-working folks at Apress. Steve Anglin got the ball rolling and Michelle Lowman handled everything in the acceptance process. Louise Corrigan helped out when others were unavailable. Mark Powers kept the book on the right track, and Gary Schwartz helped with some terrific feedback along the way. To all of the fine employees at Apress: Thank you, thank you!

A very special thanks goes out to Matthew Knott, the technical reviewer, who tested all of the code in the book and made sure that everything worked as described.

Introduction

What This Book Is

This book serves as a guide to help you make your own iPhone game. The goal is to help you create a simple 2D game from scratch using the new programming framework provided by Apple called "Sprite Kit." By using Sprite Kit to create your game, you will find that a lot of things that you would normally have to code yourself handled for you. You'll be amazed at how little code it takes to create animated characters (sprites) that can interact with each other as they move around the screen.

As you work your way through this book, you will create a fairly simple (old-school style) 2D game for the iPhone that allows users to control a character using their fingers on the touch screen. We'll add some bad guys to give the character certain challenges and some bonus items that users can collect for extra points. We won't deal with the complexity of screen scrolling (in order to keep it simple) and instead will use a stationary screen, adding ledges so that the character can have some more space in which to run around, rather than moving only along the bottom of the screen.

Each chapter is designed to highlight specific Sprite Kit features and basic game development concepts, which will help you understand how to control or interact with those features and concepts. When you're finished with the book, you will have a broad understanding of what Sprite Kit is all about, and you will have a cool game to play when you take a break from coding your soon-to-be best-selling game.

Why Buy This Book

Why not just look through the awesome sample game called "Adventure" that Apple provides for Sprite Kit developers to explore and examine? Because it can be complex and difficult for beginners to dissect and understand. It is meant for more experienced game developers to use, so that they can take their existing knowledge and use the new Sprite Kit APIs (Application Programming Interface) to make their next game quicker and easier than ever before. I believe that less experienced developers need something more straightforward as their introduction to Sprite Kit. Start simple and move on to bigger and better game development once you understand the basics.

What You Need to Know

This book assumes that you have a basic understanding of how to create applications for the iPhone using Xcode. You will not be spending any time learning programming styles or skills. You will be focusing solely on making a game using Xcode as the tool. We assume that you can download, install, and use the latest version of Xcode to create an application and run it on the iPhone Simulator.

What You Need to Have

In terms of hardware, you need an Intel-based Macintosh running Mountain Lion (OS X 10.8) or later. Regarding software, you need Xcode 5.0 or later, since that is the first version to include the Sprite Kit APIs. You can download Xcode from `http://developer.apple.com`.

What's in This Book

Here is a brief overview of the chapters in this book:

- In Chapter 1, you'll start with a template that gives you an intro screen and a main game screen that will serve as the foundation for everything else that you do with Spite Kit.

- In Chapter 2, you'll add some basic physics so that your character doesn't just float around the screen. Then you'll use some SKTextures for handling the graphical side of the animation and some SKActions for handling the timing and movement side of the animation.

- In Chapter 3, you'll work with user interaction to drive character movement.

- In Chapter 4, we introduce some ideas about how you add environmental objects with which your character can interact, like ledges to run along and boundaries so that you can handle screen wrapping.

- In Chapter 5, you'll add some bad guys and bonuses. We like bonuses!

- In Chapter 6, we'll present one way to create a sort of "cast of characters" that will handle the timing and spawning of bad guys and bonuses. You don't want everyone showing up on stage all at once!

- In Chapter 7, it's all about points, as in a score! It's all about the points, right?!

- In Chapter 8, you'll work with sprite interaction. You don't want your character just running around the screen, "floating" right through the enemies and obstacles, now do you?

- In Chapter 9, you'll add more levels. You want the game to get progressively harder as time goes on in order to keep it challenging and interesting, after all.

- In Chapter 10, we'll wrap things up and point you where you can go from here to make your game even more interesting and complex.

With all of these technical details out of the way, let's get our hands dirty with some code! Turn the page already! :)

Hello World

We Love Games

"Waka waka waka!" (Pac-Man)

My teenage years were spent playing arcade games and watching other kids play video games. Drop a quarter into the slot, and you were transported to a place that was awesome, feeling the adrenaline rush as you dodged bad guys and avoided death, fingers flying all over the controls. The best place to go was the nickel arcade, where you could pay a nominal admission fee and then each game cost a single nickel! A ten-dollar bill could last you for hours!

When the money ran out and we had to snap back into the real world, we made games. My computer had only 3KB of programmable memory, so they were very small games indeed. No wasting code-space with comments—oh no! Variable names were single letters ($x was the most common, of course). Ahhhh, those were the days!

Fast-forward 30 years and things have changed a bit. Major companies are creating games that immerse you inside a 3D world complete with story lines that put novels to shame. Mobile devices and desktop computers have more memory and graphics power than you could ever imagine back in the day. However, even with all this power and complexity dominating the gaming world, you can still find and enjoy games that are simple, easy on the eyes, and yet appealing due to the challenges they present. We call them "old school games." These games are not dead; they just reside in a different category than the newest mega-games.

Tradition

As you're probably aware, it has become somewhat of a tradition to call the first project in any programming book "Hello World." We wouldn't want to break that tradition here, lest we offend your programming finesse!

Setup

By now, you should have launched Xcode and be wondering where we will ask you to start. If you haven't yet launched Xcode, do so now.

From the Welcome to Xcode screen, you'll need to choose Create a New Xcode Project or, if you have already opened Xcode so that the Welcome screen is no longer visible, choose New Project from the File menu.

From the New Project Template sheet (see Figure 1-1), make sure that iOS - Application is selected from the list on the left, click on the Sprite Kit Game template icon, and then click the Next button. Note that your choices might be slightly different if you have different components loaded. PhoneGap, for example, is on the screen shown here, but it may not be the case on your display.

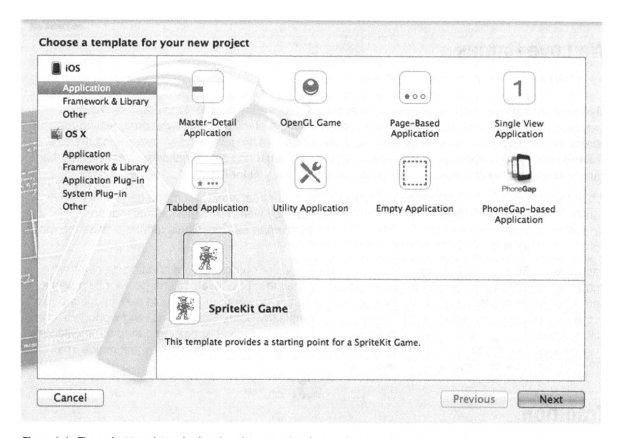

Figure 1-1. The project template selection sheet lets you select from various templates when creating a new project

Fill in the fields on the project details sheet, as shown in Figure 1-2. For Organization Name, enter your name; as the Company Identifier, enter com.*yourname*.

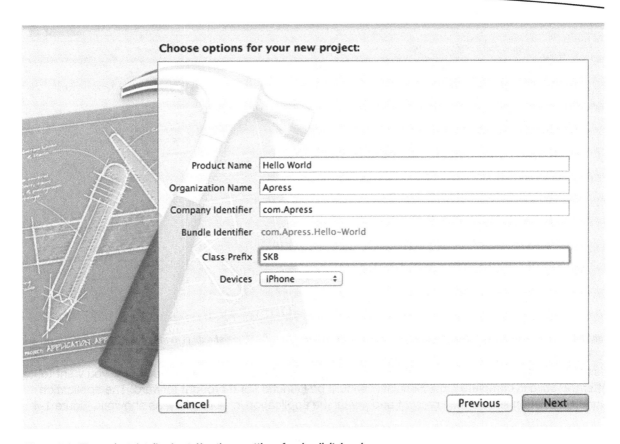

Choose options for your new project:

Product Name	Hello World
Organization Name	Apress
Company Identifier	com.Apress
Bundle Identifier	com.Apress.Hello-World
Class Prefix	SKB
Devices	iPhone ⬍

Cancel   Previous   Next

Figure 1-2. The project details sheet. Use these settings for simplicity's sake

These fields can be anything you want. We provided the data as an example, but be aware that if you choose to enter other values than what we have suggested, your code will not match the examples in the book. Also, when choosing what to enter, keep in mind that the generated bundle identifier (shown in gray) needs to be URL-compliant and unique. We choose SKB as the class prefix so that we can avoid naming conflicts with Apple (who reserves the use of all two-letter prefixes) and other developers whose code we might use. For the projects in this book, we're going to use the prefix SKB, which stands for Sprite Kit Book.

After clicking the Next button, you'll see the standard Save window, which allows you to choose where to store your new project. It's up to you whether you leave the Source Control checkbox enabled or not. If you're not familiar with what it is or how it works, feel free to uncheck it before moving on. Make your choice, and then click the Create button when you're ready.

Now that your new project has been created, saved, and opened, you will probably see some of the target settings shown in Figure 1-3.

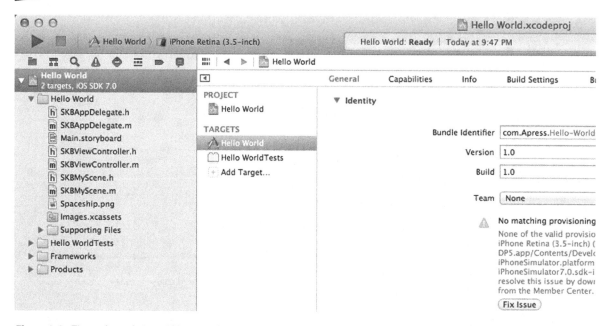

Figure 1-3. The project window. With the project selected on the left, you will see target details in the center pane

Using this template and Xcode's default settings, go ahead and run the app—you know you want to! After the build is completed, the Simulator should be launched and brought forward. The application launch animation should then present and reveal the application in all its glory, as shown in Figure 1-4.

Figure 1-4. The iOS Simulator window. Your game is running!

What you see here is not just text on a screen. It's not a standard UIView with a UILabel dropped onto it inside a storyboard, as you are probably used to already when developing iPhone apps. Instead, what we have here are four new objects that we will introduce to you.

The first object is the backdrop. It is an instance of an SKScene. Content in your game is organized into scenes, which are represented by SKScene objects. The parent of this SKScene is an SKView, which has an SKViewController as its controller.

The second object, SKLabelNode, has been dynamically created at runtime, not statically placed there using Interface Builder. A font is assigned, a size is determined, its position is declared, and the complete object is added as a child object into the scene.

The third object is an SKSpriteNode, built using an image file that's been added to the project. The point where the mouse or finger was pressed on the screen determines its position on the screen.

The fourth object is an SKAction, in this case, a rotation. The sprite object is told to run this action on itself forever. The completed sprite object is then added to the scene as a child object.

As you've probably already deduced by the naming convention, these four objects are all part of the Sprite Kit APIs. Needless to say, there are more than just these four objects to explore, but these make for a nice introduction, so let's continue.

You may be wondering about the extra information hanging out in the bottom right corner. These are there at our request, and they can be turned on and off whenever the mood strikes. They can be very useful as you begin to add more sprites to your scene, as they provide the details of the node count and the current frame rate (measured in fps, or frames per second). You can use these values to aid in determining the cause of possible sluggishness and game performance issues.

But wait, there's more!

Click anywhere on the game screen. Well, that's rather cool! A spinning spaceship should suddenly appear from out of nowhere (see Figure 1-5). Click again in a different location. Yup, another spaceship appears. If you're insatiably curious, as most programmers are by nature, by now you are clicking away all over the screen and there are spaceships spinning like crazy. Are you watching the Nodes and FPS values as they change? How many nodes are visible before the frame rate drops down to ugliness? Well, don't forget that the simulator running on your lightning-fast Mac desktop or laptop is a wee-bit faster than an actual iPhone, so don't go assuming that you can have 3,000 sprites of gigantic proportions on the screen all at once and expect to have great frame rates when your top-selling game is playing on an actual device. We're just sayin. . .

Figure 1-5. *The iOS Simulator window. Your first animated sprite appears after clicking on the game screen*

Okay, click the Stop button in Xcode to exit the game. Let's examine some of the template code. In your Project Navigator on the left side of the Xcode window, select the SKBAppDelegate.m file (see Figure 1-6).

```
//
//  SKBAppDelegate.m
//  Hello World
//
//  Created by admin on 8/20/13.
//  Copyright (c) 2013 Apress. All rights reserved.
//

#import "SKBAppDelegate.h"

@implementation SKBAppDelegate

- (BOOL)application:(UIApplication *)application didFinishLaunchingWithOptions:(NSDictionary *)launchOptions
{
    // Override point for customization after application launch.
    return YES;
}

- (void)applicationWillResignActive:(UIApplication *)application
{
    // Sent when the application is about to move from active to inactive state. This can occur for certain types of temporary
        interruptions (such as an incoming phone call or SMS message) or when the user quits the application and it begins the
        transition to the background state.
    // Use this method to pause ongoing tasks, disable timers, and throttle down OpenGL ES frame rates. Games should use this
        method to pause the game.
}

- (void)applicationDidEnterBackground:(UIApplication *)application
{
    // Use this method to release shared resources, save user data, invalidate timers, and store enough application state
        information to restore your application to its current state in case it is terminated later.
    // If your application supports background execution, this method is called instead of applicationWillTerminate: when the
        user quits.
}

- (void)applicationWillEnterForeground:(UIApplication *)application
{
    // Called as part of the transition from the background to the inactive state; here you can undo many of the changes made
        on entering the background.
}

- (void)applicationDidBecomeActive:(UIApplication *)application
{
    // Restart any tasks that were paused (or not yet started) while the application was inactive. If the application was
        previously in the background, optionally refresh the user interface.
}

- (void)applicationWillTerminate:(UIApplication *)application
{
    // Called when the application is about to terminate. Save data if appropriate. See also applicationDidEnterBackground:.
}

@end
```

Figure 1-6. The SKBAppDelegate.m file, open in the code editor

As you can see, there's not much here. There are a lot of comments that remind you of what you could put in and use here, but nothing much of interest at this point.

Select the Main.storyboard file (see Figure 1-7). Not much to see here either. One view controller and one view that we introduced earlier. This might be a good time to mention that you can use this single view controller for the entire game. You can add and switch between game scenes all you want using just this one controller.

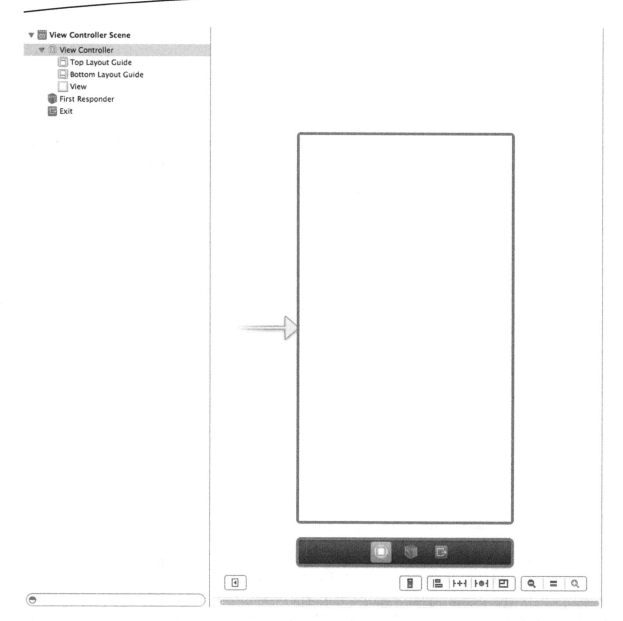

Figure 1-7. *The Main.storyboard file, open in the storyboard editor*

Next, select the SKBViewController.m file (see Figure 1-8). Now you start to get into something useful. First take a look at the viewDidLoad method. This is where the view and scene are configured, and the scene is presented in the SKView and thus is displayed on-screen.

```
//
//  SKBViewController.m
//  Hello World
//
//  Created by admin on 8/20/13.
//  Copyright (c) 2013 Apress. All rights reserved.
//

#import "SKBViewController.h"
#import "SKBMyScene.h"

@implementation SKBViewController

- (void)viewDidLoad
{
    [super viewDidLoad];

    // Configure the view.
    SKView * skView = (SKView *)self.view;
    skView.showsFPS = YES;
    skView.showsNodeCount = YES;

    // Create and configure the scene.
    SKScene * scene = [SKBMyScene sceneWithSize:skView.bounds.size];
    scene.scaleMode = SKSceneScaleModeAspectFill;

    // Present the scene.
    [skView presentScene:scene];
}

- (BOOL)shouldAutorotate
{
    return YES;
}

- (NSUInteger)supportedInterfaceOrientations
{
    if ([[UIDevice currentDevice] userInterfaceIdiom] == UIUserInterfaceIdiomPhone) {
        return UIInterfaceOrientationMaskAllButUpsideDown;
    } else {
        return UIInterfaceOrientationMaskAll;
    }
}

- (void)didReceiveMemoryWarning
{
    [super didReceiveMemoryWarning];
    // Release any cached data, images, etc that aren't in use.
}

@end
```

Figure 1-8. The SKBViewController.m file, open in the editor

Notice the following two lines inside the view configuration section:

```
skView.showsFPS = YES;
skView.showsNodeCount = YES;
```

This is where you can turn on or off the two values displayed in the bottom-right of the game screen that you saw earlier.

There is a third value (property of SKView), which is not used here but that you can add anytime you feel the urge: showsDrawCount. This value can be useful when using an SKEffectNode object, which we'll get a chance to use later in Chapter 9. Use this draw count as another piece of data when you profile your game's performance.

Other than these debugging options, you won't need to add or alter any code here in this file.

Select the SKBMyScene.m file next (see Figure 1-9).

```objc
//
//  SKBMyScene.m
//  Hello World
//
//  Created by admin on 8/20/13.
//  Copyright (c) 2013 Apress. All rights reserved.
//

#import "SKBMyScene.h"

@implementation SKBMyScene

-(id)initWithSize:(CGSize)size {
    if (self = [super initWithSize:size]) {
        /* Setup your scene here */

        self.backgroundColor = [SKColor colorWithRed:0.15 green:0.15 blue:0.3 alpha:1.0];

        SKLabelNode *myLabel = [SKLabelNode labelNodeWithFontNamed:@"Chalkduster"];

        myLabel.text = @"Hello, World!";
        myLabel.fontSize = 30;
        myLabel.position = CGPointMake(CGRectGetMidX(self.frame),
                                       CGRectGetMidY(self.frame));

        [self addChild:myLabel];
    }
    return self;
}

-(void)touchesBegan:(NSSet *)touches withEvent:(UIEvent *)event {
    /* Called when a touch begins */

    for (UITouch *touch in touches) {
        CGPoint location = [touch locationInNode:self];

        SKSpriteNode *sprite = [SKSpriteNode spriteNodeWithImageNamed:@"Spaceship"];

        sprite.position = location;

        SKAction *action = [SKAction rotateByAngle:M_PI duration:1];

        [sprite runAction:[SKAction repeatActionForever:action]];

        [self addChild:sprite];
    }
}

-(void)update:(CFTimeInterval)currentTime {
    /* Called before each frame is rendered */
}

@end
```

Figure 1-9. The SKBMyScene.m file, open in the editor

Here is the bulk of the useful code. This is where everything that you saw happened when you ran the game. The "Hello, World!" label, the debugging information, where the spaceships were spawned from, and where the spinning actions were initiated—all of this happened when the user "touched" the iPhone screen, and you clicked in the Simulator screen. That's a lot going on for two short methods, don't you think?

Let's examine it in more detail. First, take a look at the `initWithSize` method.

```
self.backgroundColor = [SKColor colorWithRed:0.15 green:0.15 blue:0.3 alpha:1.0];
```

Here, you set a background color using RGB (color) and alpha (transparency) values.

```
SKLabelNode *myLabel = [SKLabelNode labelNodeWithFontNamed:@"Chalkduster"];

myLabel.text = @"Hello, World!";
myLabel.fontSize = 30;
myLabel.position = CGPointMake(CGRectGetMidX(self.frame), CGRectGetMidY(self.frame));
```

Then you create an `SKLabelNode` object and set some important values such as its font, size, and position, as well as the text itself. For the position calculation, you might notice that some convenience methods (`CGPointMake` and `GetMidX`) are being used to determine the center of the screen using the `SKScene` frame property.

```
[self addChild:myLabel];
```

Finally, you add the `SKLabelNode` that you created as a child of the `SKScene`. This is how sprites or nodes are added to the screen: by using the `addChild` method of the `SKScene` object.

You may have noticed that all of this happened inside the scene initialization. In other words, immediately after the app launch, since this scene will be instantiated when the storyboard is loaded. This method then becomes the best place to add code to take care of whatever you want to have happen when the user starts your game. You may want to go have some sort of splash screen, or you may just get right to the point by presenting the user with several buttons from which to select: a one- or two-player game perhaps.

Finally, you have the `touchesBeganWithEvent` method. As you will infer from its name, this method will be called when the user places a finger on the screen. Not when they lift their finger off the screen (that would be the `touchesEndedWithEvent` method), as is the common method employed when using buttons, for instance. This allows the users to change their mind when making choices between buttons. But that's a different topic for a different book. When a user touches the screen in this game, you don't want to delay immediate action, so this is a better choice for method picking.

The `for` loop is used so that multiple simultaneous touches can be recognized and handled accordingly. This is a bit tricky on the simulator. However, on an actual device, try pressing two fingers down at the same time, and you'll see what you would expect: two spaceships appear where your fingers were placed.

```
CGPoint location = [touch locationInNode:self];
```

For each touch event, you first determine the position of the touch.

```
SKSpriteNode *sprite = [SKSpriteNode spriteNodeWithImageNamed:@"Spaceship"];
```

Then you create a new sprite by creating a new SKSpriteNode object. To do this, you can pass the filename of an image that you've added to the project to a convenience method of SKSpriteNode and, voila, you have a sprite. It does not appear on-screen yet, however. That comes later. Notice on the left in the Project Navigator that there is already an image file named Spaceship.png. Click on it to view it inside Xcode.

```
sprite.position = location;
```

You set the sprite's position to the location that you determined from the user's touch point. It is interesting to note that if we skipped or commented out the next two lines of code, we would have the spaceship appear on-screen and it would not be spinning.

```
SKAction *action = [SKAction rotateByAngle:M_PI duration:1];
```

Here you create a new object called SKAction. This type of object will be configured in a variety of different ways, some of which you'll discover in subsequent chapters. Once it's created and configured, it will be associated or applied to a sprite (SKSpriteNode), thereby applying that action to that sprite. That's a pretty wordy way of describing a fairly straightforward process.

In this case, you create a spinning, or rotation, action. In essence, what these parameters are saying is "rotate 180 degrees in one second." The rotateByAngle parameter expects the angle to be provided in radians not degrees, and M_PI is a C-type function provided in the math.h library that returns the value of pi, which in radians is a half circle. The duration parameter expects the value passed to it to be in seconds.

```
[sprite runAction:[SKAction repeatActionForever:action]];
```

So now that you have a configured action, this line of code attaches the action to the sprite. Not only that, but it also makes it repeat indefinitely instead of just one complete half-circle rotation (180 degrees). You could change it to that instead if you wanted to have it just rotate once and stop:

```
[sprite runAction:action];
```

Then you would add the configured sprite to the scene, which actually adds it to the screen:

```
[self addChild:sprite];
```

Summary

And that is that! Wow! Do you see that there really isn't much code needed to do all of that? Looking back several years, do you realize how much more code would have been required to perform the same thing, let alone how badly it would perform with just one spaceship that size? Not only is the iPhone amazing as far what it's capable of handling game-wise, but with the release of Sprite Kit, your job of creating the next best game becomes so much easier!

This chapter introduced you to a few Sprite Kit objects and some of the many things that you can do with them. Animation has never been easier! Ready for more? The following chapters will continue to add more exciting features. Let's get on with it.

Chapter 2

SKActions and SKTextures: Your First Animated Sprite

The "Hello World" application was a good introduction to a few Sprite Kit fundamentals such as the SKScene, SKLabelNode, SKSpriteNode, and SKAction objects, but it was seriously lacking in functionality (unless your idea of a great game is to spawn 100 spinning spaceships faster than the next developer)!

In this chapter, you're going to begin writing a game, entitled "Sewer Bros." You will start by having a splash screen presented to the user, and when the user touches the screen to start a game, you will transition to a new screen and add an animated sprite to it. Each subsequent chapter will add more features and functionality until, upon reaching the end of the book, you will have a fully functional game. You will be introduced to many Sprite Kit functions along the way and by the end, you should have enough knowledge and experience using Sprite Kit to begin writing your own best-selling 2D game to sell on the iOS App Store.

Humble Beginnings

To make things as easy as possible, you will begin with a template just as you did in the last chapter. This gives you an SKScene and the initial code that you can to use as a bare-bones foundation from which you can build the game.

So, just as before you begin, you'll need to choose Create a New Xcode Project from the Welcome to Xcode screen (if you just launched Xcode). If you have already have Xcode open so that the Welcome screen is not visible, you can choose New Project from the File menu.

From the New Project Template sheet (see Figure 1-1 from Chapter 1), make sure that iOS - Application is selected from the list on the left and click on the Sprite Kit Game template icon. Finally, click the Next button.

Fill in the fields on this sheet using the following data (see Figure 1-2 to refresh your memory):

Product Name:	Sewer Bros
Organization Name:	Your name
Company Identifier:	com.yourname
Class Prefix:	SKB
Devices:	iPhone

The next sheet is the standard Save sheet, which allows you to choose where to store your new project. Make your choice and click the Create button when you're ready.

Feel free to build and run it if you want to verify that everything is working as expected. It's always a good idea to do this often so that simple errors and problems can be addressed as soon as possible. If you wait until a lot of code has changed before building and running a program, it becomes very painful to find that illusive bug that may have been generated much earlier.

Removing Unnecessary Tidbits

Let's go back into the template-supplied code and remove some things that you won't need so that the finished product will be as slim as possible and easy to read as a future point of reference.

Begin in the SKBAppDelegate.m file.

Remove these five methods in the code (leaving just the single method called application didFinishLaunchingWithOptions):

```
- (void)applicationWillResignActive:(UIApplication *)application
{
    // ...
}

- (void)applicationDidEnterBackground:(UIApplication *)application
{
    // ...
}

- (void)applicationWillEnterForeground:(UIApplication *)application
{
    // ...
}

- (void)applicationDidBecomeActive:(UIApplication *)application
{
    // ...
}

- (void)applicationWillTerminate:(UIApplication *)application
{
    // ...
}
```

Device Orientation

You are going to support only one device orientation for the game: Landscape. There are two places where you can change this:

1. In the `SKBViewController.m` file, modify the `supportedInterfaceOrientations` method to match the following:

    ```
    - (NSUInteger)supportedInterfaceOrientations
    {
        return UIInterfaceOrientationMaskLandscape;
    }
    ```

2. Click once on the main Sewer Bros Project file in the Project Navigator window on the left. Make sure that the "Sewer Bros" target is selected, not the project. Then select the General tab across the top so that you can see and edit the Deployment Info (see Figure 2-1).

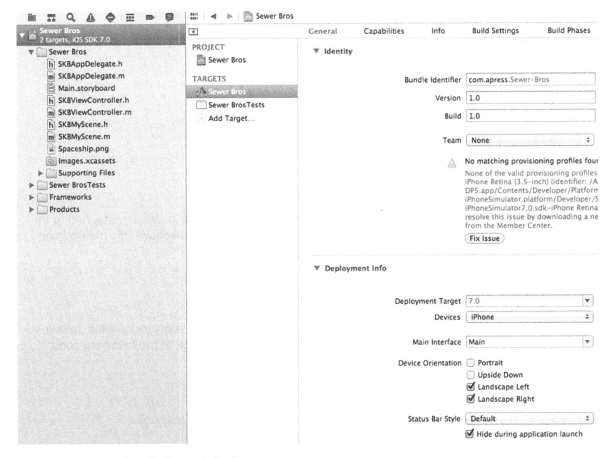

Figure 2-1. The Sewer Bros Deployment Info editor

Uncheck the Portrait checkbox listed under Device Orientation. Now if you build and run the program, you'll see that the simulator launches in landscape mode. When you try to turn the device, it will only look and function correctly in landscape mode.

Slight View Controller Changes

Because the View Controller views load in portrait by default, the size values will not be what you'd expect when your scene is added to the view. To fix this, you can set your scene along with its scaling attribute in the viewWillLayoutSubviews method instead of in the usual viewDidLoad method because by the time the view has loaded it is too late—it needs to be done before loading.

In the SKBViewController.m file, replace the viewDidLoad method with the following:

```
- (void)viewWillLayoutSubviews
{
    [super viewWillLayoutSubviews];

    // Configure the view.
    SKView * skView = (SKView *)self.view;
    if (!skView.scene) {
        skView.showsFPS = YES;
        skView.showsNodeCount = YES;

        // Create and configure the scene.
        SKScene * scene = [SKScene sceneWithSize:skView.bounds.size];
        scene.scaleMode = SKSceneScaleModeAspectFill;

        // Present the scene.
        [skView presentScene:scene];
    }
}
```

Notice that you'll also add an if() statement to check to see if the scene is already attached to the view and you'll ignore the scene creation code if it already exists. This is because this method can be called more than once.

More Unneeded Template Text

Now you'll remove the "Hello World" text from the template code. In the SKBMyScene.m file, take a look at the code inside the first initWithSize method and specifically look at the following code inside the if statement:

```
/* Set up your scene here */

self.backgroundColor = [SKColor colorWithRed:0.15 green:0.15 blue:0.3 alpha:1.0];

SKLabelNode *myLabel = [SKLabelNode labelNodeWithFontNamed:@"Chalkduster"];
```

```
myLabel.text = @"Hello, World!";
myLabel.fontSize = 30;
myLabel.position = CGPointMake(CGRectGetMidX(self.frame), CGRectGetMidY(self.frame));

[self addChild:myLabel];
```

This is where both the background color and text block is created, configured, and added to the scene. You're going to replace this with your own splash screen!

Images Available for Download

I have provided readers with a complete set of images and source code, which you can download from the Apress website. Here's a link to the book's page: http://www.apress.com/9781430264392. Look for the Source Code link in the Book Resources section on the left side of the page. Expand the archive and download the project folder to a convenient location. Inside this folder, you can browse to the folder labeled Images and look for the images whose names begin with SewerSplash. These are the files that you will now add to your game project.

From Xcode, choose Add Files to "Sewer Bros..." from the File menu. Navigate to the file SewerSplash_480.png and click once to select it. Then Shift-click on the second file called SewerSplash_568.png, so that both files are selected. Make sure that "Destination: Copy Items into Destination's Group Folder (if Needed)" is checked, then make sure that "Add to Targets: Sewer Bros" is checked. Click the Add button (see Figure 2-2).

Figure 2-2. Adding files to a project

If it's successful, you will see the files added to the Project Navigator on the left side of the window. If you wish, you can click on them one at a time to see what they look like.

Background Color

Here, you'll make the background color solid black. UIColor gives you some convenience methods to make common colors quickly by name instead of trying to determine the RGB values. For your reference, I list them here:

```
blackColor;        // 0.0 white
darkGrayColor;     // 0.333 white
lightGrayColor;    // 0.667 white
whiteColor;        // 1.0 white
grayColor;         // 0.5 white
redColor;          // 1.0, 0.0, 0.0 RGB
greenColor;        // 0.0, 1.0, 0.0 RGB
blueColor;         // 0.0, 0.0, 1.0 RGB
cyanColor;         // 0.0, 1.0, 1.0 RGB
yellowColor;       // 1.0, 1.0, 0.0 RGB
magentaColor;      // 1.0, 0.0, 1.0 RGB
orangeColor;       // 1.0, 0.5, 0.0 RGB
purpleColor;       // 0.5, 0.0, 0.5 RGB
brownColor;        // 0.6, 0.4, 0.2 RGB
clearColor;        // 0.0 white, 0.0 alpha
```

Let's modify the initWithSize method by replacing the original code with your own in the SKBMyScene.m file so that it matches the following:

```
-(id)initWithSize:(CGSize)size {
    if (self = [super initWithSize:size]) {
        /* Setup your scene here */
        self.backgroundColor = [SKColor blackColor];
    }
    return self;
}
```

Pretty straightforward—your SKScene will now have a solid black background.

The Splash Screen

You have the images inside your project that you'll use for a splash screen already, so now you add one onto the screen. You do this by adding the following code immediately after the self.backgroundColor line you just added:

```
/* Set up your scene here */
self.backgroundColor = [SKColor blackColor];
```

```
NSString *fileName = @"";
if (self.frame.size.width == 480) {
    fileName = @"SewerSplash_480";        // iPhone Retina (3.5-inch)
} else {
    fileName = @"SewerSplash_568";        // iPhone Retina (4-inch)
}
SKSpriteNode *splash = [SKSpriteNode spriteNodeWithImageNamed:fileName];
splash.name = @"splashNode";
splash.position = CGPointMake(CGRectGetMidX(self.frame), CGRectGetMidY(self.frame));

[self addChild:splash];
```

You first created an empty NSString that will hold the filename. Then you determined if the user has a 3.5-inch screen or 4-inch screen. You checked the height of the view instead of the width because, at this point in the application, the device has not yet been rotated—almost, but not yet.

Once you have determined which filename to use, you create an SKSpriteNode object using the convenience method spriteNodeWithImageNamed.

You then set the name property to give the node a string name that you can use later to reference the node as needed in other methods.

Anchor Points

By default, a sprite's frame is centered on its position and its position is the center of the graphic/frame. A sprite node's anchorPoint property can be modified to move its position to a different point on the frame. Figure 2-3 illustrates this point.

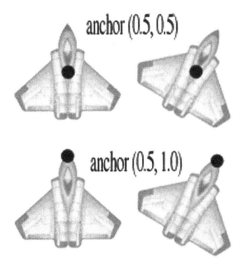

Figure 2-3. Compare two anchor point settings

In the example shown in Figure 2-3, you can see that moving the anchor point makes a big difference when the sprite is rotated, as it becomes the point of rotation. However, it can also make a difference when handling collisions and contacts, as you'll see in a later chapter. Notice that that the values used for the anchor point are in the unit coordinate system, so the bottom-left corner is (0.0, 0.0) and the upper-right corner is (1.0, 1.0), no matter the size of the sprite.

Back to the Splash Screen

When you set the position of the new sprite in the scene, you need to keep in mind that the anchor point of the sprite by default is (0.5, 0.5), meaning the center of the image. Therefore, you want the image to be centered in the scene as well. The position property expects a CGPoint, and you can use a couple of convenience methods (CGRectGetMidX and CGRectGetMidY) to determine the center of the X- and Y-axes. For those with sharp eyes, you may have noticed that you seem to have reversed the order inside the CGPointMake method. You did indeed, and this is because the device has not officially rotated into landscape mode yet, as you have already determined that you want to have happen. Thus at this point in the code, you still need to check the height of the SKView to determine both the screen size and the position of the sprite, which is drawn in landscape orientation.

Now that the sprite has been created and configured, it's time to get it into the scene and draw it, adding it as a child to the SKScene (as you did in the previous code).

Now if you build and run the program, you should see your lovely splash screen.

Moving Between Scenes

Now you'll make it so that when the users touch the screen, it doesn't spawn spinning spaceships, but instead takes them to the main game screen (the next scene).

Let's start by removing the code that you won't need anymore. Remove everything inside the for loop of the touchesBeganWithEvent method in the SKBMyScene.m file, so that it will now look like this:

```
-(void)touchesBegan:(NSSet *)touches withEvent:(UIEvent *)event {
    /* Called when a touch begins */

    for (UITouch *touch in touches) {

    }
}
```

Rename this SKScene object to better represent what it will be in your project. In the SKBMyScene.m file, near the top, double-click on SKBMyScene (found after @implementation). Then right-click on it to open a sub-menu, scroll down to Refactor and over to Rename (or select Refactor in the Edit menu and then Rename). Once the Rename sheet is displayed, you can change the name to something more descriptive, such as SKBSplashScene (see Figure 2-4). Make sure Rename Related Files is checked and click the Preview button. Review the changes if you wish and click the Save button.

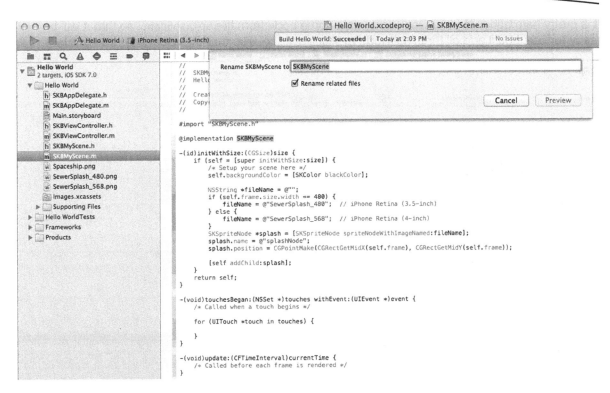

Figure 2-4. The Rename sheet

The next option is up to you. You will be given the option of having Xcode take automatic snapshots before refactoring. This would allow you, in a sense, to undo major changes like this by reverting back to a prior snapshot. Make your choice by clicking the Enable or Disable button to continue.

The object and related files have all been renamed to something more descriptive. For those with an eye for detail, you may notice that one area was not affected by the change: the comments in both file headers. Feel free to change these manually if you want to be consistent.

Creating a New Scene

Select New File from the File menu. Make sure that iOS and Cocoa Touch are selected on the left side, select Objective-C class from the list of icons, and click the Next button. Click on the drop-down arrow called Subclass of, change it to SKScene, and then give the new class the name SKBGameScene. Click the Next button, and the standard Save dialog will appear. The default location is perfect. Just verify that Targets - Sewer Bros is checked and click the Create button. Two new files—SKBGameScene.h and SKBGameScene.m—are created and shown in your Project Navigator on the left.

It is pretty bare bones isn't it? Copy and paste some code from the SplashScene, so that it will be ready for use. You'll add all three methods to SKBGameScene.m so that the end result is as follows:

```
#import "SKBGameScene.h"

@implementation SKBGameScene

-(id)initWithSize:(CGSize)size {
    if (self = [super initWithSize:size]) {
        /* Setup your scene here */
        self.backgroundColor = [SKColor blackColor];
    }
    return self;
}

-(void)touchesBegan:(NSSet *)touches withEvent:(UIEvent *)event {
    /* Called when a touch begins */
    for (UITouch *touch in touches) {

    }
}

-(void)update:(CFTimeInterval)currentTime {
    /* Called before each frame is rendered */
}

@end
```

Now you'll see how to add a fancy transition between scenes, triggered when the users touch the screen. You will use the SKAction and SKTransition classes to create some animation effects.

Animated Transitions Using SKActions

Most of the time, you get sprites to move around the scene by using actions. Most actions in Sprite Kit make changes to a node, like the SKSpriteNode you created earlier. Let's create an SKAction to describe the changes you want to apply to that node and then tell the node to run the action. When the scene is rendered, the action will be performed and it will be animated over time until the action is complete.

In the first scene implementation of SKBSplashScene.m, add one line of code right underneath the #import line at the top of the editor so that it reads like this:

```
#import "SKBSplashScene.h"
#import "SKBGameScene.h"

@implementation SKBSplashScene
```

Add the following lines of code inside the `for` loop of the `touchesBeganWithEvent` method like this:

```
for (UITouch *touch in touches) {
    SKNode *splashNode = [self childNodeWithName:@"splashNode"];
    if (splashNode != nil) {
        splashNode.name = nil;
        SKAction *zoom = [SKAction scaleTo: 4.0 duration: 1];
        [splashNode runAction: zoom completion:^{
            SKBGameScene *nextScene  = [[SKBGameScene alloc] initWithSize:self.size];
            SKTransition *doors = [SKTransition doorwayWithDuration:0.5];
            [self.view presentScene:nextScene transition:doors];
        }];
    }
}
```

Let's go over what happened here. You used a convenience method (childNodeWithName) for the SKScene object to create an SKNode named splashNode. Now you can see why you named the node when you created it in the initWithSize method; now you can create a reference object to it.

You verified that the object, which you assumed exists, in fact really does. If it doesn't, it will be a nil pointer and you can skip the touch event and continue.

If the object does exist, you set the name property to nil, because you don't want this transition to occur more than once, which could happen if the user touched the screen several times in a row.

Then you create an SKAction object, use a convenience method to create the SKAction, and set two parameters—a float value to which you want the texture (image) to be scaled up and the duration of the scaling animation in seconds. In other words, scale the texture up to 400% over a timeframe of one second.

Next you tell the node to run the action on itself. You have three method calls from which you may choose when you want a node to run an action:

- runAction—Simply execute the action.

- runAction: completion—Execute the action and call a provided block when completed.

- runAction: withKey—Execute the action and pass in a string to use as a reference to the action. This could be used later to see if a referenced action is still running.

In this case, you will use the second option, runAction: completion, and have the action execute and run a block of code when it has completed.

Looking at the code block that runs when the zoom action is finished, you see that you create an object of your own custom class SKBGameScene. Then you create an SKTransition using one of many types of transitions available (see the Xcode documentation for SKTransition for a complete listing) and set its duration to 0.5 seconds.

Finally, you tell the current scene to present the new scene you just made, using the transition you just made.

Now build and run the program. You have a splash screen, and when the screen is tapped, you have a transition to the new scene, which is solid black at this point. However, you'll notice that the zoom animation came first and then the doorway transition.

Grouping Multiple Actions

It is completely possible to group several actions to be performed at the same time. Let's add a fadeAway action to the existing zoom action to see how this is done.

Below the zoom action creation, change the following code so that it looks like this:

```
SKAction *zoom = [SKAction scaleTo: 4.0 duration: 1];
SKAction *fadeAway = [SKAction fadeOutWithDuration: 1];
SKAction *grouped = [SKAction group:@[zoom, fadeAway]];
[splashNode runAction: grouped completion:^{
```

Here you create an action that will cause the corresponding node to fade out over one second. Then you create an action that is simply an array of other actions already created. Then you tell the node to run the grouped action instead of the zoom action.

Build and run the program to see the result. You'll probably notice that, with the second scene being currently solid black, the doorway transition has become invisible. Now let's see if that changes once additional sprites are added into the game scene.

Animation Frames Using SKTextures

When you created the splash screen SKSpriteNode object, you used the convenience method spriteNodeWithImageNamed to create a static sprite that you don't plan on changing. This is fine when you want static images but not useful at all when you want sprites that have some sort of animation attached to them, like a running character with several image frames. For sprites that will use more than one frame (or image) for the purpose of animation, you need to use an SKTexture object to create the sprite.

The hero character has four frames that you will use to animate his running behavior. You will create a separate SKTexture for each of these four images, and then create an NSArray of all the textures, and finally create an SKAction that will animate the sprite using the array of textures.

First, you'll add the four images to the project. From Xcode, choose Add Files to "Sewer Bros" from the File menu. Navigate to the Player_Right1.png file and click once to select. Then Shift-click on the third file, called Player_Right4.png, so that all four files are selected. Make sure that "Destination: Copy Items Into Destination's Group Folder (if Needed)" is checked and that "Add to Targets: Sewer Bros" is checked. Click the Add button.

If it's successful, you will see the files added to the Project Navigator on the left side of the window. If you want, you can click on them one at a time to see what they look like.

Next, in the SKBGameScene.h file, you'll add a property for the player's SKSpriteNode object, right between the @interface and the @end, as shown here:

@interface SKBGameScene : SKScene

@property (strong, nonatomic) SKSpriteNode *playerSprite;

@end

Now, in the SKBGameScene.m file, add the following code to the for loop inside the touchesBeganWithEvent method, as shown here:

```
for (UITouch *touch in touches) {
        CGPoint location = [touch locationInNode:self];

        // 4 animation frames stored as textures
        SKTexture *f1 = [SKTexture textureWithImageNamed: @"Player_Right1.png"];
        SKTexture *f2 = [SKTexture textureWithImageNamed: @"Player_Right2.png"];
        SKTexture *f3 = [SKTexture textureWithImageNamed: @"Player_Right3.png"];
        SKTexture *f4 = [SKTexture textureWithImageNamed: @"Player_Right4.png"];

        // an array of these textures
        NSArray *textureArray = @[f1,f2,f3,f4];

        // our player character sprite & starting position in the scene
        _playerSprite = [SKSpriteNode spriteNodeWithTexture:f1];
        _playerSprite.position = location;

        // an Action using our array of textures with each frame lasting 0.1 seconds
        SKAction *runRightAction = [SKAction animateWithTextures:textureArray timePerFrame:0.1];

        // don't run just once but loop indefinetely
        SKAction *runForever = [SKAction repeatActionForever:runRightAction];

        // attach the completed action to our sprite
        [_playerSprite runAction:runForever];

        // add the sprite to the scene
        [self addChild:_playerSprite];
    }
```

Now if you build and run the program, tap once to dismiss the splash screen, and tap on the black scene to spawn a running character (see Figure 2-5). Multiple taps at this stage will spawn multiple player characters. You'll learn how to fix this problem later.

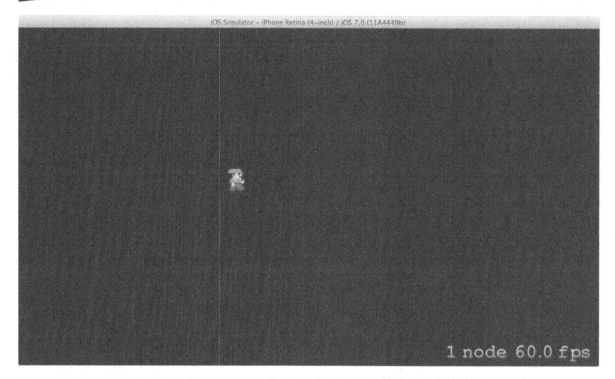

Figure 2-5. A spawned, animating sprite

Now let's elaborate on what you did.

```
CGPoint location = [touch locationInNode:self];
```

This captures the users' touch point so that you can use it later as the location where the character may spawn.

```
SKTexture *f1 = [SKTexture textureWithImageNamed: @"Player_Right1.png"];
SKTexture *f2 = [SKTexture textureWithImageNamed: @"Player_Right2.png"];
SKTexture *f3 = [SKTexture textureWithImageNamed: @"Player_Right3.png"];
SKTexture *f4 = [SKTexture textureWithImageNamed: @"Player_Right4.png"];
```

This creates four SKTexture objects—one for each animation frame. These are created from images stored inside the project, and therefore they have to be spelled exactly to avoid errors.

```
NSArray *textureArray = @[f1,f2,f3,f4];
```

You create an NSArray of the textures.

> **Note**   It's important to note that the order in which you list the textures objects in the array determines the resulting frame sequence. Also, you can use objects more than once. For example, you could have done this instead:
>
> ```
> NSArray *textureArray = @[f2,f1,f2,f3,f1,f4];
> ```
>
> In doing so, the four image frames would be displayed, in this given order, for a total of six frames drawn to the screen for each loop of the animation.

```
_playerSprite = [SKSpriteNode spriteNodeWithTexture:f1];
_playerSprite.position = location;
```

Then you create your SKSpriteNode (using the instance variable that you created with the @property statement in the interface file), applying just one of the textures. It doesn't really matter which one you use, but it kind of makes sense to use the first animation frame.

```
SKAction *runRightAction = [SKAction animateWithTextures:textureArray timePerFrame:0.1];
SKAction *runForever = [SKAction repeatActionForever:runRightAction];
```

This is where you create an SKAction using the complete set of textures inside the array and set each frame to be drawn every 0.1 seconds. Then you create another SKAction that is set to repeat the single action indefinitely.

```
[_playerSprite runAction:runForever];
[self addChild:_playerSprite];
```

This adds the repeating-forever action to the sprite and finally adds the sprite to the scene.

Summary

This chapter is designed to help you to understand a little more about the role that SKSpriteNodes, SKTextures, and SKActions have in creating visual components in your game. It's not much of a game if you don't have something visual to look at and with which to interact, right? Sprites and their associated actions are major foundational elements to every game. You will continue to use these objects as you add more game components to the game in the following chapters.

In this chapter, you also added a second SKScene and were introduced to SKTransitions, which can add some nice visual effects when switching between scenes.

In the next chapter, I will add sprite movements to go along with the running animation. You can't have your character just running in place and not going anywhere! You'll implement user touch events to determine where your character will go and add the ability to jump as well. Along the way, I will introduce you to the physics engine included with Sprite Kit, which adds major functionality to your game design. The physics engine provides the added bonus of relieving you from having to write all of the code to handle physics-based constraints and reactions in your game environment.

Chapter 3

Sprite Movement Responding to User Inputs

Run Away!

So far, once the game screen is presented (initially with a solid black background), an animated sprite appears on the screen when the user taps the screen. That's all well and good, but you've only just begun. Now you'll add some movement!

First, you'll see how to add code to detect where the user has tapped and split the screen into two zones of interest: a left zone and a right zone. When the user taps inside the left zone, you'll make the sprite move to the left, and as you would expect. When the user taps inside the right zone, you'll make the sprite move to the right. You'll determine the left and right zones in the code by taking the game screen area and dividing it by two. If the user's touch position is smaller than the resulting number, it will be a left-zone touch, and if it's greater than this number, it will be a right-zone touch.

In the SKBGameScene.m file, modify the method touchesBeganWithEvent by adding an if() statement right before the first SKTexture assignment, as shown here:

```
if (!_playerSprite) {
        // 4 animation frames stored as textures
        SKTexture *f1 = [SKTexture textureWithImageNamed: @"Player_Right1.png"];
```

Then add the following highlighted code to the end of the existing code in this same method:

```
        // add the sprite to the scene
        [self addChild:_playerSprite];
    } else if (location.x <= ( self.frame.size.width / 2 )) {
        NSLog(@"Left tap");
    } else {
        NSLog(@"Right tap");
    }
```

Now if you build and run the program, it will act as it did before, at least until you have one animated sprite on the screen. After that, each time the user taps the screen (or you click on the simulator game screen), you should be able to see a new line in the Xcode Console (see Figure 3-1). If you do not see the Console output, go back to Xcode and select View ➤ Debug Area ➤ Activate Console. Move your windows around so that you can see the Console and the Simulator screens at the same time.

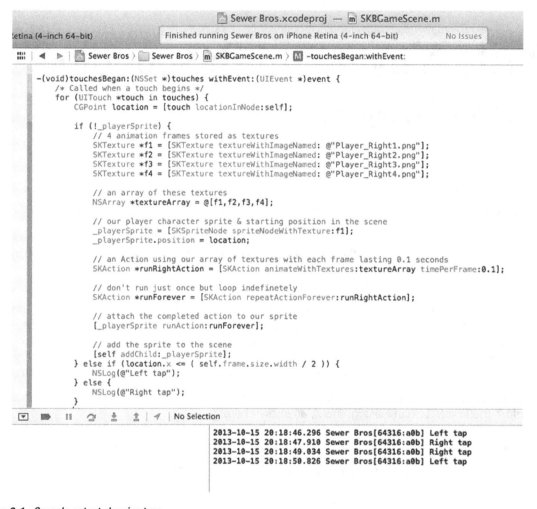

Figure 3-1. Console output showing taps

So what happened here?

First of all, you made sure that you add a sprite to the scene only if it does not already exist. This way, you end up with only one animated sprite on the screen instead of multiple sprites being spawned upon each tap.

Next, you checked the X-position of the user's tapped location and compared it to the scene's total width, cut in half. If it was less than that number, it means the user tapped the left side of the screen. If not, you assume a right-side tap.

That was fairly simple. Now you'll do something with the taps.

Modify the method touchesBeganWithEvent by adding the following six lines of code to your existing if() and else statements:

```
} else if (location.x <= ( self.frame.size.width / 2 )) {
    NSLog(@"Left tap");
    SKAction *moveLeft = [SKAction moveByX:-100 y:0 duration:1];
    SKAction *moveForever = [SKAction repeatActionForever:moveLeft];
    [self runAction:moveForever];
} else {
    NSLog(@"Right tap");
    SKAction *moveRight = [SKAction moveByX:100 y:0 duration:1];
    SKAction *moveForever = [SKAction repeatActionForever:moveRight];
    [self runAction:moveForever];
}
```

Now if you build and run it, you will see that the left and/or right taps cause the sprite to move across the screen on the horizontal or X-axis. You'll also quickly discover that once the sprite runs off the edges of the screen, it is gone for good and it will not reappear.

This behavior is expected and actually helps you by cleaning up, or getting rid of, sprites that are no longer being drawn on the screen. These sprites take up valuable space in memory, and just think of the waste if you had, say, twelve sprites on the screen, but hundreds that had left the screen! Sprite Kit does the work for you by purging sprites that are no longer being drawn on the screen, thereby keeping your precious memory cleaned up and efficient.

You probably noticed that your sprite is good at moon walking; no matter if it is moving left or right, it is always facing right. To rectify this issue, you need to add some more textures. However, before you do that, you'll see how to reorganize the code to keep it from getting out of hand.

Code Reorganization

Let's begin the reorganization by moving the texture images into their own folder. You will do this purely for organizational purposes. As you add more images to the project, it will make your life easier if you add them to a designated folder so that they are separated from the code. This keeps the project folder clean and streamlined.

Click once on the Sewer Bros folder, the second item from the top of the Project Navigator pane. Right-click on the folder and choose New Group or select New ➤ Group from the File menu (see Figure 3-2). This creates a new folder inside your project folder. It's now ready for you to provide a name for it, so call it Sprites.

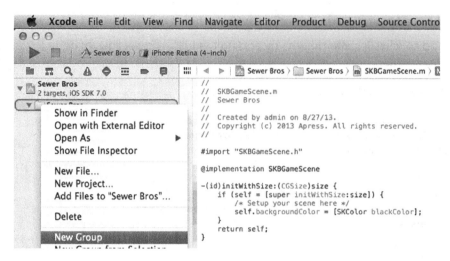

Figure 3-2. Selecting a new group

Now move both SewerSplash images and the four Player_Right images into this new folder. You can delete the Spaceship image by clicking once on it and pressing the Delete key.

If desired, you can move the Sprites folder down below the SKBObject files.

Now add another folder inside the Sprites folder to hold just the player files. You do this by following the same steps when you created the Sprites folder. Use the folder name Player for this new folder (see Figure 3-3).

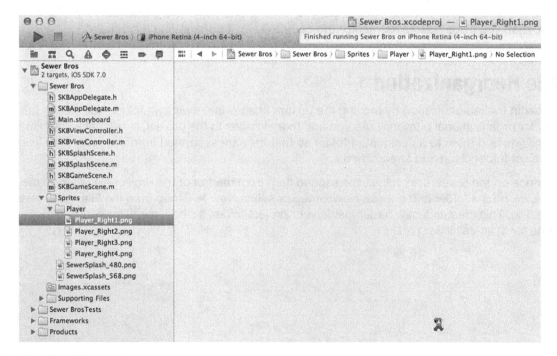

Figure 3-3. New folder structure

New Class for the Player

Next you'll create a separate class for the player and the associated code. This will make things easier when you spawn new players after they are "killed."

Select New and then File from the File menu to create a new file. Make sure that iOS and Cocoa Touch are selected on the left side, select Objective-C class from the list of icons, and click the Next button. Click on the drop-down arrow of Subclass of and change it to SKSpriteNode. (Rather than scrolling through this long list of classes, you can type SK into this drop-down menu. It will then quickly jump to the grouping of Sprite Kit classes, and then either continue typing the sprite or selecting it from the drop-down list.) Then give the new class the name SKBPlayer (see Figure 3-4). Click the Next button and the standard Save dialog will appear. The default location is perfect; just verify that Targets - Sewer Bros is checked and click the Create button. Two new files are created and shown in the Project Navigator on the left.

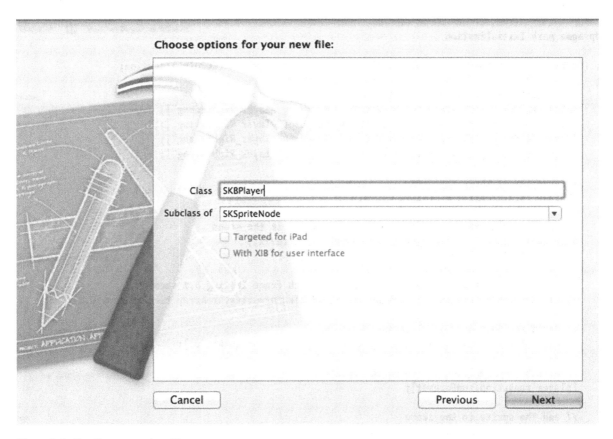

Figure 3-4. Creating a new class file

Add three new lines of code to the SKBPlayer.h file, as follows:

```
#import <SpriteKit/SpriteKit.h>

@interface SKBPlayer : SKSpriteNode

+ (SKBPlayer *)initNewPlayer:(SKScene *)whichScene startingPoint:(CGPoint)location;

- (void)runRight;
- (void)runLeft;

@end
```

Modify the SKBPlayer.m file to match the following:

```
@implementation SKBPlayer

#pragma mark Initialization

+ (SKBPlayer *)initNewPlayer:(SKScene *)whichScene startingPoint:(CGPoint)location;
{
    // 4 animation frames stored as textures
    SKTexture *f1 = [SKTexture textureWithImageNamed: @"Player_Right1.png"];
    SKTexture *f2 = [SKTexture textureWithImageNamed: @"Player_Right2.png"];
    SKTexture *f3 = [SKTexture textureWithImageNamed: @"Player_Right3.png"];
    SKTexture *f4 = [SKTexture textureWithImageNamed: @"Player_Right4.png"];

    // an array of these textures
    NSArray *textureArray = @[f1,f2,f3,f4];

    // our player character sprite & starting position in the scene
    SKBPlayer *player = [SKBPlayer spriteNodeWithTexture:f1];
    player.position = location;

    // an Action using our array of textures with each frame lasting 0.1 seconds
    SKAction *runRightAction = [SKAction animateWithTextures:textureArray timePerFrame:0.1];

    // don't run just once but loop indefinetely
    SKAction *runForever = [SKAction repeatActionForever:runRightAction];

    // attach the completed action to our sprite
    [player runAction:runForever];

    // add the sprite to the scene
    [whichScene addChild:player];
    return player;
}
```

```
#pragma mark Movement

- (void)runRight
{
    NSLog(@"run Right");
    SKAction *moveRight = [SKAction moveByX:100 y:0 duration:1];
    SKAction *moveForever = [SKAction repeatActionForever:moveRight];
    [self runAction:moveForever];
}

- (void)runLeft
{
    NSLog(@"run Left");
    SKAction *moveLeft = [SKAction moveByX:-100 y:0 duration:1];
    SKAction *moveForever = [SKAction repeatActionForever:moveLeft];
    [self runAction:moveForever];
}

@end
```

You'll notice that all you've done is moved the existing code from the touchesBeganWithEvent method into the new Player class. The lines of code beginning with #pragma mark are solely for organizational purposes and have no effect on the game code. To see what they accomplish, try clicking on the drop-down menu just to the right of the class file shown at the top of the editor, and you'll see that the pragma marks (Initialization and Movement) are highlighted there (see Figure 3-5).

Figure 3-5. *Pragma marks displayed in the class method list*

Now you can modify the SKBGameScene.h file to use the new code instead:

```
#import <SpriteKit/SpriteKit.h>
#import "SKBPlayer.h"

@interface SKBGameScene : SKScene
```

```
@property (strong, nonatomic) SKBPlayer *playerSprite;

@end
```

Modify the SKBGameScene.m file to match the following:

```
-(void)touchesBegan:(NSSet *)touches withEvent:(UIEvent *)event {
    /* Called when a touch begins */
    for (UITouch *touch in touches) {
        CGPoint location = [touch locationInNode:self];

        if (!_playerSprite) {
            _playerSprite = [SKBPlayer initNewPlayer:self startingPoint:location];
        } else if (location.x <= ( self.frame.size.width / 2 )) {
            [_playerSprite runLeft];
        } else {
            [_playerSprite runRight];
        }
    }
}
```

Now if you build and run the program, you will see that everything still works the same, but in a much more organized fashion. You moved the images into folders, and your methods dealing with sprite movement have been placed in a separate class that deals exclusively with the player's sprite.

Replacing Static Values

Now, you'll get rid of static values in the code. It's easy to add static values in code as you develop your game, but this makes it very difficult to change small details later when the number of lines of code increases dramatically. Instead of searching pages and pages of code—because you need to change how far the sprite moves in each draw cycle for example—it would be much easier if you had values like these at the top of your class code.

To do this, add a line to the top of the SKBPlayer.h file as follows:

```
#import <SpriteKit/SpriteKit.h>

#define kPlayerRunningIncrement      100

@interface SKBPlayer : SKSpriteNode
```

Then change the two static values that you used for "running" speed in the SKBPlayer.m file, like so:

```
- (void)runRight
{
    NSLog(@"run Right");
    SKAction *moveRight = [SKAction moveByX:kPlayerRunningIncrement y:0 duration:1];
    SKAction *moveForever = [SKAction repeatActionForever:moveRight];
    [self runAction:moveForever];
}
```

```
- (void)runLeft
{
    NSLog(@"run Left");
    SKAction *moveLeft = [SKAction moveByX:-kPlayerRunningIncrement y:0 duration:1];
    SKAction *moveForever = [SKAction repeatActionForever:moveLeft];
    [self runAction:moveForever];
}
```

When you want to change the speed of the player, you have only one place in the code to change it. That's much better!

New Class for Your Textures

You have cleaned up the code tremendously, but there is one more change to make before you add textures: create a new class to handle all of the player textures. After all, you are going to be adding a lot more textures before you're through, so this will make a centralized place to handle all the particulars.

Just as you did for the player class, you'll create a new file and class for the textures. Select New File from the File menu. Make sure that iOS and Cocoa Touch are selected on the left side, select Objective-C Class from the list of icons, and click the Next button. Click on the drop-down arrow of Subclass of, and change it to NSObject. Then give the new class the name SKBSpriteTextures. Click the Next button and the standard Save dialog will appear. The default location is perfect; just verify that Targets - Sewer Bros is checked and click the Create button. Two new files are created and shown in the Project Navigator on the left.

Now you can modify the SKBSpriteTextures.h file to match the following:

```
#import <Foundation/Foundation.h>
#import <SpriteKit/SpriteKit.h>

#define kPlayerRunRight1FileName            @"Player_Right1.png"
#define kPlayerRunRight2FileName            @"Player_Right2.png"
#define kPlayerRunRight3FileName            @"Player_Right3.png"
#define kPlayerRunRight4FileName            @"Player_Right4.png"

@interface SKBSpriteTextures : NSObject

@property (nonatomic, strong) NSArray *playerRunRightTextures;

- (void)createAnimationTextures;

@end
```

Now modify the SKBSpriteTextures.m file to match the following:

```
@implementation SKBSpriteTextures

- (void)createAnimationTextures
{
    // animation arrays
```

```
//    right, running
SKTexture *f1 = [SKTexture textureWithImageNamed:kPlayerRunRight1FileName];
SKTexture *f2 = [SKTexture textureWithImageNamed:kPlayerRunRight2FileName];
SKTexture *f3 = [SKTexture textureWithImageNamed:kPlayerRunRight3FileName];
SKTexture *f4 = [SKTexture textureWithImageNamed:kPlayerRunRight4FileName];
_playerRunRightTextures = @[f1,f2,f3,f4];
}
```

```
@end
```

Notice that you replaced the static filenames with defined variables here, just like you did with the player run speed earlier. This makes things easier if you change graphics later, and it helps you to remain consistent and organized.

Now modify the SKBPlayer.h file to add an instance variable to hold the array of textures using the new texture class:

```
#import <SpriteKit/SpriteKit.h>
#import "SKBSpriteTextures.h"

#define kPlayerRunningIncrement       100

@interface SKBPlayer : SKSpriteNode

@property (nonatomic, strong) SKBSpriteTextures *spriteTextures;

+ (SKBPlayer *)initNewPlayer:(SKScene *)whichScene startingPoint:(CGPoint)location;
```

Now modify the SKBPlayer.m file to use the new texture class:

```
+ (SKBPlayer *)initNewPlayer:(SKScene *)whichScene startingPoint:(CGPoint)location;
{
    // initialize and create our sprite textures
    SKBSpriteTextures *playerTextures = [[SKBSpriteTextures alloc] init];
    [playerTextures createAnimationTextures];

    // initial frame
    SKTexture *f1 = [SKTexture textureWithImageNamed: kPlayerRunRight1FileName];

    // our player character sprite & starting position in the scene
    SKBPlayer *player = [SKBPlayer spriteNodeWithTexture:f1];
    player.position = location;
    player.spriteTextures = playerTextures;

    // add the sprite to the scene
    [whichScene addChild:player];
    return player;
}
```

```
- (void)runRight
{
    NSLog(@"run Right");

    SKAction *walkAnimation = [SKAction animateWithTextures:_spriteTextures.playerRunRightTextures
timePerFrame:0.05];
    SKAction *walkForever = [SKAction repeatActionForever:walkAnimation];
    [self runAction:walkForever];

    SKAction *moveRight = [SKAction moveByX:kPlayerRunningIncrement y:0 duration:1];
    SKAction *moveForever = [SKAction repeatActionForever:moveRight];
    [self runAction:moveForever];
}

- (void)runLeft
{
    NSLog(@"run Left");

    SKAction *walkAnimation = [SKAction animateWithTextures:_spriteTextures.playerRunRightTextures
timePerFrame:0.05];
    SKAction *walkForever = [SKAction repeatActionForever:walkAnimation];
    [self runAction:walkForever];

    SKAction *moveLeft = [SKAction moveByX:-kPlayerRunningIncrement y:0 duration:1];
    SKAction *moveForever = [SKAction repeatActionForever:moveLeft];
    [self runAction:moveForever];
}
```

One slight change that results from these modifications is that when the sprite is first spawned onto the screen, it is now motionless. Once a tap takes place and movement begins, the four animation frames begin and run indefinitely.

Reorganization has been accomplished, so now you can add more textures so that the sprite can run in both directions.

Adding Textures

First, let's add the four left-facing player images and the two standing-still images to the project. To add them automatically into the folder already created for all of the texture files, select the folder you want by clicking once on the Player folder that's inside the Sprites folder. Choose Add Files to "Sewer Bros" from the File menu. Navigate to the file called Player_Left1.png and click once to select. Then Shift-click on the last desired file, Player_Left4.png, so that all four files are selected (see Figure 3-6).

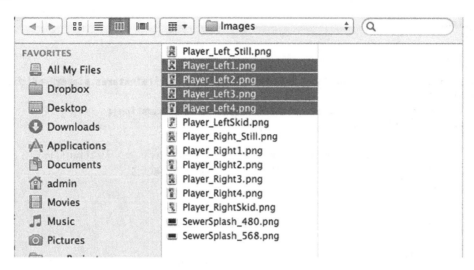

Figure 3-6. Selecting more than one file when adding images

Make sure that Destination: Copy Items into Destination's Group Folder (if Needed) is checked, make sure that Add to Targets: Sewer Bros is checked and click the Add button. Do the same thing for the other two images called Player_Right_Still and Player_Left_Still.

Then you add the filename constants, right below kPlayerRunRight4FileName in the SKBSpriteTextures.h file:

```
#define kPlayerRunRight4FileName         @"Player_Right4.png"
#define kPlayerStillRightFileName        @"Player_Right_Still.png"

#define kPlayerRunLeft1FileName          @"Player_Left1.png"
#define kPlayerRunLeft2FileName          @"Player_Left2.png"
#define kPlayerRunLeft3FileName          @"Player_Left3.png"
#define kPlayerRunLeft4FileName          @"Player_Left4.png"
#define kPlayerStillLeftFileName         @"Player_Left_Still.png"
```

Now add an instance variable for the left-facing textures and standing-still textures:

```
@property (nonatomic, strong) NSArray *playerRunRightTextures, *playerStillFacingRightTextures;
@property (nonatomic, strong) NSArray *playerRunLeftTextures, *playerStillFacingLeftTextures;
```

Now switch to the SKBSpriteTextures.m file and add the new array-generating code below the existing playerRunRightTextures array:

```
_playerRunRightTextures = @[f1,f2,f3,f4];

//   right, still
f1 = [SKTexture textureWithImageNamed:kPlayerStillRightFileName];
_playerStillFacingRightTextures = @[f1];
```

```
//   left, running
f1 = [SKTexture textureWithImageNamed:kPlayerRunLeft1FileName];
f2 = [SKTexture textureWithImageNamed:kPlayerRunLeft2FileName];
f3 = [SKTexture textureWithImageNamed:kPlayerRunLeft3FileName];
f4 = [SKTexture textureWithImageNamed:kPlayerRunLeft4FileName];
_playerRunLeftTextures = @[f1,f2,f3,f4];

//   left, still
f1 = [SKTexture textureWithImageNamed:kPlayerStillLeftFileName];
_playerStillFacingLeftTextures = @[f1];
```

Now all you need to do is to make one small change to the existing player runLeft method in the SKBPlayer.m file:

```
SKAction *walkAnimation = [SKAction animateWithTextures:self.spriteTextures.playerRunLeftTextures
timePerFrame:0.05];
```

When you build and run it, the player sprite will now change the way it faces when it's moving left and right. To do this, you have two arrays being stored in a texture class that holds the animation frames. When you want the sprite to run left, you'll create a repeating action using the array of left-facing textures. When you want it to run right, you'll create a repeating action using the array of right-facing textures.

Changing Direction

The sprite's current behavior doesn't look right when it changes directions. If it is running to the right and you click on the left side of the screen, the sprite stops moving, which is good, but the running animation continues and it runs in place. That's not quite what you want. You want the sprite to stop all animation when standing still.

To do this, you need to keep track of what the sprite is currently doing. You'll create an instance variable and an enumerated list to do this.

Add these to the SKBPlayer.h file as follows:

```
#define kPlayerRunningIncrement       100

typedef enum : int {
    SBPlayerFacingLeft = 0,
    SBPlayerFacingRight,
    SBPlayerRunningLeft,
    SBPlayerRunningRight
} SBPlayerStatus;

@interface SKBPlayer : SKSpriteNode

@property (nonatomic, strong) SKBSpriteTextures *spriteTextures;
@property SBPlayerStatus playerStatus;

+ (SKBPlayer *)initNewPlayer:(SKScene *)whichScene startingPoint:(CGPoint)location;
```

Now capture the two running statuses inside the runLeft and runRight methods inside SKBPlayer.m:

```
NSLog(@"run Right");
_playerStatus = SBPlayerRunningRight;

SKAction *walkAnimation = [SKAction animateWithTextures:_spriteTextures.playerRunRightTextures
timePerFrame:0.05];




.
.
.


NSLog(@"run Left");
_playerStatus = SBPlayerRunningLeft;

SKAction *walkAnimation = [SKAction animateWithTextures:_spriteTextures.playerRunLeftTextures
timePerFrame:0.05];
```

Finally, the biggest change will be in touchesBeganWithEvent, inside the SKBGameScene.m file:

```
if (!_playerSprite) {
    playerSprite = [SKBPlayer initNewPlayer:self startingPoint:location];
} else if (location.x <= ( self.frame.size.width / 2 )) {
    // user touched left side of screen
    if (_playerSprite.playerStatus == SBPlayerRunningRight) {
        _playerSprite.playerStatus = SBPlayerFacingRight;

        // stop running by switching to a single frame
        [_playerSprite removeAllActions];
        SKAction *standingFrame = [SKAction animateWithTextures:
                _playerSprite.spriteTextures.playerStillFacingRightTextures timePerFrame:0.05];
        SKAction *standForever = [SKAction repeatActionForever:standingFrame];
        [_playerSprite runAction:standForever];
    } else {
        [_playerSprite runLeft];
    }
} else {
    // user touched right side of screen
    if (_playerSprite.playerStatus == SBPlayerRunningLeft) {
        _playerSprite.playerStatus = SBPlayerFacingLeft;

        // stop running by switching to a single frame
        [_playerSprite removeAllActions];
        SKAction *standingFrame = [SKAction animateWithTextures:
                _playerSprite.spriteTextures.playerStillFacingLeftTextures timePerFrame:0.05];
        SKAction *standForever = [SKAction repeatActionForever:standingFrame];
        [_playerSprite runAction:standForever];
    } else {
        [_playerSprite runRight];
    }
}
```

What you did here is best described with an example. Say that the sprite is running to the right and the user presses the left side of the screen. The sprite's status will be SBPlayerRunningRight, so you change its status to SBPlayerFacingRight. You use a SpriteNode method called removeAllActions to remove all previous actions (the animation and the movement along the X-axis), which makes the sprite come to a halt; that is, it freezes in place. Then you create a new action using a single frame of animation and apply the action to the sprite. You do this so that you can control which animation frame is used when the sprite is standing still. If you just used the removeAllActions method to cause the sprite to stop and stand still, it would be drawn in whatever was the last frame when it was running. Instead, you'll force the frame you want it to use for standing still.

If you build and run the program now, you'll see that the running animation and direction changes look much better. There is, however, another minor change that you should make. Touching the left side of the screen while the sprite is already running to the left causes its speed to double, and the same goes for the right side of the screen while running right. You don't want the sprite to have super powers, so let's take that special ability away from it.

Add two if() statements to final else clauses in both the left- and right-screen touch sections, so that the complete if() statement looks like this:

```
if (!_playerSprite) {
    _playerSprite = [SKBPlayer initNewPlayer:self startingPoint:location];
} else if (location.x <= ( self.frame.size.width / 2 )) {
    // user touched left side of screen
    if (_playerSprite.playerStatus == SBPlayerRunningRight) {
        _playerSprite.playerStatus = SBPlayerFacingRight;

        // stop running by switching to a single frame
        [_playerSprite removeAllActions];
        SKAction *standingFrame = [SKAction animateWithTextures:
                _playerSprite.spriteTextures.playerStillFacingRightTextures timePerFrame:0.05];
        SKAction *standForever = [SKAction repeatActionForever:standingFrame];
        [_playerSprite runAction:standForever];
    } else if (_playerSprite.playerStatus != SBPlayerRunningLeft) {
            [_playerSprite runLeft];
    }
} else {
    // user touched right side of screen
    if (_playerSprite.playerStatus == SBPlayerRunningLeft) {
        _playerSprite.playerStatus = SBPlayerFacingLeft;

        // stop running by switching to a single frame
        [_playerSprite removeAllActions];
        SKAction *standingFrame = [SKAction animateWithTextures:
                _playerSprite.spriteTextures.playerStillFacingLeftTextures timePerFrame:0.05];
        SKAction *standForever = [SKAction repeatActionForever:standingFrame];
        [_playerSprite runAction:standForever];
    } else if (_playerSprite.playerStatus != SBPlayerRunningRight) {
            [_playerSprite runRight];
        }
    }
```

Now when the player is running right and the user presses right, nothing happens.

Skidding to a Stop

Instead of stopping on a dime, you'll have the player skid a short distance before coming to a complete rest. This will bring about a little challenge when you introduce some bad guys to the game.

You need to add two additional images and instance variables to the Texture class. As you've done before, choose Add Files to "Sewer Bros" from the File menu and select Player_RightSkid.png. Do the same thing for the second image named Player_LeftSkid.png.

Add the highlighted code to the SKBSpriteTextures.h file:

```
#define kPlayerRunRight4FileName            @"Player_Right4.png"
#define kPlayerSkidRightFileName            @"Player_RightSkid.png"
#define kPlayerStillRightFileName           @"Player_Right_Still.png"
.
.
.
#define kPlayerRunLeft4FileName             @"Player_Left4.png"
#define kPlayerSkidLeftFileName             @"Player_LeftSkid.png"
#define kPlayerStillLeftFileName            @"Player_Left_Still.png"
.
.
.
@property (nonatomic, strong) NSArray *playerRunRightTextures, *playerSkiddingRightTextures,
                                                   *playerStillFacingRightTextures;
@property (nonatomic, strong) NSArray *playerRunLeftTextures, *playerSkiddingLeftTextures,
                                                   *playerStillFacingLeftTextures;
```

Then add the highlighted code to the SKBSpriteTextures.m file:

```
_playerRunRightTextures = @[f1,f2,f3,f4];

//   right, skidding
f1 = [SKTexture textureWithImageNamed:kPlayerSkidRightFileName];
_playerSkiddingRightTextures = @[f1];

//   right, still
.
.
.
_playerRunLeftTextures = @[f1,f2,f3,f4];

//   left, skidding
f1 = [SKTexture textureWithImageNamed:kPlayerSkidLeftFileName];
_playerSkiddingLeftTextures = @[f1];

//   left, still
```

Next you will add two more values for keeping track of the sprite's current status. In the SKBPlayer.h file, modify the enum definition as follows:

```
typedef enum : int {
    SBPlayerFacingLeft = 0,
    SBPlayerFacingRight,
    SBPlayerRunningLeft,
    SBPlayerRunningRight,
    SBPlayerSkiddingLeft,
    SBPlayerSkiddingRight
} SBPlayerStatus;
```

You'll also add a static value to hold the distance of each skid:

```
#define kPlayerRunningIncrement      100
#define kPlayerSkiddingIncrement      20
```

One more change in this file involves adding two new public methods:

```
- (void)runRight;
- (void)runLeft;
- (void)skidRight;
- (void)skidLeft;
```

Now you move over to the SKBPlayer.m file to add the new method implementations. Insert them after the existing runLeft method:

```
- (void)skidRight
{
    NSLog(@"skid Right");
    [self removeAllActions];
    _playerStatus = SBPlayerSkiddingRight;

    NSArray *playerSkidTextures = _spriteTextures.playerSkiddingRightTextures;
    NSArray *playerStillTextures = _spriteTextures.playerStillFacingRightTextures;

    SKAction *skidAnimation = [SKAction animateWithTextures:playerSkidTextures timePerFrame:1];
    SKAction *skidAwhile = [SKAction repeatAction:skidAnimation count:0.2];

    SKAction *moveLeft = [SKAction moveByX:kPlayerSkiddingIncrement y:0 duration:0.2];
    SKAction *moveAwhile = [SKAction repeatAction:moveLeft count:1];

    SKAction *stillAnimation = [SKAction animateWithTextures:playerStillTextures timePerFrame:1];
    SKAction *stillAwhile = [SKAction repeatAction:stillAnimation count:0.1];

    SKAction *sequence = [SKAction sequence:@[skidAwhile, moveAwhile, stillAwhile]];
    [self runAction:sequence completion:^{
        NSLog(@"skid ended, still facing right");
        _playerStatus = SBPlayerFacingRight;
    }];
}
```

```
- (void)skidLeft
{
    NSLog(@"skid Left");
    [self removeAllActions];
    _playerStatus = SBPlayerSkiddingLeft;

    NSArray *playerSkidTextures = _spriteTextures.playerSkiddingLeftTextures;
    NSArray *playerStillTextures = _spriteTextures.playerStillFacingLeftTextures;

    SKAction *skidAnimation = [SKAction animateWithTextures:playerSkidTextures timePerFrame:1];
    SKAction *skidAwhile = [SKAction repeatAction:skidAnimation count:0.2];

    SKAction *moveLeft = [SKAction moveByX:-kPlayerSkiddingIncrement y:0 duration:0.2];
    SKAction *moveAwhile = [SKAction repeatAction:moveLeft count:1];

    SKAction *stillAnimation = [SKAction animateWithTextures:playerStillTextures timePerFrame:1];
    SKAction *stillAwhile = [SKAction repeatAction:stillAnimation count:0.1];

    SKAction *sequence = [SKAction sequence:@[skidAwhile, moveAwhile, stillAwhile]];
    [self runAction:sequence completion:^{
        NSLog(@"skid ended, still facing left");
        _playerStatus = SBPlayerFacingLeft;
    }];
}
```

So what did you do here?

```
[self removeAllActions];
```

First you cleared out all currently running actions using the removeAllActions method.

```
NSArray *playerSkidTextures = _spriteTextures.playerSkiddingLeftTextures;
NSArray *playerStillTextures = _spriteTextures.playerStillFacingLeftTextures;
```

You created two sets of texture arrays: one for the skidding and one for the standing-still frames. As you can see in the Textures class, these are actually single-frame textures, at least for now.

```
SKAction *skidAnimation = [SKAction animateWithTextures:playerSkidTextures timePerFrame:1];
SKAction *skidAwhile = [SKAction repeatAction:skidAnimation count:0.2];
```

You use the skid texture array to create a new SKAction, then create another action to handle animating the frames. Technically, you could probably remove the second SKAction, but it would break things if you changed your mind later and added more frames. Keeping it here may save you time and trouble later.

```
SKAction *moveLeft = [SKAction moveByX:-kPlayerSkiddingIncrement y:0 duration:0.2];
SKAction *moveAwhile = [SKAction repeatAction:moveLeft count:1];
```

You created another set of SKActions to handle to actual movement while skidding.

```
SKAction *stillAnimation = [SKAction animateWithTextures:playerStillTextures timePerFrame:1];
SKAction *stillAwhile = [SKAction repeatAction:stillAnimation count:0.1];
```

Then you created a new action set for the conclusion of the skid, when the sprite will be standing still. As you will see in a moment, this method handles both the skidding and the still frames when the skidding is finished.

```
SKAction *sequence = [SKAction sequence:@[skidAwhile, moveAwhile, stillAwhile]];
```

Now I'll introduce you to a new method for actions: the sequence. A *sequence* is a set of actions that run consecutively. When an SKNode runs a sequence, the actions are triggered in consecutive order. When one action completes, the next action starts immediately. When the last action in the sequence completes, the sequence action also completes. Thus you built an array of the three actions you just created. SkidAwhile will run for its defined 0.2 seconds, then moveAwhile will run for 1 second, and finally stillAwhile for 0.1 seconds.

```
[self runAction:sequence completion:^{
    NSLog(@"skid ended, still facing left");
    _playerStatus = SBPlayerFacingLeft;
}];
```

The runAction:completion: method is identical to the runAction: method, but after the action completes, your block is called. This callback is called only if the action runs to completion. If the action is removed before it completes, the completion handler is never called. Thus when the sequence runs its course and the sprite is standing still, the callback block sends a message to the console and changes the status accordingly.

Your last change is in the SKBGameScene.m file. (Several lines have been deleted, so modify the touchesBeganWithEvent method to match the following.)

```
if (!_playerSprite) {
    _playerSprite = [SKBPlayer initNewPlayer:self startingPoint:location];
} else if (location.x <= ( self.frame.size.width / 2 )) {
    // user touched left side of screen
    if (_playerSprite.playerStatus == SBPlayerRunningRight) {
        [_playerSprite skidRight];
    } else if (_playerSprite.playerStatus != SBPlayerRunningLeft) {
        [_playerSprite runLeft];
    }
} else {
    // user touched right side of screen
    if (_playerSprite.playerStatus == SBPlayerRunningLeft) {
        [_playerSprite skidLeft];
    } else if (_playerSprite.playerStatus != SBPlayerRunningRight) {
        [_playerSprite runRight];
    }
}
```

When you build and run the program now, you'll have fluid sprite reactions to your user's inputs. When coming to a stop, the sprite will skid a short distance. Things are really beginning to take shape.

Summary

This chapter presented ideas on how to handle user's input in order to produce desired reactions. The user needs to do something other than just watch some predetermined series of animations— this isn't a movie after all. In this case, you had the user controlling the actions of a running character or sprite.

Along the way, you learned some methods for organizing your growing code base. You created some custom classes to hold important data, and you tried to eliminate hard-coded static values that you may elect to change later.

The end result is that you had a game character appear on the screen and, when the user touches the screen, it reacts to the user's control inputs and runs around the screen. Well, back and forth at least.

In the next chapter, I'll introduce you to the powerful physics engine that comes with Sprite Kit. You will learn how this engine allows you to interact easily with other objects, such as the "ground" that you'll add so that your player has something solid to plant its running feet. You'll add some floating ledges and then give the sprite the ability to jump so that it can reach those ledges. Let's do it!

Chapter 4

Edges, Boundaries, and Ledges

Physics

You can probably imagine the amount code work needed to add complicated sprites that interact with each other and with the game world you create. In this game, you'll want basic physics principles like gravity to affect every character that you add to the game. You'll also want your sprites to have some walls or ledges to run along. However, all of the coding required to handle all of these physics-based interactions is daunting. Luckily, Sprite Kit comes with a built-in physics world. Let's start exploring this option with your sprite and its world.

Add one line of code to the `SKBPlayer.m` file in the `initNewPlayer` method:

```
player.position = location;
player.spriteTextures = playerTextures;
```

`// physics`
`player.physicsBody = [SKPhysicsBody bodyWithRectangleOfSize:player.size];`

```
// add the sprite to the scene
```

Build and run. When clicking the screen to add your sprite, you might want to choose a location near the top of the screen. Now quit and run it again. It doesn't stay on the screen for very long!

So what is happening here and why? Well, you have applied the Sprite Kit Physics engine to your game, and the physics world has gravity in it. So the sprite "materializes" into thin air and immediately begins falling. As you learned earlier, when the sprite runs or falls beyond the boundaries of the screen, it ceases to exist, as revealed by the node count displayed on the screen.

```
player.physicsBody = [SKPhysicsBody bodyWithRectangleOfSize:player.size];
```

When creating an SKPhysicsBody for a volume-based node like your sprite, you have three options: bodyWithRectangleOfSize, bodyWithCircleOfRadius, and bodyWithPolygonFromPath. You want to choose the option that matches the basic size and shape of your sprite. With sprites as small as this one, the circle or rectangle options are going to be much easier to use.

Now create another SKPhysicsBody and apply it to your scene. Modify the initWithSize method in your SKBGameScene.m file like this:

```
-(id)initWithSize:(CGSize)size {
    if (self = [super initWithSize:size]) {
        /* Setup your scene here */
        self.backgroundColor = [SKColor blackColor];
        self.physicsBody = [SKPhysicsBody bodyWithEdgeLoopFromRect:self.frame];
    }
    return self;
}
```

When creating an SKPhysicsBody for an edge-based node like the scene borders, you have four options: bodyWithEdgeLoopFromRect, bodyWithEdgeFromPoint:toPoint, bodyWithEdgeLoopFromPath, and bodyWithEdgeChainFromPath. Again, this example uses the simpler rectangle variety to create an edge along all four sides of the game screen, or scene.

Build and run. This time the sprite cannot run or fall outside the border. With two lines of code you have drastically changed the game!

Properties of a Physics Body

There are several properties you can mess around with for every SKPhysicsBody that you have associated with your sprites or SKNodes. Real world attributes like mass, density, friction, linear damping, and others are included and available to change however you see fit. You can, of course, explore the Xcode documentation for full details, but let's tweak a few to see how and what happens.

Add these three lines to the initNewPlayer method inside of the SKBPlayer.m file:

```
// physics
player.physicsBody = [SKPhysicsBodybodyWithRectangleOfSize:player.size];
player.physicsBody.density = 0.1;
player.physicsBody.linearDamping = 1.0;
player.physicsBody.restitution = 1.0;
```

Build and run. Your little sprite becomes light as a feather and as springy as a superball. Play with these values; just keep in mind that these properties expect values between 0.0 and 1.0. When you're finished, just change them back to defaults:

```
// physics
player.physicsBody = [SKPhysicsBody bodyWithRectangleOfSize:player.size];
player.physicsBody.density = 1.0;
player.physicsBody.linearDamping = 0.1;
player.physicsBody.restitution = 0.2;
```

Adding a Backdrop

Since the sprite has started to run around a much more realistic world than it experienced previously, you should probably add some scenery to its environment. It's not floating around in space shooting down aliens or asteroids; instead it is running around underground in the sewers. Let's add a background image to reflect this.

As you've done many times before, add the two images named Backdrop_568.png and Backdrop_480.png to your project and move them into your Sprites folder.

Now modify the initWithSize method in the SKBGameScene.m file like this:

```
    self.backgroundColor = [SKColor blackColor];
    self.physicsBody = [SKPhysicsBody bodyWithEdgeLoopFromRect:self.frame];

    NSString *fileName = @"";
    if (self.frame.size.width == 480) {
        fileName = @"Backdrop_480";        // iPhone Retina (3.5-inch)
    } else {
        fileName = @"Backdrop_568";        // iPhone Retina (4-inch)
    }
    SKSpriteNode *backdrop = [SKSpriteNode spriteNodeWithImageNamed:fileName];
    backdrop.name = @"backdropNode";
    backdrop.position = CGPointMake(CGRectGetMidX(self.frame), CGRectGetMidY(self.frame));

    [self addChild:backdrop];
}
return self;
```

Build and run to see this new game world.

Contacts and Collisions

One of the features you'll add to this game is the ability to wrap around both the left and right sides of the screen. This gives it an old-style video game feel and makes the game world feel bigger than it really is. In other words, when the sprite runs to the left and eventually runs into the left-side wall, you'll wrap it around immediately, so that it instantly reappears on the right side of the screen as if it were continuously running without restrictions.

In order to do this, you need to set up the physicsBody attributes of both the edge and character SpriteNode, so that they will handle each other's contact events. Using a bitmask, you can set every SpriteNode to allow or handle contacts and/or collisions with each other. You will want some sprites to "pass through" other sprites (no contact or collision) and some to collide with each other.

You'll begin by creating some constants for bitmasking. Since they need to be available to several classes, you'll add them to the AppDelegate. Add these three lines to the SKBAppDelegate.h file:

```
#import <UIKit/UIKit.h>

// Global project constants
static const uint32_t kPlayerCategory =          0x1 << 0;
static const uint32_t kWallCategory =            0x1 << 1;

@interface SKBAppDelegate : UIResponder <UIApplicationDelegate>
```

Two of the existing classes (SKBGameScene and SKBPlayer) need access to these constants, so you need to be sure that they have access to the AppDelegate. Therefore, add this line of code to the SKBGameScene.h file:

```
#import <SpriteKit/SpriteKit.h>
#import "SKBAppDelegate.h"
#import "SKBPlayer.h"
```

And add the same line of code to the SKBPlayer.h file:

```
#import <SpriteKit/SpriteKit.h>
#import "SKBAppDelegate.h"
#import "SKBSpriteTextures.h"
```

Now you add contact attributes to your player in the SKBPlayer.m file:

```
// physics
player.physicsBody = [SKPhysicsBody bodyWithRectangleOfSize:player.size];
player.physicsBody.categoryBitMask = kPlayerCategory;
player.physicsBody.contactTestBitMask = kWallCategory;
player.physicsBody.density = 1.0;
player.physicsBody.linearDamping = 0.1;
player.physicsBody.restitution = 0.2;
```

The categoryBitMask tells the Physics engine that this node is of this type kPlayerCategory. The contactTestBitMask tells the Physics engine that this node can make contact with the provided types of nodes. Any node types not listed in the contactTestBitMask will be ignored. Even though you have provided only one type of node here in the contactTestBitMask, you can pass in any number of node types with which you want the engine to be concerned (using the pipe | character as a delimiter). You will add more later.

In order to process contacts and collisions, you need a delegate to handle them. You'll designate the SKBGameScene to have the honors. Add the SKPhysicsContactDelegate protocol to the SKBGameScene.h file:

```
@interface SKBGameScene : SKScene <SKPhysicsContactDelegate>
```

Now you add a categoryBitMask attribute to the edge and set the contactDelegate to SKBGameScene in the initWithSize method of the SKBGameScene.m file:

```
self.backgroundColor = [SKColor blackColor];
self.physicsBody = [SKPhysicsBody bodyWithEdgeLoopFromRect:self.frame];
self.physicsBody.categoryBitMask = kWallCategory;
self.physicsWorld.contactDelegate = self;
```

Then you can add the delegate method didBeginContact to handle the contacts and collisions (add it to the SKBGameScene.m file):

```
- (void)didBeginContact:(SKPhysicsContact *)contact
{
    SKPhysicsBody *firstBody, *secondBody;

    if (contact.bodyA.categoryBitMask < contact.bodyB.categoryBitMask)
    {
        firstBody = contact.bodyA;
        secondBody = contact.bodyB;
    }
    else {
        firstBody = contact.bodyB;
        secondBody = contact.bodyA;
    }

    // Player / sideWalls
    if ((((firstBody.categoryBitMask & kPlayerCategory) != 0) && ((secondBody.categoryBitMask &
kWallCategory) != 0)))
    {
        NSLog(@"player contacted edge");
    }
}
```

When this method is called, it is passed an SKPhysicsContact object, which describes the particulars. There are four properties available for use: bodyA, bodyB, contactPoint, and collisionImpulse. For now, you are not much interested in the exact position (or point) of contact or how hard they struck each other, but you are interested in determining which two sprites were involved so that you can act accordingly.

The first if() statement used here makes the order that you used in your category constant declarations (kPlayerCategory and kWallCategory) determine the order of the variables firstBody and secondBody. In other words, if the player sprite contacts a wall, the player sprite will always be set as firstBody and the wall will always be set as secondBody. They will never be reversed. This makes it so that you can use a lot fewer if() statements as you go along, checking on which sprite contacted which other sprite.

The second if() statement checks to see if firstBody is the player and secondBody is the wall. If so, you'll post a console message.

Build and run. Watch the console as you try various inputs to see when this contact is triggered.

Adding a Brick Base

You may have noticed that when the sprite fell and landed on the bottom of the screen, it triggered a contact event with the edge. Let's add an image that will act as a raised base for it to run along, so that you'll end up with only left- and right-side edge contact events.

Add the image Base_600.png to the project and move it into the Sprites folder.

You need an additional bitmask constant in the SKBAppDelegate.h file, and since you are inserting it before the existing kWallCategory, you need to change its value as well (they need to be sequential):

```
// Global project constants
static const uint32_t kPlayerCategory =          0x1 << 0;
static const uint32_t kBaseCategory =            0x1 << 1;
static const uint32_t kWallCategory =            0x1 << 2;
```

You need the SKBPlayer.m file updated so that the player can process contacts with the new base:

```
player.physicsBody.categoryBitMask = kPlayerCategory;
player.physicsBody.contactTestBitMask = kBaseCategory | kWallCategory;
player.physicsBody.density = 1.0;
```

Then you add the applicable code to the initWithSize method of the SKBGameScene.m file to add the base as a new SKNode:

```
    backdrop.position = CGPointMake(CGRectGetMidX(self.frame), CGRectGetMidY(self.frame));

    [self addChild:backdrop];

    // brick base
    SKSpriteNode *brickBase = [SKSpriteNode spriteNodeWithImageNamed:@"Base_600"];
    brickBase.name = @"brickBaseNode";
    brickBase.position = CGPointMake(CGRectGetMidX(self.frame), brickBase.size.height/2);
    brickBase.physicsBody = [SKPhysicsBody bodyWithRectangleOfSize:brickBase.size];
    brickBase.physicsBody.categoryBitMask = kBaseCategory;
    brickBase.physicsBody.dynamic = NO;

    [self addChild:brickBase];
}
return self;
```

You had to create this node as a volume-based node (bodyWithRectangleOfSize), not an edge-based node (bodyWithEdgeLoopFromRect), because edge nodes allow movement from inside their borders (like the wall you created in the last section), not outside. This volume-based node acts as a solid brick wall that has volume. You should take note that you defined the physicsBody.dynamic property on this object and set it to NO. This is so that it will not be affected by gravity and will not budge when the character collides with it when falling; it becomes an immoveable object.

Build and run it to see how this image becomes a solid surface for the player to run along (see Figure 4-1).

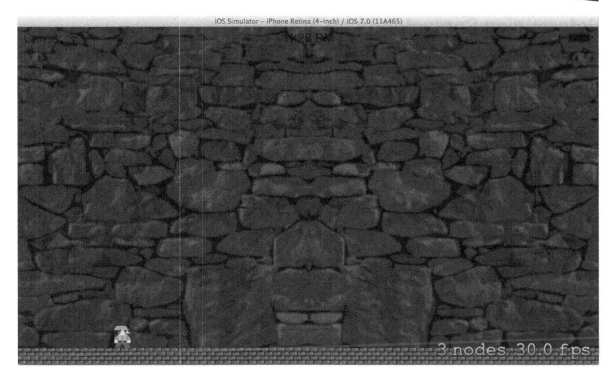

Figure 4-1. *The player standing on the brick base*

Even though it's not necessary at this point, you could add an if() statement to the delegate didBeginContact method (as shown next) so that you can use it later if necessary, and to be consistent with handling all contact events. It's not a requirement and nothing would fail if you left it out—consider it a placeholder that can be used later.

```
// Player / Base
if ((((firstBody.categoryBitMask & kPlayerCategory) != 0) &&
        ((secondBody.categoryBitMask & kBaseCategory) != 0)))
{
    // Not interested in this contact event
}

// Player / sideWalls
if ((((firstBody.categoryBitMask & kPlayerCategory) != 0) &&
        ((secondBody.categoryBitMask & kWallCategory) != 0)))
{
    NSLog(@"player contacted edge");
}
```

Determining Contact with an Edge

In order to handle wrapping properly when the sprite contacts the left or right edge, you need to determine which side was contacted. You'll modify the didBeginContact method (in the SKBGameScene.m file) so that you can determine this:

```
// Player / sideWalls
    if (((((firstBody.categoryBitMask & kPlayerCategory) != 0) && ((secondBody.categoryBitMask &
                            kWallCategory) != 0))) {
        if (firstBody.node.position.x < 100) {
            NSLog(@"player contacted left edge");
        } else {
            NSLog(@"player contacted right edge");
        }
    }
```

You test the sprite's position along the horizontal or X-axis (position.x) to see if it is currently on the left or right side of the screen. This code compared its x-position to a value of less than 100, but you could have used 50, 200, or even 300. It won't trigger an edge contact along the bottom of the screen any more because it's running along the brick base, keeping it from touching the base. Thus you know by the fact that it contacted the edge that its position.x value is going to be fairly large or fairly small.

Build and run it to see the change. The console should accurately respond to the applicable left- and right-edge contact.

Handling Sprite Wrapping

Now you can add the wrapping handlers so that your sprites can wrap from both edges of the screen over to the other edge. To help now and in the future, you are going to use the name property of an SKNode to hold a unique string that can be used in identifying the affected nodes inside the various methods. So add one to your initNewPlayer method in your SKBPlayer.m file:

```
// our player character sprite & starting position in the scene
SKBPlayer *player = [SKBPlayer spriteNodeWithTexture:f1];
player.name = @"player1";
player.position = location;
player.spriteTextures = playerTextures;
```

Now you need to insert a new wrapPlayer:where method between the initNewPlayer and runRight methods:

```
#pragma mark Screen wrap

- (void)wrapPlayer:(CGPoint)where
{
    SKPhysicsBody *storePB = self.physicsBody;
    self.physicsBody = nil;
    self.position = where;
    self.physicsBody = storePB;
}
```

I'll stop here and explain this interesting method. What I discovered as I developed this game is that attempting to simply change a sprite's position doesn't work as expected. However, I also discovered that a quick and easy way to get past this restriction is to remove the physics body from the sprite (storing it in a temporary variable), change the position, and then restore the physics body. Looking at the code that you just added, you can see that this is what I have just done. Sneaky, but it gets you what you need; that is, instant teleportation to another point on the screen. You'll see this as soon as you run the game at the end of this section. You need to make a few more changes first, however.

To continue, you need to make this method public so that you can call it from the SKScene class. To do this, add this line to the SKBPlayer.h file:

```
+ (SKBPlayer *)initNewPlayer:(SKScene *)whichScene startingPoint:(CGPoint)location;

- (void)wrapPlayer:(CGPoint)where;

- (void)runRight;
```

Now, over in the SKBGameScene.m file in the didBeginContact method, add a variable to hold the firstBody contact name:

```
else {
    firstBody = contact.bodyB;
    secondBody = contact.bodyA;
}

// contact body name
NSString *firstBodyName = firstBody.node.name;

// Player / Base
```

You can then use this name to verify that the affected contact is actually the player's sprite and, if so, call the wrapPlayer:where method to handle the actual wrapping:

```
// Player / sideWalls
    if ((((firstBody.categoryBitMask & kPlayerCategory) != 0) && ((secondBody.categoryBitMask &
        kWallCategory) != 0))) {
        if ([firstBodyName isEqualToString: @"player1"]) {
            if (_playerSprite.position.x < 20) {
                NSLog(@"player contacted left edge");
                [_playerSprite wrapPlayer:CGPointMake(self.frame.size.width-10,
                                                    _playerSprite.position.y)];
            } else {
                NSLog(@"player contacted right edge");
                [_playerSprite wrapPlayer:CGPointMake(10, _playerSprite.position.y)];
            }
        }
    }
```

You might notice that when you are calculating the x-axis point that you want to send to the wrapPlayer:where method, you add or subtract 10 points from it. This is roughly half the width of the player sprite and this extra buffer helps make it so that the sprite doesn't trigger another edge contact event when it appears on the other side of the screen.

Build and run it to see the new screen wrapping in all its glory!

Jumping

You will soon add some ledges that your player can jump up on and run along. In order to do that, the sprite needs the ability to jump, so let's work on that.

Jumping requires an additional input from the user, but from where? You already split the screen into two zones for left and right inputs, and you need to change this somehow. You'll split the screen into three areas by splitting the bottom half split into left and right zones (see Figure 4-2).

Figure 4-2. *Three input zones*

You need to modify the touchesBegan:withEvent method in the SKBGameScene.m file to handle this change:

```
if (!_playerSprite) {
    _playerSprite = [SKBPlayer initNewPlayer:self startingPoint:location];
} else if (location.y >= (self.frame.size.height / 2 )) {
    // user touched upper half of the screen (zero = bottom of screen)
    NSLog(@"jump");
} else if (location.x <= ( self.frame.size.width / 2 )) {
```

This triggers a jump message to the console when the user touches anywhere on the screen where the y-axis position is greater than half the height of the screen (the upper half).

Now that the input is handled as desired, you can make the sprite launch itself off of the ground. To do this, you will use one of the SKPhysicsWorld methods for applying forces or impulses to a physics body. You have six from which to choose: applyForce, applyTorque, applyForce:atPoint, applyImpulse, applyAngularImpulse, and applyImpulse:atPoint. Impulses are typically used for immediate changes to a body's velocity, while forces are used for continuous effects. According to the Sprite Kit documentation, using applyImpulse applies an impulse uniformly to a physics body, while using applyForce:atPoint applies an impulse to a specific point of a physics body. Thus it seems that the best choice for a jumping ability is applyImpulse.

Add a static value to the SKBPlayer.h file:

```
#define kPlayerSkiddingIncrement    20
#define kPlayerJumpingIncrement     10
```

In the same file, you also need a public declaration of the new jump method:

```
- (void)skidRight;
- (void)skidLeft;
- (void)jump;

@end
```

Then you can add the new jump method to the SKBPlayer.m file, inserting it after the existing skidLeft method:

```
- (void)jump
{
    NSLog(@"jump");
    [self.physicsBody applyImpulse:CGVectorMake(0, kPlayerJumpingIncrement)];
}
```

Then you modify the touchesBegan:withEvent method in the SKBGameScene.m file:

```
} else if (location.y >= (self.frame.size.height / 2 )) {
    // user touched upper half of the screen (zero = bottom of screen)
    [_playerSprite jump];
} else if (location.x <= ( self.frame.size.width / 2 )) {
```

Build and run it to try out the new jumping ability. The sprite has amazing muscles, eh? Wow!

After playing around with this jumping ability, you will notice some small details that need some tuning. You need to change the animation during the jump so that the sprite doesn't continue "running" while airborne, and you need to remove its ability to initiate another powerful jump before completing the prior one.

You're going to use a single frame for the jumping animation, so start by adding the Player_LeftJump.png and Player_RightJump.png images to the project; move them into the Player folder.

You then add two instance variables to the SKBSpriteTextures.h file:

```
@property (nonatomic, strong) NSArray *playerRunRightTextures, *playerJumpRightTextures;
@property (nonatomic, strong) NSArray *playerSkiddingRightTextures, *playerStillFacingRightTextures;
@property (nonatomic, strong) NSArray *playerRunLeftTextures, *playerJumpLeftTextures;
@property (nonatomic, strong) NSArray *playerSkiddingLeftTextures, *playerStillFacingLeftTextures;
```

You also add two more static filenames to the SKBSpriteTextures.h file:

```
#define kPlayerRunRight4FileName          @"Player_Right4.png"
#define kPlayerJumpRightFileName          @"Player_RightJump.png"
#define kPlayerSkidRightFileName          @"Player_RightSkid.png"
    .
    .
    .
#define kPlayerRunLeft4FileName           @"Player_Left4.png"
#define kPlayerJumpLeftFileName           @"Player_LeftJump.png"
#define kPlayerSkidLeftFileName           @"Player_LeftSkid.png"
```

Then you modify the createAnimationTextures method in the SKBSpriteTextures.m file:

```
//   right, skidding
f1 = [SKTexture textureWithImageNamed:kPlayerSkidRightFileName];
_playerSkiddingRightTextures = @[f1];
_playerRunRightTextures = @[f1,f2,f3,f4];

//   right, jumping
f1 = [SKTexture textureWithImageNamed:kPlayerJumpRightFileName];
_playerJumpRightTextures = @[f1];

//   right, still
f1 = [SKTexture textureWithImageNamed:kPlayerStillRightFileName];
_playerStillFacingRightTextures = @[f1];
    .
    .
    .
//   left, skidding
f1 = [SKTexture textureWithImageNamed:kPlayerSkidLeftFileName];
_playerSkiddingLeftTextures = @[f1];

//   left, jumping
f1 = [SKTexture textureWithImageNamed:kPlayerJumpLeftFileName];
_playerJumpLeftTextures = @[f1];

//   left, still
f1 = [SKTexture textureWithImageNamed:kPlayerStillLeftFileName];
_playerStillFacingLeftTextures = @[f1];
```

You add some more status values to the enumerated list in the SKBPlayer.h file:

```
typedef enum : int {
    SBPlayerFacingLeft = 0,
    SBPlayerFacingRight,
    SBPlayerRunningLeft,
    SBPlayerRunningRight,
    SBPlayerSkiddingLeft,
    SBPlayerSkiddingRight,
    SBPlayerJumpingLeft,
    SBPlayerJumpingRight,
    SBPlayerJumpingUpFacingLeft,
    SBPlayerJumpingUpFacingRight
} SBPlayerStatus;
```

By slightly modifying the touchesBeganWithEvent method in the SKBGameScene.m file, you can remove the sprite's ability to jump until it has completed the previous jump:

```
for (UITouch *touch in touches) {
    CGPoint location = [touch locationInNode:self];
    SBPlayerStatus status = _playerSprite.playerStatus;

    if (!_playerSprite) {
        _playerSprite = [SKBPlayer initNewPlayer:self startingPoint:location];
    } else if (location.y >= (self.frame.size.height / 2 )) {
        // user touched upper half of the screen (zero = bottom of screen)
        if (status != SBPlayerJumpingLeft && status != SBPlayerJumpingRight && status !=
                SBPlayerJumpingUpFacingLeft && status != SBPlayerJumpingUpFacingRight) {
            [_playerSprite jump];
        }
    } else if (location.x <= ( self.frame.size.width / 2 )) {
        // user touched left side of screen
        if (status == SBPlayerRunningRight) {
            [_playerSprite skidRight];
        } else if (status == SBPlayerFacingLeft || status == SBPlayerFacingRight) {
            [_playerSprite runLeft];
        }
    } else {
        // user touched right side of screen
        if (status == SBPlayerRunningLeft) {
            [_playerSprite skidLeft];
        } else if (status == SBPlayerFacingLeft || status == SBPlayerFacingRight) {
            [_playerSprite runRight];
        }
    }
}
```

Finally, you make these major changes to the jump method in the SKBPlayer.m file:

```objc
- (void)jump
{
    NSArray *playerJumpTextures = nil;
    SBPlayerStatus nextPlayerStatus = 0;

    // determine direction and next phase
    if (self.playerStatus == SBPlayerRunningLeft || self.playerStatus == SBPlayerSkiddingLeft) {
        NSLog(@"jump left");
        self.playerStatus = SBPlayerJumpingLeft;
        playerJumpTextures = _spriteTextures.playerJumpLeftTextures;
        nextPlayerStatus = SBPlayerRunningLeft;
    } else if (self.playerStatus == SBPlayerRunningRight || self.playerStatus ==
                SBPlayerSkiddingRight) {
        NSLog(@"jump right");
        self.playerStatus = SBPlayerJumpingRight;
        playerJumpTextures = _spriteTextures.playerJumpRightTextures;
        nextPlayerStatus = SBPlayerRunningRight;
    } else if (self.playerStatus == SBPlayerFacingLeft) {
        NSLog(@"jump up, facing left");
        self.playerStatus = SBPlayerJumpingUpFacingLeft;
        playerJumpTextures = _spriteTextures.playerJumpLeftTextures;
        nextPlayerStatus = SBPlayerFacingLeft;
    } else if (self.playerStatus == SBPlayerFacingRight) {
        NSLog(@"jump up, facing right");
        self.playerStatus = SBPlayerJumpingUpFacingRight;
        playerJumpTextures = _spriteTextures.playerJumpRightTextures;
        nextPlayerStatus = SBPlayerFacingRight;
    } else {
        NSLog(@"SKBPlayer::jump encountered invalid value...");
    }

    // applicable animation
    SKAction *jumpAnimation = [SKAction animateWithTextures:playerJumpTextures timePerFrame:1];
    SKAction *jumpAwhile = [SKAction repeatAction:jumpAnimation count:1.0];

    // run jump action and when completed handle next phase
    [self runAction:jumpAwhile completion:^{
        if (nextPlayerStatus == SBPlayerRunningLeft) {
            [self removeAllActions];
            [self runLeft];
        } else if (nextPlayerStatus == SBPlayerRunningRight) {
            [self removeAllActions];
            [self runRight];
        } else if (nextPlayerStatus == SBPlayerFacingLeft) {
            NSArray *playerStillTextures = _spriteTextures.playerStillFacingLeftTextures;
            SKAction *stillAnimation = [SKAction animateWithTextures:playerStillTextures
                                                         timePerFrame:1];
            SKAction *stillAwhile = [SKAction repeatAction:stillAnimation count:0.1];
            [self runAction:stillAwhile];
            self.playerStatus = SBPlayerFacingLeft;
```

```
        } else if (nextPlayerStatus == SBPlayerFacingRight) {
            NSArray *playerStillTextures = _spriteTextures.playerStillFacingRightTextures;
            SKAction *stillAnimation = [SKAction animateWithTextures:playerStillTextures
                                                        timePerFrame:1];
            SKAction *stillAwhile = [SKAction repeatAction:stillAnimation count:0.1];
            [self runAction:stillAwhile];
            self.playerStatus = SBPlayerFacingRight;
        } else {
            NSLog(@"SKBPlayer::jump completion block encountered invalid value...");
        }
    }];

    // jump impulse applied
    [self.physicsBody applyImpulse:CGVectorMake(0, kPlayerJumpingIncrement)];
}
```

Let's examine what was done here.

```
NSArray *playerJumpTextures = nil;
SBPlayerStatus nextPlayerStatus = 0;
```

You create two local variables to hold an animation texture array and the status that will be used when the jump animation has completed.

```
if (self.playerStatus == SBPlayerRunningLeft || self.playerStatus == SBPlayerSkiddingLeft) {
    NSLog(@"jump left");
    self.playerStatus = SBPlayerJumpingLeft;
    playerJumpTextures = _spriteTextures.playerJumpLeftTextures;
    nextPlayerStatus = SBPlayerRunningLeft;
```

If the player is running or skidding to the left, you log a message to the console that a jump to the left has been triggered and you alter the status to reflect this. Then you set the jumping animation texture array to the applicable set of textures. When the animation has completed, the player will continue running to the left.

```
else if (self.playerStatus == SBPlayerRunningRight || self.playerStatus == SBPlayerSkiddingRight) {
    NSLog(@"jump right");
    self.playerStatus = SBPlayerJumpingRight;
    playerJumpTextures = _spriteTextures.playerJumpRightTextures;
    nextPlayerStatus = SBPlayerRunningRight;
```

This handles the running and skidding conditions for right-facing directions that you just completed for the left.

```
else if (self.playerStatus == SBPlayerFacingLeft) {
    NSLog(@"jump up, facing left");
    self.playerStatus = SBPlayerJumpingUpFacingLeft;
    playerJumpTextures = _spriteTextures.playerJumpLeftTextures;
    nextPlayerStatus = SBPlayerFacingLeft;
```

This applies the applicable status and textures for jumping while standing still so that no sideways movement will be applied. The player will complete the jump by standing still and facing to the left.

```
else if (self.playerStatus == SBPlayerFacingRight) {
    NSLog(@"jump up, facing right");
    self.playerStatus = SBPlayerJumpingUpFacingRight;
    playerJumpTextures = _spriteTextures.playerJumpRightTextures;
    nextPlayerStatus = SBPlayerFacingRight;
```

This handles jumping from a standing still position for the right-facing direction that you just completed for the left-facing direction.

```
else {
    NSLog(@"SKBPlayer::jump encountered invalid value...");
}
```

This line was not entirely necessary, but it will help you debug potential problems later if you missed some programming logic. Adding extra lines of code like this can pay off later by saving you the time of having to go back and look over code to determine why you're getting strange or unexpected results.

```
// applicable animation
SKAction *jumpAnimation = [SKAction animateWithTextures:playerJumpTextures timePerFrame:1];
SKAction *jumpAwhile = [SKAction repeatAction:jumpAnimation count:1.0];
```

This creates the jump animation textures used while the sprite is jumping. This frame of animation is used for a full second before the animation switches to something else. There isn't a callback in the code for when the impulse has been completed and the sprite has fallen back onto the base. Thus, this time-based action allows you to determine roughly a set amount of time to allow for the jump before running another set of actions.

```
// run jump action and when completed handle next phase
 [self runAction:jumpAwhile completion:^{
```

This initiates the animation and a one-second waiting period for the jump animation, even though you have not yet triggered the jumping impulse that starts it rocketing toward the top of the screen. Notice that the completion block option of the SKAction runAction method is used, as it allows you to run some code when this action completes.

```
if (nextPlayerStatus == SBPlayerRunningLeft) {
    [self removeAllActions];
    [self runLeft];
} else if (nextPlayerStatus == SBPlayerRunningRight) {
    [self removeAllActions];
    [self runRight];
```

This if() block tests for the value you set as the next status to apply when the jump has completed; these two expressions test for running left or right. If the sprite should be running, it removes all previous actions and sets the sprite to run in the applicable direction. (If you didn't call the removeAllActions method and the sprite was already running when another runLeft or runRight method call was triggered, its speed would double.)

```
else if (nextPlayerStatus == SBPlayerFacingLeft) {
    NSArray *playerStillTextures = _spriteTextures.playerStillFacingLeftTextures;
    SKAction *stillAnimation = [SKAction animateWithTextures:playerStillTextures timePerFrame:1];
    SKAction *stillAwhile = [SKAction repeatAction:stillAnimation count:0.1];
    [self runAction:stillAwhile];
    self.playerStatus = SBPlayerFacingLeft;
} else if (nextPlayerStatus == SBPlayerFacingRight) {
    NSArray *playerStillTextures = _spriteTextures.playerStillFacingRightTextures;
    SKAction *stillAnimation = [SKAction animateWithTextures:playerStillTextures timePerFrame:1];
    SKAction *stillAwhile = [SKAction repeatAction:stillAnimation count:0.1];
    [self runAction:stillAwhile];
    self.playerStatus = SBPlayerFacingRight;
```

These two expressions handle standing still after the running is completed. They both work similarly, with slight changes in regard to left or right directions. They create the standing-still texture arrays, attach these arrays to an SKAction to display them for a period of time (unmoving until a new action is triggered), and then set the applicable player status.

```
else {
    NSLog(@"SKBPlayer::jump completion block encountered invalid value...");
}
```

Again this line was not entirely necessary, but it will help you debug potential problems later if you missed some programming logic.

```
// jump impulse applied
[self.physicsBody applyImpulse:CGVectorMake(0, kPlayerJumpingIncrement)];
```

Finally, you initiate the impulse that launches the sprite into the sky.

Build and run it. You'll see that the sprite's jumping ability has taken on the desired traits and that you fixed the minor problems noted earlier. There were a lot of code changes, but hopefully now it all makes perfect sense.

To tidy things up, you'll fix the sprite's starting texture and status so that, upon creation, it spawns facing to the right with the correct properties. Modify the initNewPlayer method in the SKBPlayer.m file:

```
// initial frame
SKTexture *f1 = [SKTexture textureWithImageNamed: kPlayerStillRightFileName];

// our player character sprite & starting position in the scene
SKBPlayer *player = [SKBPlayer spriteNodeWithTexture:f1];
player.name = @"player1";
player.position = location;
player.spriteTextures = playerTextures;
player.playerStatus = SBPlayerFacingRight;
```

Ledges and Joints

So far, the player runs along the brick base, wraps around to the other side of the screen when it reaches the far edge, and jumps with amazing muscle power. The sprite needs a bit more to interact with in order to make this more exciting. To accomplish this, you are going to add several more levels above the sprite for it to run along. This will also create a path for bad guys to run along when you add them later.

Instead of creating solid ledges for the underground sewer environment, you are going to create flexible blocks that will all be joined together so that you will have the digital equivalent of rope bridges when you're finished. This will help you gain a good understanding of Sprite Kit's SKPhysicsJoint capability, which allows you to join different PhysicsBodies together so that they will be simulated together in the physics world.

There are five joint types that you can use when connecting bodies: SKPhysicsJointFixed, SKPhysicsJointSliding, SKPhysicsJointSpring, SKPhysicsJointLimit, and SKPhysicsJointPin. You are going to use the SKPhysicsJointPin type for the ledges so that they can be connected at a single anchor point, as if they were pinned together (see Figure 4-3).

Figure 4-3. *Three SKPhysicsJointPin connections between four SKSpriteNodes*

You are going to create several ledges made from many single blocks, so you need to create a separate class to handle all of the details.

As you've done a few times already, go ahead and create a new class named SKBLedge as a subclass of NSObject. Modify the SKBLedge.h file to match the following:

```
#import <Foundation/Foundation.h>
#import <SpriteKit/SpriteKit.h>
#import "SKBAppDelegate.h"
#define kLedgeBrickFileName          @"LedgeBrick.png"
#define kLedgeBrickSpacing           9
#define kLedgeSideBufferSpacing      4


@interface SKBLedge : NSObject


- (void)createNewSetOfLedgeNodes:(SKScene *)whichScene startingPoint:(CGPoint)leftSide
             withHowManyBlocks:(int)blockCount startingIndex:(int)indexStart;


@end
```

Add the LedgeBrick.png to the project and move it into the Sprites folder.

Now you add the createNewSetOfLedgeNodes method to the new SKBLedge.m file:

```
- (void)createNewSetOfLedgeNodes:(SKScene *)whichScene startingPoint:(CGPoint)leftSide
            withHowManyBlocks:(int)blockCount startingIndex:(int)indexStart
{
    // ledge nodes
    SKTexture *ledgeBrickTexture = [SKTexture textureWithImageNamed:kLedgeBrickFileName];

    CGPoint where = leftSide;

    // nodes, equally spaced
    for (int index=0; index < blockCount; index++) {
        SKSpriteNode *theNode = [SKSpriteNode spriteNodeWithTexture:ledgeBrickTexture];
        theNode.name = [NSString stringWithFormat:@"ledgeBrick%d", indexStart+index];
        NSLog(@"%@ created", theNode.name);
        theNode.position = where;
        theNode.anchorPoint = CGPointMake(0.5,0.5);
        where.x += kLedgeBrickSpacing;

        [whichScene addChild:theNode];
    }
}
```

You load up the texture that you will use for all of the blocks. The left side of the ledge is where you begin, and the method parameter tells you where to begin. You create a for() loop, beginning at zero and going until you reach the blockCount parameter that was passed in. Each pass through the loop creates a node using the texture, gives it a unique name by appending the for() loop index value to the end of a ledgeBrick string, logs the name to the console, sets its position and its anchor point, increments the position of the next block, and adds the node as a child to the scene.

Now you modify the SKBGameScene.h file so you can reference and use the new class:

```
#import "SKBPlayer.h"
#import "SKBLedge.h"

@interface SKBGameScene : SKScene <SKPhysicsContactDelegate>
```

Append the initWithSize method in the SKBGameScene.m file to create the ledge as the scene is initially created:

```
[self addChild:brickBase];

// ledge
SKBLedge *sceneLedge = [[SKBLedge alloc] init];
[sceneLedge createNewSetOfLedgeNodes:self startingPoint:CGPointMake(kLedgeSideBufferSpacing, 80)
                                              withHowManyBlocks:23 startingIndex:0];
```

This creates a new SKBLedge object, calls its createNewSetOfLedgeNodes method with its left edge almost to the edge of the screen (80 points up from the bottom and composed of 23 blocks), and it begins its index at zero.

Build and run it to see the new ledge (see Figure 4-4).

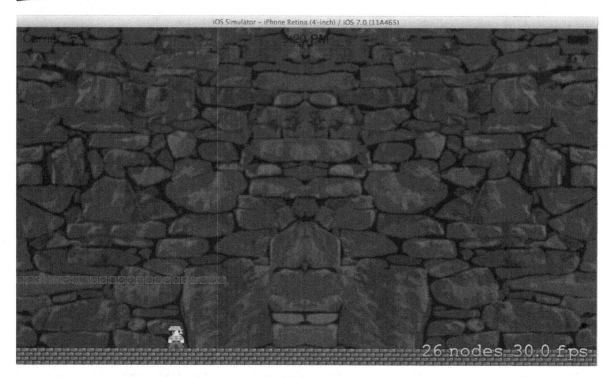

Figure 4-4. Ledge of 23 blocks

The sprite will not be able to interact with it yet; it just acts as part of the background for now. Glancing at the console, you can see the unique names being generated for each node block as they're created and added to the scene.

Now you'll add a new bitmask value to the SKBAppDelegate.h file so that you can handle contact events with the ledge blocks:

```
static const uint32_t kBaseCategory =          0x1 << 1;
static const uint32_t kWallCategory =          0x1 << 2;
static const uint32_t kLedgeCategory =         0x1 << 3;
```

Each ledge node block needs a physics body, so add that inside the for() loop of the createNewSetOfLedgeNodes method in the SKBLedge.m file:

```
where.x += kLedgeBrickSpacing;

// physicsBody
theNode.physicsBody = [SKPhysicsBody bodyWithRectangleOfSize:theNode.size];
theNode.physicsBody.categoryBitMask = kLedgeCategory;

[theLedge addChild:theNode];
```

Build and run it to see what you've done by adding the physics body to each node. Kind of humorous, huh? Certainly not what you were expecting, but do you understand why it is acting this way? Each block is reacting to the same gravity and physics properties as the player.

Let's change things a bit by changing the `affectedByGravity` property of the ledge node's physics body, which defaults to YES:

```
theNode.physicsBody.categoryBitMask = kLedgeCategory;
theNode.physicsBody.affectedByGravity = NO;

[theLedge addChild:theNode];
```

Build and run it again. This time the blocks won't fall to the ground. Now have the player jump up onto them; you'll see some drastic results!

Blocks go flying everywhere, with each one reacting to external forces that are being applied when the other objects contact and collide with them. Like balls on a pool table being struck by a cue stick, the blocks immediately react to forces, all handled by the Physics engine. As for the player sprite, it also reacts to all of the forces being applied, and it has probably ended up on its side with undesired results, since none of the animations or edge handlers was prepared for all of these possibilities.

Now you'll add joints between the node blocks to see what they can do for you.

```
- (void)createNewSetOfLedgeNodes:(SKScene *)whichScene startingPoint:(CGPoint)leftSide
withHowManyBlocks:(int)blockCount startingIndex:(int)indexStart
{
    // ledge nodes
    SKTexture *ledgeBrickTexture = [SKTexture textureWithImageNamed:kLedgeBrickFileName];

    NSMutableArray *nodeArray = [[NSMutableArray alloc] initWithCapacity:blockCount-1];
    CGPoint where = leftSide;

    // nodes, equally spaced
    for (int index=0; index < blockCount; index++) {
        SKSpriteNode *theNode = [SKSpriteNode spriteNodeWithTexture:ledgeBrickTexture];
        theNode.name = [NSString stringWithFormat:@"ledgeBrick%d", indexStart+index];
        NSLog(@"%@ created", theNode.name);
        theNode.position = where;
        theNode.anchorPoint = CGPointMake(0.5,0.5);
        where.x += kLedgeBrickSpacing;

        // physicsBody
        theNode.physicsBody = [SKPhysicsBody bodyWithRectangleOfSize:theNode.size];
        theNode.physicsBody.categoryBitMask = kLedgeCategory;
        theNode.physicsBody.affectedByGravity = NO;

        [nodeArray insertObject:theNode atIndex:index];
        [whichScene addChild:theNode];
    }

    // joints between nodes
    for (int index=0; index <= (blockCount-2); index++) {
        SKSpriteNode *nodeA = [nodeArray objectAtIndex:index];
        SKSpriteNode *nodeB = [nodeArray objectAtIndex:index+1];
        SKPhysicsJointPin *theJoint = [SKPhysicsJointPin jointWithBodyA:nodeA.physicsBody
```

```
            bodyB:nodeB.physicsBody anchor:CGPointMake(nodeB.position.x, nodeB.position.y)];
    [whichScene.physicsWorld addJoint:theJoint];
  }
}
```

You add an array that holds onto all of the nodes as you create them, inserting them during each run through the loop, so that you can use them later for joint creation. Once the nodes are created and added to the scene, you can start to create the joints. Start with the first joint between blocks 1 and 2. The first node block becomes nodeA and the second node becomes nodeB. You create the SKPhysicsJointPin object and add it to the scene.

Build and run it as before. Have the player jump onto or into the ledge blocks to see the changes. Now the ledge is treated as a set of blocks connected by rubber bands. This should start to give you an idea of at least one of the many applications of joints.

As cool as this behavior is, it is not quite what you want as the finished result. You want the ledge to react to physics, yet pretty much stay in place and not go floating around the screen. To fix this, you'll need to lock the two end pieces in place.

Modify the createNewSetOfLedgeNodes method to match this code:

```
theNode.physicsBody.categoryBitMask = kLedgeCategory;
theNode.physicsBody.affectedByGravity = NO;

// designate left & right edge pieces
if (index == 0) {
    // first node stays solidly in place; anchor point
    theNode.physicsBody.dynamic = NO;
} else if (index == (blockCount-1)) {
    // last node stays solidly in place; anchor point
    theNode.physicsBody.dynamic = NO;
} else {
    // all the other nodes inbetween the edge pieces
    theNode.physicsBody.dynamic = YES;
}

[nodeArray insertObject:theNode atIndex:index];
[whichScene addChild:theNode];
```

By setting the physicsBody property to NO (it is set to YES by default), the physics body ignores all of the forces and impulses applied to it.

Build and run it. As before, have the sprite jump into or onto the ledge blocks. This time the end points are locked in place so that the ledge doesn't move from its location, yet all of the blocks in between react to the physics forces as before. As a side effect of this change, the character can now run along the tops of the ledge blocks. But an obvious problem is that the player easily tips over, which tends to mess things up. You can fix this with one line of code.

Add this line of code to the SKBPlayer.m method initNewPlayer:

```
player.physicsBody.restitution = 0.2;
player.physicsBody.allowsRotation = NO;
```

```
// add the sprite to the scene
[whichScene addChild:player];
```

Build and run it. You'll see that you are indeed making good progress.

To make the ledge block's joint movement seem sluggish and yet still act like a rope bridge, you'll add some more dynamic properties to the SKBLedge.m file:

```
theNode.physicsBody.categoryBitMask = kLedgeCategory;
theNode.physicsBody.affectedByGravity = NO;
theNode.physicsBody.linearDamping = 1.0;
theNode.physicsBody.angularDamping = 1.0;
.
.
.
SKPhysicsJointPin *theJoint = [SKPhysicsJointPin jointWithBodyA:nodeA.physicsBody
        bodyB:nodeB.physicsBody anchor:CGPointMake(nodeB.position.x, nodeB.position.y)];
theJoint.frictionTorque = 1.0;
theJoint.shouldEnableLimits = YES;
theJoint.lowerAngleLimit = 0.0000;
theJoint.upperAngleLimit = 0.0000;
[whichScene.physicsWorld addJoint:theJoint];
```

Build and run it to see these changes in action. Kind of like a sluggish rope bridge, right? Sweet!

Before adding another ledge, modify the existing ledge-generating code slightly in the SKBGameScene.m method initWithSize:

```
// Ledges
SKBLedge *sceneLedge = [[SKBLedge alloc] init];
int ledgeIndex = 0;

// ledge, bottom left
int howMany = 0;
if (CGRectGetMaxX(self.frame) < 500)
    howMany = 18;
else
    howMany = 23;
[sceneLedge createNewSetOfLedgeNodes:self startingPoint:CGPointMake(kLedgeSideBufferSpacing,
                brickBase.position.y+80) withHowManyBlocks:howMany startingIndex:ledgeIndex];
ledgeIndex = ledgeIndex + howMany;
```

You add an integer variable to track the ledge index value as more ledge blocks are added. You add a screen size check so that you can condense the ledge sizes for smaller screens.

Now you can add more ledges a bit easier. Insert these lines right after the previously modified lines in the initWithSize method:

```
// ledge, bottom right
if (CGRectGetMaxX(self.frame) < 500)
    howMany = 18;
else
```

```
    howMany = 23;
[sceneLedge createNewSetOfLedgeNodes:self startingPoint:CGPointMake(CGRectGetMaxX(self.frame)-
        kLedgeSideBufferSpacing-((howMany-1)*kLedgeBrickSpacing), brickBase.position.y+80)
        withHowManyBlocks:howMany startingIndex:ledgeIndex];
ledgeIndex = ledgeIndex + howMany;
```

The only difficult thing here is determining the left side of the new ledge. Using the kLedgeBrickSpacing and howMany values, you can determine the total width of the new ledge and then subtract it from the far-right edge of the screen frame. The rest of the code is the same as before.

Build and run it to see the two ledges (see Figure 4-5).

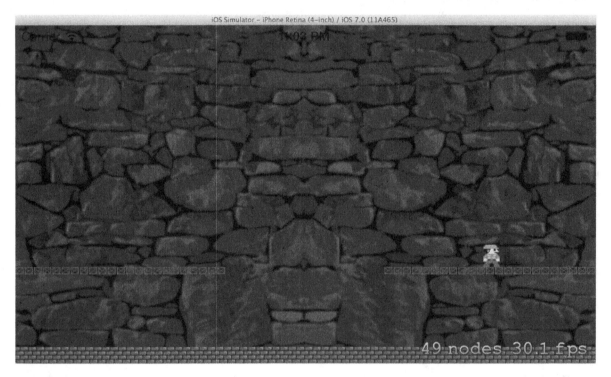

Figure 4-5. Two ledges

Now you'll add the rest of the game ledges—seven in all (see Figure 4-6). Insert these below the others:

```
// ledge, middle left
        if (CGRectGetMaxX(self.frame) < 500)
            howMany = 6;
        else
            howMany = 8;
        [sceneLedge createNewSetOfLedgeNodes:self startingPoint:CGPointMake(CGRectGetMinX
                (self.frame)+kLedgeSideBufferSpacing, brickBase.position.y+142)
                withHowManyBlocks:howMany startingIndex:ledgeIndex];
        ledgeIndex = ledgeIndex + howMany;
```

```
// ledge, middle middle
if (CGRectGetMaxX(self.frame) < 500)
    howMany = 31;
else
    howMany = 36;
[sceneLedge createNewSetOfLedgeNodes:self startingPoint:CGPointMake(CGRectGetMidX
        (self.frame)-((howMany * kLedgeBrickSpacing) / 2), brickBase.position.y+152)
        withHowManyBlocks:howMany startingIndex:ledgeIndex];
ledgeIndex = ledgeIndex + howMany;

// ledge, middle right
if (CGRectGetMaxX(self.frame) < 500)
    howMany = 6;
else
    howMany = 9;
[sceneLedge createNewSetOfLedgeNodes:self startingPoint:CGPointMake(CGRectGetMaxX
        (self.frame)-kLedgeSideBufferSpacing-((howMany-1)*kLedgeBrickSpacing),
        brickBase.position.y+142) withHowManyBlocks:howMany startingIndex:ledgeIndex];
ledgeIndex = ledgeIndex + howMany;

// ledge, top left
if (CGRectGetMaxX(self.frame) < 500)
    howMany = 23;
else
    howMany = 28;
[sceneLedge createNewSetOfLedgeNodes:self startingPoint:CGPointMake(CGRectGetMinX
        (self.frame)+kLedgeSideBufferSpacing, brickBase.position.y+224)
        withHowManyBlocks:howMany startingIndex:ledgeIndex];
ledgeIndex = ledgeIndex + howMany;

// ledge, top right
if (CGRectGetMaxX(self.frame) < 500)
    howMany = 23;
else
    howMany = 28;
[sceneLedge createNewSetOfLedgeNodes:self startingPoint:CGPointMake(CGRectGetMaxX
        (self.frame)-kLedgeSideBufferSpacing-((howMany-1)*kLedgeBrickSpacing),
        brickBase.position.y+224) withHowManyBlocks:howMany startingIndex:ledgeIndex];
ledgeIndex = ledgeIndex + howMany;
```

Build and run it (see Figure 4-6). Very nice. Lots of space in which the game's characters can run around. You do have one little problem, and that is the top edge. Hitting it causes an unexpected teleport to one side or the other.

Figure 4-6. Seven ledges

You can make some minor tweaks to make things a little bit more like the finished product and see if you can fix the top edge issue as well.

First off, change the sprite's jumping height in the SKBPlayer.h file:

```
#define kPlayerRunningIncrement      100
#define kPlayerSkiddingIncrement      20
#define kPlayerJumpingIncrement        8
```

Next, make its time spent jumping a bit shorter in the jump method inside the SKBPlayer.m file:

```
/ applicable animation
SKAction *jumpAnimation = [SKAction animateWithTextures:playerJumpTextures timePerFrame:0.2];
    SKAction *jumpAwhile = [SKAction repeatAction:jumpAnimation count:4.0];
```

You can tweak these two values until you end up as close as possible to a finished result.

Finally, adjust the edge of the scene that is created in the `initWithSize` of the `SKBGameScene.m` file:

```
self.backgroundColor = [SKColor blackColor];

CGRect edgeRect = CGRectMake(0.0, 0.0, 568.0, 420.0);

self.physicsBody = [SKPhysicsBody bodyWithEdgeLoopFromRect:edgeRect];
self.physicsBody.categoryBitMask = kWallCategory;
```

This makes a rectangle that is 100 points taller than the game screen and still has an origin at the bottom-left of the screen. This in effect raises the ceiling by 100 points. This will make it fairly impossible for the player to bang his head on this raised ceiling.

Summary

You started this chapter with a quick dive right into the `PhysicsWorld` scene and `PhysicsBody` node. You got to see the power and versatility of these two elements first hand, without much work. You made some adjustments to some of the properties of these objects, including density, linear damping, and restitution, and then saw their effects. You began exploring how to set up and handle contact events so that you could implement screen wrapping. Then you triggered an impulse on the player's sprite that caused it to jump on command and updated its animations to match its actions. Finally, you added some ledges to run along by making a set of brick blocks interconnected by joints that acted like rubber bands when they were added to the Physics engine in the scene.

You got a lot accomplished as a result. Your sprite has a large world and several obstacles to run around and with which it can interact. But it is a bit lonely and longs for more to do. The next chapter should fulfill the sprite's desires nicely by teaching you how to add more sprites to the game screen!

Chapter 5

More Animated Sprites: "Enemies" and "Bonuses"

The Opposition

So far, this game is a solo endeavor of running and jumping endlessly without any apparent objective. In the words of my little cousin, "It's lame!" That's just a wee bit pessimistic, but it is a fairly accurate assessment.

Well, it's time to change all that. In this chapter, you'll generate some bad guys to liven things up a bit.

Before doing so, you need to move some code around to increase readability and organization. You'll pull the ledge and brick base creation out of the initWithSize method and into a separate method called createSceneContents, which is located in the SKBGameScene.m file and inserted immediately below initWithSize:

```
    [self addChild:backdrop];

    [self createSceneContents];
  }
  return self;
}

#pragma mark Scene creation
```

```objc
- (void)createSceneContents
{
    // brick base
    SKSpriteNode *brickBase = [SKSpriteNode
                                spriteNodeWithImageNamed:@"Base_600"];
    brickBase.name = @"brickBaseNode";
    brickBase.position = CGPointMake(CGRectGetMidX(self.frame),
                            brickBase.size.height/2);
    brickBase.physicsBody = [SKPhysicsBody
                            bodyWithRectangleOfSize:brickBase.size];
    brickBase.physicsBody.categoryBitMask = kBaseCategory;
    brickBase.physicsBody.dynamic = NO;

    [self addChild:brickBase];

    // Ledges
    SKBLedge *sceneLedge = [[SKBLedge alloc] init];
    int ledgeIndex = 0;

    // ledge, bottom left
    int howMany = 0;
    if (CGRectGetMaxX(self.frame) < 500)
        howMany = 18;
    else
        howMany = 23;
    [sceneLedge createNewSetOfLedgeNodes:self
                startingPoint:CGPointMake(kLedgeSideBufferSpacing,
                brickBase.position.y+80) withHowManyBlocks:howMany
                startingIndex:ledgeIndex];
    ledgeIndex = ledgeIndex + howMany;

    // ledge, bottom right
    .
    .
    .

    // ledge, top right
    if (CGRectGetMaxX(self.frame) < 500)
        howMany = 23;
    else
        howMany = 28;
    [sceneLedge createNewSetOfLedgeNodes:self
                startingPoint:CGPointMake(CGRectGetMaxX(self.frame)-
                kLedgeSideBufferSpacing-((howMany-1)*kLedgeBrickSpacing),
                brickBase.position.y+224) withHowManyBlocks:howMany
                startingIndex:ledgeIndex];
    ledgeIndex = ledgeIndex + howMany;
}
```

Optimizing Texture Generation

The sprite textures are currently being created when you spawn the player onto the scene. Move this into the scene's `initWithSize` method and pass the textures onto sprites as they are spawned. As you begin to add more sprites and characters into the game, the sprite textures will contain those for all of these sprites, so you might as well initialize the sprite textures at launch in the game scene, instead of when the player sprite is spawned.

Add an instance variable for the finished sprites in the `SKBGameScene.h` file:

```
@interface SKBGameScene : SKScene <SKPhysicsContactDelegate>

@property (strong, nonatomic) SKBPlayer *playerSprite;
@property (strong, nonatomic) SKBSpriteTextures *spriteTextures;
```

In the `SKBGameScene.m` file, modify `initWithSize` to include this change:

```
self.physicsWorld.contactDelegate = self;

// initialize and create our sprite textures
_spriteTextures = [[SKBSpriteTextures alloc] init];
[_spriteTextures createAnimationTextures];

NSString *fileName = @"";
```

Then remove that same block of code from the `initNewPlayer` method of the `SKBPlayer.m` file, along with the assignment into the local instance variable:

```
// initialize and create our sprite textures
SKBSpriteTextures *playerTextures = [[SKBSpriteTextures alloc] init];
[playerTextures createAnimationTextures];

// initial frame
SKTexture *f1 = [SKTexture textureWithImageNamed: kPlayerStillRightFileName];

// our player character sprite & starting position in the scene
SKBPlayer *player = [SKBPlayer spriteNodeWithTexture:f1];
player.name = @"player1";
player.position = location;
player.spriteTextures = playerTextures;
player.playerStatus = SBPlayerFacingRight;
```

Since you will soon need to reference the game scene in the `Player` class, you should add the necessary #import method to the `SKBPlayer.m` file:

```
#import "SKBPlayer.h"
#import "SKBGameScene.h"

@implementation SKBPlayer
```

Now you add a method to the SKBPlayer class to take care of adding the existing sprite textures to newly spawned player sprites. First you add a public method declaration in the SKBPlayer.h file:

```
+ (SKBPlayer *)initNewPlayer:(SKScene *)whichScene
                         startingPoint:(CGPoint)location;
- (void)spawnedInScene:(SKScene *)whichScene;

- (void)wrapPlayer:(CGPoint)where;
```

Then you insert the method into the SKBPlayer.m file, immediately below the initNewPlayer method:

```
// add the sprite to the scene
    [whichScene addChild:player];
    return player;
}

- (void)spawnedInScene:(SKScene *)whichScene
{
    SKBGameScene *theScene = (SKBGameScene *)whichScene;
    _spriteTextures = theScene.spriteTextures;
}
```

To finish this change to the player sprite, modify the touchesBegan method in the SKBGameScene.m file to call this new method at the applicable time:

```
if (!_playerSprite) {
        _playerSprite = [SKBPlayer initNewPlayer:self startingPoint:location];
        [_playerSprite spawnedInScene:self];
} else if (location.y >= (self.frame.size.height / 2 )) {
```

As far as the user is concerned, nothing has changed; but under the hood, you now have a foundation in place to make it much easier to add more sprites. Your code is also easier to read and understand.

Enemy "Ratz" Class

The new enemy sprite, called a "ratz," has its own set of animation frames. You'll add those to the project and get them moved into the Sprites folder. You also might want to add a new Group (folder) inside the Sprites folder specifically for the new character. Add the 10 images from the Images folder all prefixed with Ratz_.

Now you can use them in the texture-generation method in the SKBSpriteTexture class. First, you need some header additions (SKBSpriteTextures.h):

```
#define kPlayerStillLeftFileName          @"Player_Left_Still.png"

#define kRatzRunRight1FileName            @"Ratz_Right1.png"
#define kRatzRunRight2FileName            @"Ratz_Right2.png"
#define kRatzRunRight3FileName            @"Ratz_Right3.png"
#define kRatzRunRight4FileName            @"Ratz_Right4.png"
#define kRatzRunRight5FileName            @"Ratz_Right5.png"
```

```
#define kRatzRunLeft1FileName                    @"Ratz_Left1.png"
#define kRatzRunLeft2FileName                    @"Ratz_Left2.png"
#define kRatzRunLeft3FileName                    @"Ratz_Left3.png"
#define kRatzRunLeft4FileName                    @"Ratz_Left4.png"
#define kRatzRunLeft5FileName                    @"Ratz_Left5.png"

@interface SKBSpriteTextures : NSObject

@property (nonatomic, strong) NSArray *playerRunRightTextures,
                                       *playerJumpRightTextures;
@property (nonatomic, strong) NSArray *playerSkiddingRightTextures,
                                       *playerStillFacingRightTextures;

@property (nonatomic, strong) NSArray *playerRunLeftTextures,
                                       *playerJumpLeftTextures;
@property (nonatomic, strong) NSArray *playerSkiddingLeftTextures,
                                       *playerStillFacingLeftTextures;

@property (nonatomic, strong) NSArray *ratzRunLeftTextures,
                                       *ratzRunRightTextures;

- (void)createAnimationTextures;
```

Then you change the createAnimationTextures method in the SKBSpriteTextures.m file:

```
//   left, still
f1 = [SKTexture textureWithImageNamed:kPlayerStillLeftFileName];
_playerStillFacingLeftTextures = @[f1];

// Ratz

//  right, running
f1 = [SKTexture textureWithImageNamed:kRatzRunRight1FileName];
f2 = [SKTexture textureWithImageNamed:kRatzRunRight2FileName];
f3 = [SKTexture textureWithImageNamed:kRatzRunRight3FileName];
f4 = [SKTexture textureWithImageNamed:kRatzRunRight4FileName];
SKTexture *f5 = [SKTexture textureWithImageNamed:kRatzRunRight5FileName];
_ratzRunRightTextures = @[f1,f2,f3,f4,f5];

//  left, running
f1 = [SKTexture textureWithImageNamed:kRatzRunLeft1FileName];
f2 = [SKTexture textureWithImageNamed:kRatzRunLeft2FileName];
f3 = [SKTexture textureWithImageNamed:kRatzRunLeft3FileName];
f4 = [SKTexture textureWithImageNamed:kRatzRunLeft4FileName];
f5 = [SKTexture textureWithImageNamed:kRatzRunLeft5FileName];
_ratzRunLeftTextures = @[f1,f2,f3,f4,f5];
```

You also need another bitmask category in the SKBAppDelegate.h file:

```
static const uint32_t kLedgeCategory =          0x1 << 3;
static const uint32_t kRatzCategory =           0x1 << 4;
```

With that done, you'll create a custom subclass of SKSpriteNode for the first bad guy type, just like you did for the main player sprite. Create a new class named SKBRatz as a subclass of SKSpriteNode. Modify the SKBRatz.h file to match the following:

```
#import <SpriteKit/SpriteKit.h>
#import "SKBAppDelegate.h"
#import "SKBSpriteTextures.h"

#define kRatzRunningIncrement        40

typedef enum : int {
    SBRatzRunningLeft = 0,
    SBRatzRunningRight
} SBRatzStatus;

@interface SKBRatz : SKSpriteNode

@property int ratzStatus;
@property (nonatomic, strong) SKBSpriteTextures *spriteTextures;

+ (SKBRatz *)initNewRatz:(SKScene *)whichScene startingPoint:(CGPoint)location
                                                ratzIndex:(int)index;
- (void)spawnedInScene:(SKScene *)whichScene;
- (void)wrapRatz:(CGPoint)where;

- (void)runRight;
- (void)runLeft;

@end
```

Now you'll add the initial code for the Ratz sprite all at once, including the methods for initializing, wrapping, and running in both directions:

```
#import "SKBRatz.h"
#import "SKBGameScene.h"

@implementation SKBRatz

#pragma mark Initialization

+ (SKBRatz *)initNewRatz:(SKScene *)whichScene startingPoint:(CGPoint)location ratzIndex:(int)index
{
    SKTexture *ratzTexture = [SKTexture
                        textureWithImageNamed:kRatzRunRight1FileName];
    SKBRatz *ratz = [SKBRatz spriteNodeWithTexture:ratzTexture];
    ratz.name = [NSString stringWithFormat:@"ratz%d", index];
```

```
    ratz.position = location;
    ratz.physicsBody = [SKPhysicsBody bodyWithRectangleOfSize:ratz.size];
    ratz.physicsBody.categoryBitMask = kRatzCategory;
    ratz.physicsBody.contactTestBitMask = kWallCategory | kBaseCategory ;
    ratz.physicsBody.density = 1.0;
    ratz.physicsBody.linearDamping = 0.1;
    ratz.physicsBody.restitution = 0.2;
    ratz.physicsBody.allowsRotation = NO;

    [whichScene addChild:ratz];
    return ratz;
}

- (void)spawnedInScene:(SKScene *)whichScene
{
    SKBGameScene *theScene = (SKBGameScene *)whichScene;
    _spriteTextures = theScene.spriteTextures;

    // set initial direction and start moving
    if (self.position.x < CGRectGetMidX(whichScene.frame))
        [self runRight];
    else
        [self runLeft];
}

#pragma mark Screen wrap

- (void)wrapRatz:(CGPoint)where
{

    SKPhysicsBody *storePB = self.physicsBody;
    self.physicsBody = nil;
    self.position = where;
    self.physicsBody = storePB;
}

#pragma mark Movement

- (void)runRight
{
    _ratzStatus = SBRatzRunningRight;

    SKAction *walkAnimation = [SKAction
                animateWithTextures:_spriteTextures.ratzRunRightTextures
                timePerFrame:0.05];
    SKAction *walkForever = [SKAction repeatActionForever:walkAnimation];
    [self runAction:walkForever];

    SKAction *moveRight = [SKAction moveByX:kRatzRunningIncrement y:0
                                                    duration:1];
    SKAction *moveForever = [SKAction repeatActionForever:moveRight];
    [self runAction:moveForever];
}
```

```
- (void)runLeft
{
    _ratzStatus = SBRatzRunningLeft;

    SKAction *walkAnimation = [SKAction
                animateWithTextures:_spriteTextures.ratzRunLeftTextures
                timePerFrame:0.05];
    SKAction *walkForever = [SKAction repeatActionForever:walkAnimation];
    [self runAction:walkForever];

    SKAction *moveLeft = [SKAction moveByX:-kRatzRunningIncrement y:0 duration:1];
    SKAction *moveForever = [SKAction repeatActionForever:moveLeft];
    [self runAction:moveForever];
}

@end
```

You'll probably notice that most of this code is identical to the player sprite with just a few minor changes.

Timing

Now you have to decide where and when to spawn your new enemy sprite. For now, you will have him fall down into the sewer area from the top of the screen and maybe from the left side. Its appearance will coincide with the appearance of the player, which currently happens when the user touches the screen. To introduce the waitForDuration method of an SKAction, you'll add a four-second lag before the enemy sprite spawns and after the player appears.

You need to reference the new class in the game scene, so add the necessary #import to the SKBGameScene.h file:

```
#import "SKBPlayer.h"
#import "SKBRatz.h"

#define kEnemySpawnEdgeBufferX        60
```

Add these five lines of code to the touchesBegan method in the SKBGameScene.m file:

```
if (!_playerSprite) {
    _playerSprite = [SKBPlayer initNewPlayer:self startingPoint:location];
    [_playerSprite spawnedInScene:self];

    SKAction *spawnDelay = [SKAction waitForDuration:4];
    [self runAction:spawnDelay completion:^{
        SKBRatz *newEnemy = [SKBRatz initNewRatz:self
                                       startingPoint:CGPointMake(50, 280)
                                                                    ratzIndex:0];

        [newEnemy spawnedInScene:self];
    }];

} else if (location.y >= (self.frame.size.height / 2 )) {
```

Build and run the program to see the new enemy sprite appears four seconds after the player (see Figure 5-1).

Figure 5-1. Enemy sprite has spawned

Just like other SKActions that you've used previously, waitForDuration is useful for timing events in your game. You combined it with a completion block to trigger specific code to run when the wait timer completed. This is just a temporary way of spawning the bad guy so that you can quickly see the result of all of the code you just modified and added. In the next chapter, you will create a better solution for spawning bad guys.

Wrapping

You may have noticed that one of the next things you need to take into account is enemy sprite screen wrapping. You have the code in place to handle wrapping, but you haven't added the necessary code in the didBeginContact method to trigger it. You'll add that now to the SKBGameScene.m file:

```
            NSLog(@"player contacted right edge");
            [_playerSprite wrapPlayer:CGPointMake(10,
                                    _playerSprite.position.y)];
        }
    }
}

// Ratz / sideWalls
if (((((firstBody.categoryBitMask & kWallCategory) != 0) && ((secondBody.categoryBitMask &
kRatzCategory) != 0))) {
    SKBRatz *theRatz = (SKBRatz *)secondBody.node;
```

```
    if (theRatz.position.x < 100) {
        [theRatz wrapRatz:CGPointMake(self.frame.size.width-11,
                                                    theRatz.position.y)];
    } else {
        [theRatz wrapRatz:CGPointMake(11, theRatz.position.y)];
    }
}
```

Build and run the program to see enemy screen wrapping successfully implemented.

The Update Method

There's a method you can use during each loop through Sprite Kit's rendering cycle, called update. You can use this method to implement game logic or artificial intelligence (A.I.) for enemies. This is a good place to handle the spawning of enemy sprites without tying them up inside a touch or contact event. So you'll move the sprite spawning process there.

You need a couple instance variables, so you'll add those to the SKBGameScene.h file first:

```
@property (strong, nonatomic) SKBPlayer *playerSprite;
@property (strong, nonatomic) SKBSpriteTextures *spriteTextures;

@property int spawnedEnemyCount;
@property BOOL enemyIsSpawningFlag;

@end
```

In the SKBGameScene.m file, remove the old enemy sprite spawning code so that the modified touchesBegan method looks like the following:

```
if (!_playerSprite) {
    _playerSprite = [SKBPlayer initNewPlayer:self startingPoint:location];
    [_playerSprite spawnedInScene:self];
} else if (location.y >= (self.frame.size.height / 2 )) {
    // user touched upper half of the screen (zero = bottom of screen)
    if (status != SBPlayerJumpingLeft && status != SBPlayerJumpingRight && status !=
                SBPlayerJumpingUpFacingLeft && status != SBPlayerJumpingUpFacingRight) {
        [_playerSprite jump];
    }
} else . . .
```

Add some variable initializers at the top of the createSceneContents method:

```
- (void)createSceneContents
{
    // Initialize Enemies & Schedule
    _spawnedEnemyCount = 0;
    _enemyIsSpawningFlag = NO;

    // brick base
    SKSpriteNode *brickBase = [SKSpriteNode spriteNodeWithImageNamed:@"Base_600"];
```

Then you can complete the change by adding spawning code to the provided update method:

```
-(void)update:(CFTimeInterval)currentTime {
    /* Called before each frame is rendered */

    if (!_enemyIsSpawningFlag && _spawnedEnemyCount < 5) {
        _enemyIsSpawningFlag = YES;
        int castIndex = _spawnedEnemyCount;

        int scheduledDelay = 5;
        int startX = 50;
        int startY = 280;

        // begin delay & when completed spawn new enemy
        SKAction *spacing = [SKAction waitForDuration:scheduledDelay];
        [self runAction:spacing completion:^{
            // Create & spawn the new Enemy
            _enemyIsSpawningFlag = NO;
            _spawnedEnemyCount = _spawnedEnemyCount + 1;

            SKBRatz *newEnemy = [SKBRatz initNewRatz:self
                                startingPoint:CGPointMake(startX, startY)

                                ratzIndex:castIndex];
            [newEnemy spawnedInScene:self];
        }];
    }
}
```

Build and run the program to verify that you now get a total of five enemies spawning every five seconds, without regard to the player spawning when the screen is touched. So how did you do that?

```
_spawnedEnemyCount = 0;
_enemyIsSpawningFlag = NO;
```

When the scene is first created, these two variables are set.

```
if (!_enemyIsSpawningFlag && _spawnedEnemyCount < 5) {
```

The first time the update method is called, this if() expression returns true so it runs.

```
_enemyIsSpawningFlag = YES;
int castIndex = _spawnedEnemyCount;
```

You immediately set the enemyIsSpawningFlag to true so that the next update method call won't trigger the if() statement again. You will be using the spawnedEnemyCount to keep track of how many enemies have already been spawned.

```
int scheduledDelay = 5;
int startX = 50;
int startY = 280;
```

These determine the length of time (in seconds) between spawns and set the starting positions.

```
// begin delay & when completed spawn new enemy
        SKAction *spacing = [SKAction waitForDuration:scheduledDelay];
        [self runAction:spacing completion:^{
            // Create & spawn the new Enemy
            _enemyIsSpawningFlag = NO;
            _spawnedEnemyCount = _spawnedEnemyCount + 1;

            SKBRatz *newEnemy = [SKBRatz initNewRatz:self startingPoint:CGPointMake(startX, startY)
ratzIndex:castIndex];
            [newEnemy spawnedInScene:self];
        }];
```

This is similar to what you used in the touchesBegan event before. You create an SKAction that does nothing for the delay period of five seconds, and when completed it triggers an enemy spawn. As this is taking place, you reset the enemyIsSpawningFlag to false so that the next update method call will start the next enemy spawn. You also increment the enemy count by one. That's all fairly straightforward.

Now you can have a little fun! Change the scheduledDelay to 2 and the max enemy limiter to 25:

```
if (!_enemyIsSpawningFlag && _spawnedEnemyCount < 25) {
        _enemyIsSpawningFlag = YES;
        int castIndex = _spawnedEnemyCount;

        int scheduledDelay = 2;
        int startX = 50;
```

Build and run the program. Suddenly you have a lemmings-like result. Notice over time that they run on top of each other, in the same way that the player and ratz sprites all run along the tops of the ledges (see Figure 5-2).

Figure 5-2. Walking all over each other

Collisions

You can add one line of code to change the erratic walking. Insert this line into the
SKBRatz.m initNewRatz method:

```
ratz.physicsBody.categoryBitMask = kRatzCategory;
ratz.physicsBody.contactTestBitMask = kWallCategory | kBaseCategory ;
ratz.physicsBody.collisionBitMask = kBaseCategory | kWallCategory |
                                        kLedgeCategory ;
ratz.physicsBody.density = 1.0;
ratz.physicsBody.linearDamping = 0.1;
```

Now build and run your program. There is no more running on top of each other. As a matter of fact,
you can also see another result of this change—they no longer collide against each other. They can
pass right through each other.

You specified the node types with which you were interested in colliding. Any type not included
suddenly has no effect on collisions of those types.

Add this line to the initNewPlayer method in the SKBPlayer.m file:

```
player.physicsBody.contactTestBitMask = kBaseCategory | kWallCategory;
player.physicsBody.collisionBitMask = kBaseCategory | kWallCategory |
                                        kLedgeCategory ;
player.physicsBody.density = 1.0;
```

Build and run the program now, and try running the player through the waves of enemies. No effect whatsoever.

While on the topic of contacts and collisions, you might as well get rid of the kBaseCategory contact bitmask for both the player and enemy sprites because you do not need to handle contact events for the kBaseCategory types of nodes. You need them for the kWallCategory events only:

```
player.physicsBody.contactTestBitMask = kWallCategory;
.
.
ratz.physicsBody.contactTestBitMask = kWallCategory ;
```

> **Note**   Notice that keeping these bitmasks as clean as possible helped increase the frame rates slightly.

Now you'll change things so that the enemies alternate sides when spawning. First a couple of constants are needed in the SKBGameScene.h file:

```
#import "SKBRatz.h"

#define kEnemySpawnEdgeBufferX        60
#define kEnemySpawnEdgeBufferY        60

@interface SKBGameScene : SKScene <SKPhysicsContactDelegate>
```

Then you change the starting point in the update method of the SKBGameScene.m file:

```
int scheduledDelay = 2;
int leftSideX = CGRectGetMinX(self.frame)+kEnemySpawnEdgeBufferX;
int rightSideX = CGRectGetMaxX(self.frame)-kEnemySpawnEdgeBufferX;
int topSideY = CGRectGetMaxY(self.frame)-kEnemySpawnEdgeBufferY;

int startX = 0;
// alternate sides for every other spawn
if (castIndex % 2 == 0)
    startX = leftSideX;
else
    startX = rightSideX;
int startY = topSideY;

// begin delay & when completed spawn new enemy
SKAction *spacing = [SKAction waitForDuration:scheduledDelay];
```

Build and run the program to see that you now alternate sides when spawning enemy sprites. The direction with which they begin is already handled in the SpawnedInScene method in the SKBRatz class:

```
// set initial direction and start moving
    if (self.position.x < CGRectGetMidX(whichScene.frame))
        [self runRight];
    else
        [self runLeft];
```

You simply used a math function (the modulo operator %) that causes the if() statement to be true when the castIndex value is an even number. When it is true, the enemy sprite spawns on the left side of the screen; when it's not true, it spawns on the right. Easy peasy.

Now that you have enemies running in different directions, you can deal with collisions. At this point, everyone can run through each other as if they were all ghosts. However, you want them to change directions when running into each other. How can you do this? Well, you will use the existing didBeginContact method inside the SKBGameScene.m file to check for collisions and handle them appropriately.

To begin, you add the kRatzCategory to the contactTestBitMask and collisionBitMask properties for the enemy sprites, inside the initNewRatz method of the SKBRatz.m file:

```
ratz.physicsBody.contactTestBitMask = kWallCategory | kRatzCategory ;
ratz.physicsBody.collisionBitMask = kBaseCategory | kWallCategory |
                                    kLedgeCategory | kRatzCategory ;
ratz.physicsBody.density = 1.0;
```

You want some specific code to run when a collision occurs, so add two methods to your enemy class. You need public method declarations in the SKBRatz.h file:

```
- (void)runRight;
- (void)runLeft;
- (void)turnRight;
- (void)turnLeft;

@end
```

Then you add the methods to the SKBRatz.m file, inserting them after the runLeft method:

```
    [self runAction:moveForever];
}

- (void)turnRight
{
    self.ratzStatus = SBRatzRunningRight;
    [self removeAllActions];
    SKAction *moveRight = [SKAction moveByX:5 y:0 duration:0.4];
    [self runAction:moveRight completion:^{[self runRight];}];
}

- (void)turnLeft
{
    self.ratzStatus = SBRatzRunningLeft;
    [self removeAllActions];
    SKAction *moveLeft = [SKAction moveByX:-5 y:0 duration:0.4];
    [self runAction:moveLeft completion:^{[self runLeft];}];
}

@end
```

Then you add an `if()` statement to the `didBeginContact` method in the `SKBGameScene.m` file, inserting it after the "Ratz/Sidewalls" `if()` statement:

```
// Ratz / sideWalls
    if (((((firstBody.categoryBitMask & kWallCategory) != 0) &&
                ((secondBody.categoryBitMask & kRatzCategory) != 0))) {
        SKBRatz *theRatz = (SKBRatz *)secondBody.node;
        if (theRatz.position.x < 100) {
            [theRatz wrapRatz:CGPointMake(self.frame.size.width-11,
                                            theRatz.position.y)];
        } else {
            [theRatz wrapRatz:CGPointMake(11, theRatz.position.y)];
        }
    }

    // Ratz / Ratz
    if (((((firstBody.categoryBitMask & kRatzCategory) != 0) &&
                ((secondBody.categoryBitMask & kRatzCategory) != 0))) {
        SKBRatz *theFirstRatz = (SKBRatz *)firstBody.node;
        SKBRatz *theSecondRatz = (SKBRatz *)secondBody.node;

        NSLog(@"%@ & %@ have collided...", theFirstRatz.name,
                theSecondRatz.name);

        // cause first Ratz to turn and change directions
        if (theFirstRatz.ratzStatus == SBRatzRunningLeft) {
            [theFirstRatz turnRight];
        } else if (theFirstRatz.ratzStatus == SBRatzRunningRight) {
            [theFirstRatz turnLeft];
        }
        // cause second Ratz to turn and change directions
        if (theSecondRatz.ratzStatus == SBRatzRunningLeft) {
            [theSecondRatz turnRight];
        } else if (theSecondRatz.ratzStatus == SBRatzRunningRight) {
            [theSecondRatz turnLeft];
        }
    }
}
```

Build and run the program to see these changes in action. The enemy sprites no longer pass through each other, and when they bump into each other, they pause and turn around (see Figure 5-3).

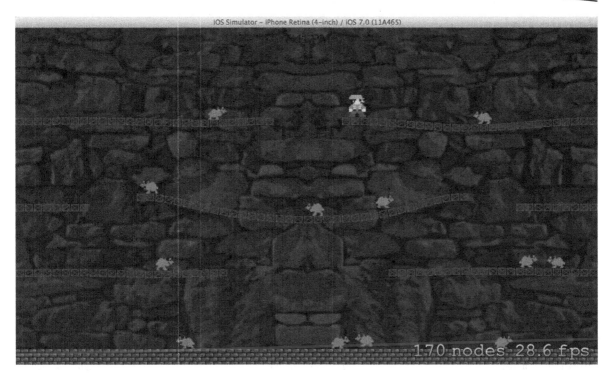

Figure 5-3. *Alternating spawning points and collision bouncing*

```
- (void)turnRight
{
    self.ratzStatus = SBRatzRunningRight;
    [self removeAllActions];
    SKAction *moveRight = [SKAction moveByX:5 y:0 duration:0.4];
    [self runAction:moveRight completion:^{[self runRight];}];
}
```

If you glance at the code of the turnRight and turnLeft methods, you can see that you created an SKAction that moves them slightly apart from each other. When completed, it triggers them to run in the opposite direction.

```
NSLog(@"%@ & %@ have collided...", theFirstRatz.name, theSecondRatz.name);
```

You added an NSLog method call when this is triggered inside the didBeginContact method so that you can see which enemies were affected in the console. Feel free to comment out any of these NSLogs at any time, as they can rapidly become a bit too much data to which you must pay attention. They are used only to help you understand any new code snippets you add and for debugging purposes.

Bonus Coins

Besides being chased around the screen by enemies, our hero needs some goodies to collect; that is, some bonus coins. Humans wandering around up on ground level (above this sewer playing area) are always dropping loose change, and when the money rolls down into the sewer, the player can try to collect it. This will be similar to adding the enemy sprite, and these coins will have a few animation frames. You'll add those animation frames now to the project and move them into the Sprites folder. You also might want to add a new Group (folder) inside the Sprites folder specifically for the new sprite. Add the three images from the Images folder all prefixed with Coin_.

Now you can use them in the texture-generation method in the SKBSpriteTexture class. First you need some header additions (SKBSpriteTextures.h):

```
#define kRatzRunLeft4FileName            @"Ratz_Left4.png"
#define kRatzRunLeft5FileName            @"Ratz_Left5.png"

#define kCoin1FileName                   @"Coin1.png"
#define kCoin2FileName                   @"Coin2.png"
#define kCoin3FileName                   @"Coin3.png"

@interface SKBSpriteTextures : NSObject

@property (nonatomic, strong) NSArray *playerRunRightTextures, *playerJumpRightTextures;
@property (nonatomic, strong) NSArray *playerSkiddingRightTextures, *playerStillFacingRightTextures;

@property (nonatomic, strong) NSArray *playerRunLeftTextures, *playerJumpLeftTextures;
@property (nonatomic, strong) NSArray *playerSkiddingLeftTextures, *playerStillFacingLeftTextures;

@property (nonatomic, strong) NSArray *ratzRunLeftTextures, *ratzRunRightTextures;

@property (nonatomic, strong) NSArray *coinTextures;
```

Then you add to the createAnimationTextures method to the SKBSpriteTextures.m file:

```
    _ratzRunLeftTextures = @[f1,f2,f3,f4,f5];


    // Coins
    f1 = [SKTexture textureWithImageNamed:kCoin1FileName];
    f2 = [SKTexture textureWithImageNamed:kCoin2FileName];
    f3 = [SKTexture textureWithImageNamed:kCoin3FileName];
    _coinTextures = @[f1,f2,f3,f2];
}

@end
```

With the animation textures completed, you can create a new custom subclass of SKSpriteNode for the bonus coin type, just as you did for the main player and enemy sprites. Create a new class named SKBCoin as a subclass of SKSpriteNode. Modify the SKBCoin.h file to match the following:

```
#import <SpriteKit/SpriteKit.h>
#import "SKBAppDelegate.h"
#import "SKBSpriteTextures.h"

#define kCoinRunningIncrement        40

typedef enum : int {
    SBCoinRunningLeft = 0,
    SBCoinRunningRight
} SBCoinStatus;

@interface SKBCoin : SKSpriteNode

@property int coinStatus;
@property (nonatomic, strong) SKBSpriteTextures *spriteTextures;

+ (SKBCoin *)initNewCoin:(SKScene *)whichScene startingPoint:(CGPoint)location
                                                coinIndex:(int)index;
- (void)spawnedInScene:(SKScene *)whichScene;

- (void)wrapCoin:(CGPoint)where;

- (void)runRight;
- (void)runLeft;
- (void)turnRight;
- (void)turnLeft;

@end
```

You also need another bitmask category in the SKBAppDelegate.h file. You'll notice that you inserted this one between the ledge and ratz entries, but the order does *not* matter here as long as they are unique values! (It's just a personal preference, or in layman's terms, an "OCD" issue.)

```
static const uint32_t kLedgeCategory =          0x1 << 3;
static const uint32_t kCoinCategory =           0x1 << 4;
static const uint32_t kRatzCategory =           0x1 << 5;
```

As you did for the Ratz class, add the initial code for the Coin sprite all at once, including methods for initializing, wrapping, and running in both directions:

```
#import "SKBCoin.h"
#import "SKBGameScene.h"

@implementation SKBCoin
```

```objc
#pragma mark Initialization

+ (SKBCoin *)initNewCoin:(SKScene *)whichScene startingPoint:(CGPoint)location
                                                    coinIndex:(int)index
{
    SKTexture *coinTexture = [SKTexture textureWithImageNamed:kCoin1FileName];
    SKBCoin *coin = [SKBCoin spriteNodeWithTexture:coinTexture];
    coin.name = [NSString stringWithFormat:@"coin%d", index];
    coin.position = location;
    coin.physicsBody = [SKPhysicsBody bodyWithRectangleOfSize:coin.size];
    coin.physicsBody.categoryBitMask = kCoinCategory;
    coin.physicsBody.contactTestBitMask = kWallCategory | kCoinCategory ;
    coin.physicsBody.collisionBitMask = kBaseCategory | kWallCategory |
                                        kLedgeCategory | kCoinCategory ;
    coin.physicsBody.density = 1.0;
    coin.physicsBody.linearDamping = 0.1;
    coin.physicsBody.restitution = 0.2;
    coin.physicsBody.allowsRotation = NO;

    [whichScene addChild:coin];
    return coin;
}

- (void)spawnedInScene:(SKScene *)whichScene
{
    SKBGameScene *theScene = (SKBGameScene *)whichScene;
    _spriteTextures = theScene.spriteTextures;

    // set initial direction and start moving
    if (self.position.x < CGRectGetMidX(whichScene.frame))
        [self runRight];
    else
        [self runLeft];
}

#pragma mark Screen wrap

- (void)wrapCoin:(CGPoint)where
{
    SKPhysicsBody *storePB = self.physicsBody;
    self.physicsBody = nil;
    self.position = where;
    self.physicsBody = storePB;
}

#pragma mark Movement

- (void)runRight
{
    _coinStatus = SBCoinRunningRight;

    SKAction *walkAnimation = [SKAction
        animateWithTextures:_spriteTextures.coinTextures timePerFrame:0.05];
```

```objc
    SKAction *walkForever = [SKAction repeatActionForever:walkAnimation];
    [self runAction:walkForever];

    SKAction *moveRight = [SKAction moveByX:kCoinRunningIncrement y:0
        duration:1];
    SKAction *moveForever = [SKAction repeatActionForever:moveRight];
    [self runAction:moveForever];
}

- (void)runLeft
{
    _coinStatus = SBCoinRunningLeft;

    SKAction *walkAnimation = [SKAction
        animateWithTextures:_spriteTextures.coinTextures timePerFrame:0.05];
    SKAction *walkForever = [SKAction repeatActionForever:walkAnimation];
    [self runAction:walkForever];

    SKAction *moveLeft = [SKAction moveByX:-kCoinRunningIncrement y:0
        duration:1];
    SKAction *moveForever = [SKAction repeatActionForever:moveLeft];
    [self runAction:moveForever];
}

- (void)turnRight
{
    self.coinStatus = SBCoinRunningRight;
    [self removeAllActions];
    SKAction *moveRight = [SKAction moveByX:5 y:0 duration:0.4];
    [self runAction:moveRight completion:^{[self runRight];}];
}

- (void)turnLeft
{
    self.coinStatus = SBCoinRunningLeft;
    [self removeAllActions];
    SKAction *moveLeft = [SKAction moveByX:-5 y:0 duration:0.4];
    [self runAction:moveLeft completion:^{[self runLeft];}];
}

@end
```

As you can see by glancing over the Coin class code, there are a lot of similarities to the other sprite classes you created, with minor changes that are specific to the type of sprite.

Now that you have everything in place to spawn bonus coins, you need to figure out when to spawn them. To do this quickly, you can simply make every fifth enemy spawn a coin. Import the new class into the SKBGameScene.h file like this:

```objc
#import "SKBPlayer.h"
#import "SKBCoin.h"
#import "SKBRatz.h"
```

Then modify the update method in the SKBGameScene.m file like this:

```
[self runAction:spacing completion:^{
    // Create & spawn the new Enemy
    _enemyIsSpawningFlag = NO;
    _spawnedEnemyCount = _spawnedEnemyCount + 1;

    if (castIndex % 5 == 0) {
        SKBCoin *newCoin = [SKBCoin initNewCoin:self
                                  startingPoint:CGPointMake(startX, startY)
                                      coinIndex:castIndex];
        [newCoin spawnedInScene:self];
    } else {
        SKBRatz *newEnemy = [SKBRatz initNewRatz:self
                                   startingPoint:CGPointMake(startX, startY)
                                       ratzIndex:castIndex];
        [newEnemy spawnedInScene:self];
    }
}];
```

The coins need to be able to wrap, so modify the didBeginContact method of the SKBGameScene.m file as follows:

```
    } else if (theSecondRatz.ratzStatus == SBRatzRunningRight) {
            [theSecondRatz turnLeft];
    }
}


    // Coin / sideWalls
    if ((((firstBody.categoryBitMask & kWallCategory) != 0) &&
            ((secondBody.categoryBitMask & kCoinCategory) != 0))) {
        SKBCoin *theCoin = (SKBCoin *)secondBody.node;
        if (theCoin.position.x < 100) {
            [theCoin wrapCoin:CGPointMake(self.frame.size.width-6,
                                                theCoin.position.y)];
        } else {
            [theCoin wrapCoin:CGPointMake(6, theCoin.position.y)];
        }
    }
}
```

Build and run the program. The game now spawns a bonus coin every fifth enemy spawn (see Figure 5-4).

Figure 5-4. *Coins spawned every fifth occurance*

As with your enemy sprites, you need to add contact detection to the spawned coins so that when they bump into each other, they will turn around. You already have most of the code in place for this to happen; you just need to insert the contact-check into the didBeginContact method of the SKBGameScene.m file:

```
    } else {
        [theCoin wrapCoin:CGPointMake(6, theCoin.position.y)];
    }
}

// Coin / Coin
if ((((firstBody.categoryBitMask & kCoinCategory) != 0) &&
        ((secondBody.categoryBitMask & kCoinCategory) != 0))) {
    SKBCoin *theFirstCoin = (SKBCoin *)firstBody.node;
    SKBCoin *theSecondCoin = (SKBCoin *)secondBody.node;

    NSLog(@"%@ & %@ have collided...", theFirstCoin.name,
            theSecondCoin.name);

    // cause first Coin to turn and change directions
    if (theFirstCoin.coinStatus == SBCoinRunningLeft) {
        [theFirstCoin turnRight];
    } else if (theFirstCoin.coinStatus == SBCoinRunningRight) {
        [theFirstCoin turnLeft];
    }
```

```
    // cause second Coin to turn and change directions
    if (theSecondCoin.coinStatus == SBCoinRunningLeft) {
        [theSecondCoin turnRight];
    } else if (theSecondCoin.coinStatus == SBCoinRunningRight) {
        [theSecondCoin turnLeft];
    }
}
```

Enemy and Coin Collisions

Now that you have enemies bouncing off each other and coins bouncing off each other, you can change the code so that enemy sprites and coins react to each other as well. Not many changes will be required to implement this effect.

You need to add a single bitmask value to the categoryBitMask and collisionTestBitMask properties of both of the affected classes. First, in the initNewRatz method of the SKBRatz.m file:

```
ratz.physicsBody.categoryBitMask = kRatzCategory;
ratz.physicsBody.contactTestBitMask = kWallCategory | kRatzCategory |
                            kCoinCategory ;
ratz.physicsBody.collisionBitMask = kBaseCategory | kWallCategory |
                            kLedgeCategory | kRatzCategory | kCoinCategory ;
ratz.physicsBody.density = 1.0;
```

Second, in the initNewCoin method of the SKBCoin.m file:

```
coin.physicsBody.categoryBitMask = kCoinCategory;
coin.physicsBody.contactTestBitMask = kWallCategory | kCoinCategory |
                            kRatzCategory ;
coin.physicsBody.collisionBitMask = kBaseCategory | kWallCategory |
                            kLedgeCategory | kCoinCategory | kRatzCategory ;
coin.physicsBody.density = 1.0;
```

Then all that's needed is to add an if() statement to the didBeginContact method in the SKBGameScene.m file:

```
    } else if (theSecondCoin.coinStatus == SBCoinRunningRight) {
        [theSecondCoin turnLeft];
    }
}

// Coin / Ratz
if (((((firstBody.categoryBitMask & kCoinCategory) != 0) &&
            ((secondBody.categoryBitMask & kRatzCategory) != 0)))) {
    SKBCoin *theCoin = (SKBCoin *)firstBody.node;
    SKBRatz *theRatz = (SKBRatz *)secondBody.node;

    NSLog(@"%@ & %@ have collided...", theCoin.name, theRatz.name);
```

```
    // cause Coin to turn and change directions
    if (theCoin.coinStatus == SBCoinRunningLeft) {
        [theCoin turnRight];
    } else if (theCoin.coinStatus == SBCoinRunningRight) {
        [theCoin turnLeft];
    }
    // cause Ratz to turn and change directions
    if (theRatz.ratzStatus == SBRatzRunningLeft) {
        [theRatz turnRight];
    } else if (theRatz.ratzStatus == SBRatzRunningRight) {
        [theRatz turnLeft];
    }
}
```

Build and run the program again. The enemies and coins now interact with each other in the desired fashion.

Summary

This chapter introduced you to the important concept of collision and/or contact events and how to use them. In every game, you will add characters, walls, enemies, bonuses, and various other objects to the screen, and you will always want these various objects to interact with each other. You now should have a better understanding of how you can go about doing that.

You added two types of sprites (ratz and coins) to the screen to create additional elements with which your player can interact, besides the walls and ledges. You still have a ways to go before this game will start to feel complete, but it's quickly coming along.

In the next chapter, you will learn how to change the way you introduce (spawn) the enemy and coin sprites. Instead of creating a static pattern of spawning as you currently do, you will create a "cast of characters" that provides a more dynamic way of spawning sprites into the playing area. So turn the page already!

Chapter 6

Creating a Cast of Characters

Static vs. Dynamic Characters

The solution to enemy spawning thus far has been to use the update method in the SKBGameScene class to create new sprites in a repeating loop until hitting a statically defined maximum. While this works fine for viewing immediate results when adding new enemy classes, it's not an elegant or efficient solution in the long term. You need a way of introducing characters into play in such a way that you can easily change your mind without having to change the code, thereby forcing you to rebuild the project every time you add, remove, or modify your spawning ideas. In other words, you need a dynamic "cast of characters."

You do this by having the spawning data reside in a file that is not compiled during the build process. If this were a desktop game, you might think of this solution as a separate data file that could be loaded at runtime that contains the spawning data. This might also open up the possibility of allowing the end user to create and modify the data in a way similar to a level editor.

You won't do anything quite that complex at this time, but hopefully this gives you a clearer understanding of what you will learn to do in this chapter.

File Format

Since this is an iOS application, you will store this file in the local sandbox. This will allow you to know where the file is and what it's called. The next thing is to determine the format of this external file. One of the easiest ways to save and retrieve data from a file is to use the property list (plist) format, which is just an XML file under the hood. When you use this format, you don't need to write a lot of code to parse the data once you've read it from disk. You just treat it as a NSDictionary, which keeps things nice and simple.

CREATING THE FILE

1. Select New File from the File menu.

2. Make sure that iOS and Resource are selected on the left side, select Property List from the list of icons to choose from, and click the Next button.

3. The standard Save dialog will appear. Give it the title CastOfCharacters.

4. The default location is fine as it is. Verify that the Targets - Sewer Bros is checked and click the Create button.

You will now be viewing the Property List Editor in the center pane. It shows the default entry with the Root key, the Dictionary type, and a value of 0 items (see Figure 6-1).

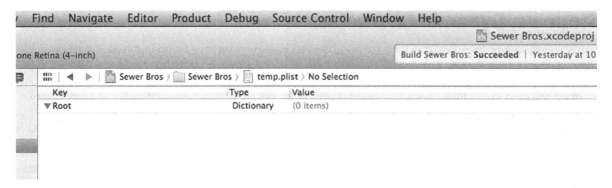

Figure 6-1. Property List Editor

Entering values in this editor can be a little bit confusing at first, but it starts to reveal its underlying logic as you use it more and more, so just be a little patient with it. What you get when adding a new element is based in part on the status of the disclosure triangle. (In the example in Figure 6-1, it is the arrow to the immediate left of the Root key, which in this case is pointing down.) To add an element, you have to move your mouse so that it points anywhere along the line in which you want to add an element (see Figure 6-2).

Figure 6-2. Hovering your mouse over the Root line reveals the + button

When your mouse is hovering over a line, the + and – buttons (the minus button appears only if the element can be deleted) appear to the right side of the Key column (see Figure 6-3).

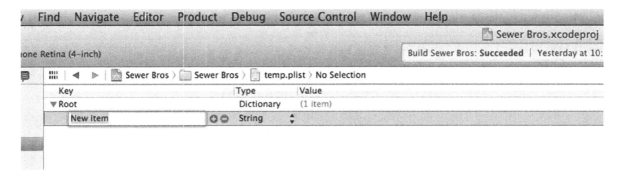

Figure 6-3. New element inside the Root dictionary

Click the + button to add an element, as shown in Figure 6-3. Change the name from New Item to Level. Then change the type from String to Dictionary and click on the disclosure arrow so that it opens the dictionary (arrow pointing down, as shown in Figure 6-4).

Figure 6-4. Editing a new element

While hovering your mouse on the Level element line, click twice on the + button to create two new elements inside the Level dictionary (see Figure 6-5).

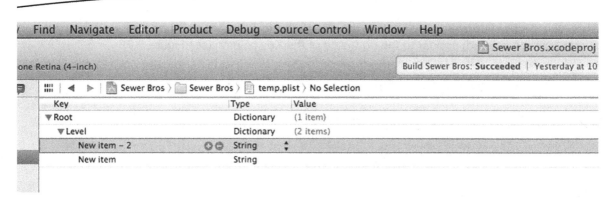

Figure 6-5. Two new elements in the Level element

Change the name (double-click on it) of the first new element from New Item - 2 to One and change the type from String to Array. Click on the disclosure arrow so that it opens the array (see Figure 6-6). Likewise, change the name of the second new element from New Item to Two and change the type from String to Array. Click on the disclosure arrow so that it opens the array (see Figure 6-6).

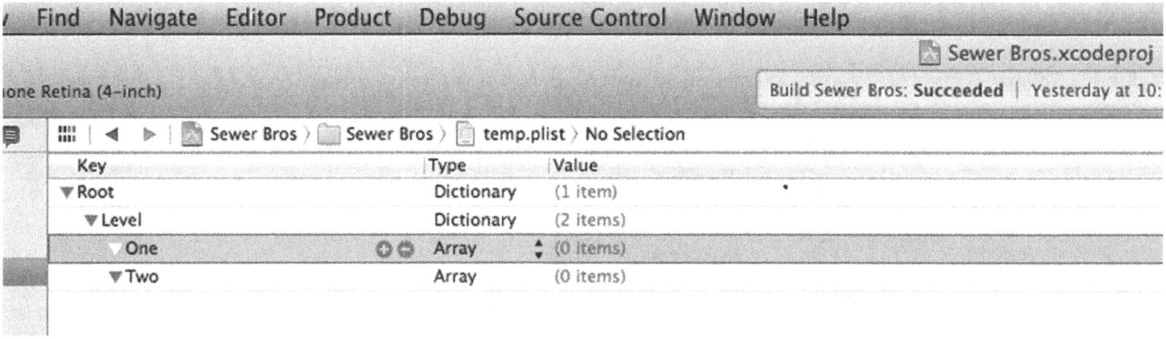

Figure 6-6. Two new array elements in the Level dictionary

While hovering your mouse on the new One Array line, click six times on the + button to create six new elements inside the One Array (see Figure 6-7). Then, while hovering your mouse on the new Two Array line, click once on the + button to create one new element inside the Two Array (see Figure 6-7).

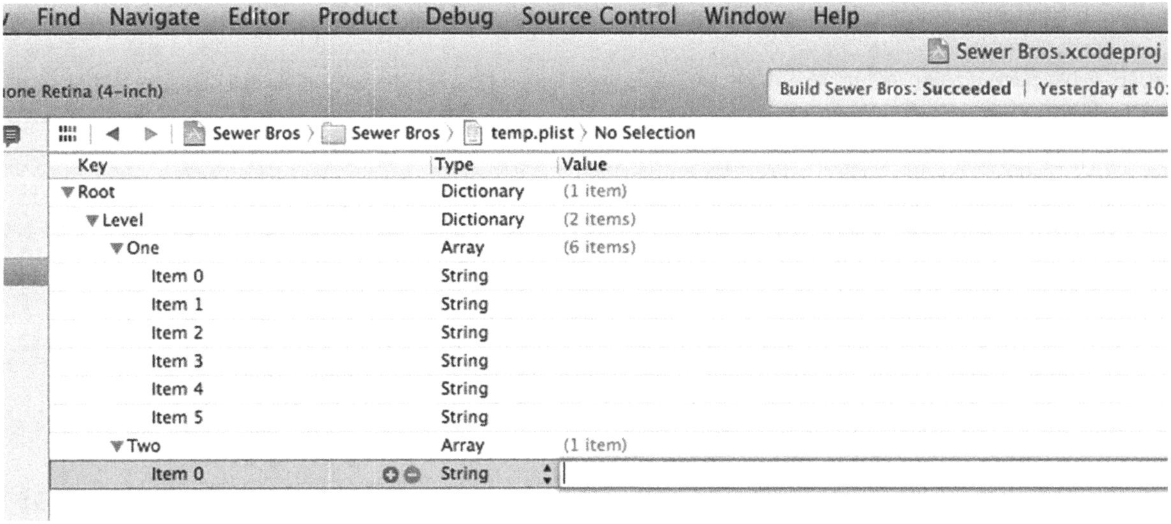

Figure 6-7. Seven new elements: six in level one and one in level two

Change all seven new elements from String to Dictionary, and on each one, click the disclosure triangle (pointing down) to open them all (see Figure 6-8).

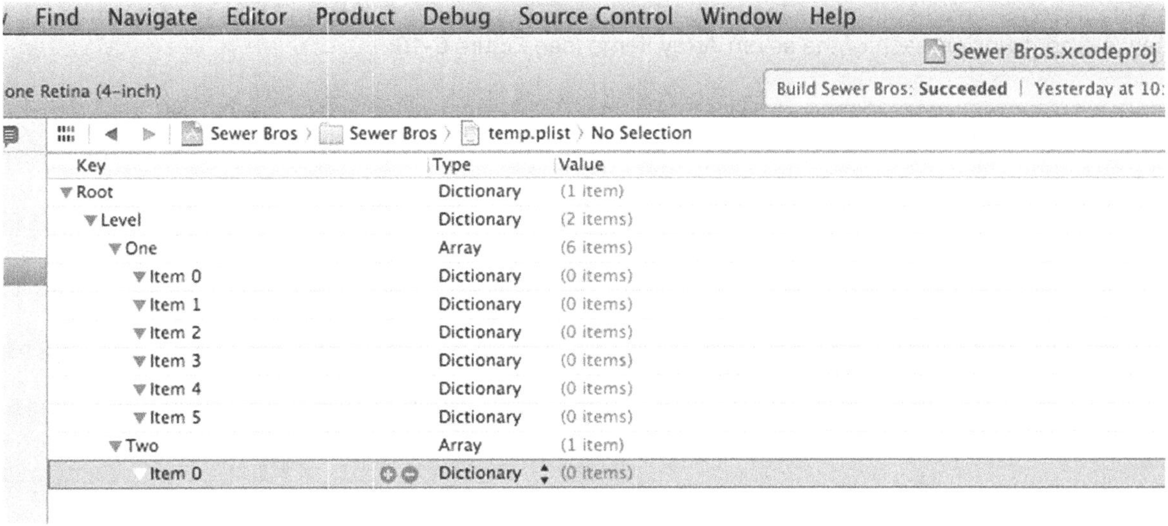

Figure 6-8. Seven new elements, all changed to the Dictionary type

While hovering your mouse on the new Item 0 Dictionary line (immediately below the One key), click three times on the + button to create three new elements inside the Item 0 Dictionary (see Figure 6-9).

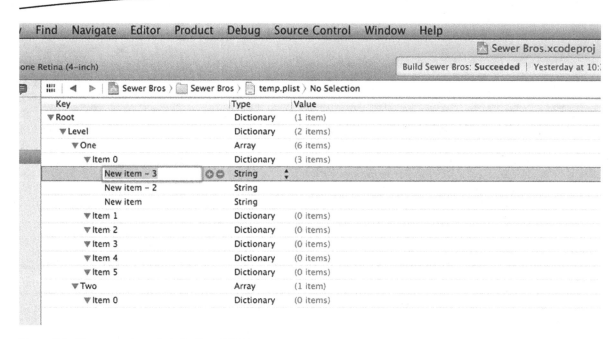

Figure 6-9. Three new elements in the Item 0 dictionary

While hovering your mouse on the new Item 1 Dictionary line, click three times on the + button to create three new elements inside the Item 1 Dictionary. Repeat this five more times to create three new elements inside each of the seven Array items (see Figure 6-10).

Figure 6-10. Three new elements inside each item

Change all 21 new elements from String to Number. For each of the three new number elements, change the key strings from New Item – 3 to Type, New Item – 2 to Delay, and New Item to StartXindex (see Figure 6-11).

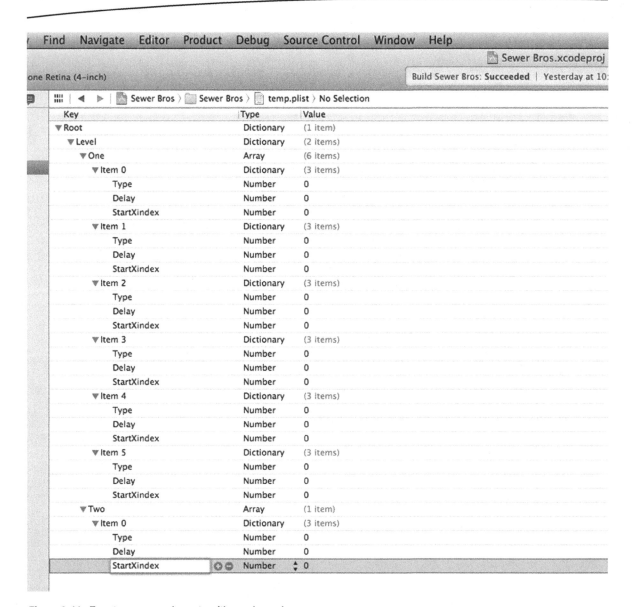

Figure 6-11. *Twenty-one new elements with new key values*

Now for the Number values. In Level One, Item 0, change the three Number values to 1, 3, and 0 (see Figure 6-12).

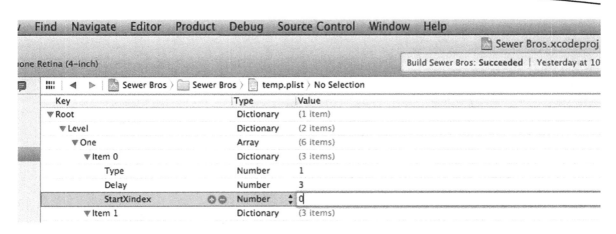

Figure 6-12. Level One Item 0 values

In Level One, Item 1, change the three Number values to 1, 3, and 1.

In Level One, Item 2, change the three Number values to 0, 3, and 0.

In Level One, Item 3, change the three Number values to 1, 3, and 1.

In Level One, Item 4, change the three Number values to 1, 3, and 0.

In Level One, Item 5, change the three Number values to 0, 3, and 1.

In Level One, Item 0, change the three Number values to 1, 3, and 0.

The finished result is shown in Figure 6-13.

| Find | Navigate | Editor | Product | Debug | Source Control | Window | Help |

Sewer Bros.xcodeproj

one Retina (4-inch)   Build Sewer Bros: **Succeeded** | Yesterda

Sewer Bros ⟩ Sewer Bros ⟩ CastOfCharacters.plist ⟩ No Selection

Key	Type	Value
▼ Root	Dictionary	(1 item)
▼ Level	Dictionary	(2 items)
▼ One	Array	(6 items)
▼ Item 0	Dictionary	(3 items)
Type	Number	1
Delay	Number	3
StartXindex	Number	0
▼ Item 1	Dictionary	(3 items)
Type	Number	1
Delay	Number	3
StartXindex	Number	1
▼ Item 2	Dictionary	(3 items)
Type	Number	0
Delay	Number	3
StartXindex	Number	0
▼ Item 3	Dictionary	(3 items)
Type	Number	1
Delay	Number	3
StartXindex	Number	1
▼ Item 4	Dictionary	(3 items)
Type	Number	1
Delay	Number	3
StartXindex	Number	0
▼ Item 5	Dictionary	(3 items)
Type	Number	0
Delay	Number	3
StartXindex	Number	1
▼ Two	Array	(1 item)
▼ Item 0	Dictionary	(3 items)
Type	Number	1
Delay	Number	3
StartXindex	Number	0

Figure 6-13. Finished file, with all additions and changes

XML Format

Opening this file in another application that can read XML files reveals the actual data being saved (see Figure 6-14). This should appear very familiar to you if you've worked with XML files before. You could have created this file in a basic text editor, as long as you adhered to the exact format. The Property List Editor built into Xcode provides an adequate way of creating this type of file without having to pay close attention to opening and closing tags (see Figure 6-14).

```
000                              CastOfCharacters.plist
<?xml version="1.0" encoding="UTF-8"?>
<!DOCTYPE plist PUBLIC "-//Apple//DTD PLIST 1.0//EN" "http://www.apple.com/DTDs/PropertyList-1.0.dtd">
<plist version="1.0">
<dict>
        <key>Level</key>
        <dict>
                <key>One</key>
                <array>
                        <dict>
                                <key>Type</key>
                                <integer>1</integer>
                                <key>Delay</key>
                                <integer>3</integer>
                                <key>StartXindex</key>
                                <integer>0</integer>
                        </dict>
                        <dict>
                                <key>Type</key>
                                <integer>1</integer>
                                <key>Delay</key>
                                <integer>3</integer>
                                <key>StartXindex</key>
                                <integer>1</integer>
                        </dict>
                        <dict>
                                <key>Type</key>
                                <integer>0</integer>
                                <key>Delay</key>
                                <integer>3</integer>
                                <key>StartXindex</key>
                                <integer>0</integer>
                        </dict>
                        <dict>
                                <key>Type</key>
                                <integer>1</integer>
                                <key>Delay</key>
                                <integer>3</integer>
                                <key>StartXindex</key>
                                <integer>1</integer>
                        </dict>
                        <dict>
                                <key>Type</key>
                                <integer>1</integer>
                                <key>Delay</key>
                                <integer>3</integer>
                                <key>StartXindex</key>
                                <integer>0</integer>
                        </dict>
                        <dict>
                                <key>Type</key>
                                <integer>0</integer>
                                <key>Delay</key>
                                <integer>3</integer>
                                <key>StartXindex</key>
                                <integer>1</integer>
                        </dict>
                </array>
                <key>Two</key>
                <array>
                        <dict>
                                <key>Type</key>
                                <integer>1</integer>
                                <key>Delay</key>
                                <integer>3</integer>
                                <key>StartXindex</key>
                                <integer>0</integer>
                        </dict>
                </array>
        </dict>
</dict>
</plist>
```

Figure 6-14. *The property list file viewed as standard XML*

Loading the File

Now that the file has been generated with all of the data that you need to use for spawning sprites in the game, you need to load the data from the file into your code.

First, create a new method called `loadCastOfCharacters` in the `SKBGameScene.m` file and call it from within the `initWithSize` method:

```
SKSpriteNode *backdrop = [SKSpriteNode spriteNodeWithImageNamed:fileName];
backdrop.name = @"backdropNode";
backdrop.position = CGPointMake(CGRectGetMidX(self.frame),
                                    CGRectGetMidY(self.frame));

// add backdrop image to screen
[self addChild:backdrop];

// add surfaces to screen
[self createSceneContents];

// compose cast of characters from propertyList
[self loadCastOfCharacters];
}
return self;
```

You insert the new method between the existing `createSceneContents` and `didBeginContact` methods:

```
[sceneLedge createNewSetOfLedgeNodes:self
             startingPoint:CGPointMake(CGRectGetMaxX(self.frame)-
             kLedgeSideBufferSpacing-((howMany-1)*kLedgeBrickSpacing),
             brickBase.position.y+224) withHowManyBlocks:howMany
             startingIndex:ledgeIndex];
    ledgeIndex = ledgeIndex + howMany;
}

#pragma mark

- (void)loadCastOfCharacters
{

}

#pragma mark Contact / Collision / Touches

- (void)didBeginContact:(SKPhysicsContact *)contact
{
    SKPhysicsBody *firstBody, *secondBody;
```

To keep from having static filenames in the bulk of your code, add a constant to your
SKBAppDelegate.h file:

```
#import <UIKit/UIKit.h>

#define kCastOfCharactersFileName
@"CastOfCharacters"

// Global project constants
static const uint32_t kPlayerCategory =            0x1 << 0;
```

Once you load the data from the file, you need to store the resulting data into some instance
variables, so you need to add some properties to your SKBGameScene.h file:

```
@property (strong, nonatomic) SKBPlayer *playerSprite;
@property (strong, nonatomic) SKBSpriteTextures *spriteTextures;
@property (strong, nonatomic) NSArray *cast_TypeArray, *cast_DelayArray,
                                       *cast_StartXindexArray;
@property int spawnedEnemyCount;
@property BOOL enemyIsSpawningFlag;
```

Then you can add the code to read the data from disk in the new loadCastOfCharacters
method in the SKBGameScene.m file:

```
- (void)loadCastOfCharacters
{
    // load cast from plist file
    NSString *path = [[NSBundle mainBundle]
                pathForResource:kCastOfCharactersFileName ofType:@"plist"];
    NSDictionary *plistDictionary = [NSDictionary
                dictionaryWithContentsOfFile:path];
    if (plistDictionary) {
        NSLog(@"Got our data from disk: %@", plistDictionary);
    } else {
        NSLog(@"No plist loaded from '%@'", kCastOfCharactersFileName);
    }
}
```

Build and run the program. If no errors occur, you will see the console detailing the internal data
extracted from the plist file (see Figure 6-15). The plist data has no effect on the game thus
far, but it is a good time to determine if all of your changes and the plist data have been entered
correctly and are being read as desired. The if() statement verifies that the NSDictionary was
created as directed and, if successful, the data will be presented in the console. If not, if will display
an error message in the console.

```
2013-11-19 14:06:49.107 Sewer Bros[29313:a0b] Got our data from disk: {
    Level =     {
        One =           (
                    {
            Delay = 3;
            StartXindex = 0;
            Type = 1;
        },
                    {
            Delay = 3;
            StartXindex = 1;
            Type = 1;
        },
                ƒ
```

Figure 6-15. Data extracted from the plist file into the local dictionary, shown in the console

Parsing the Data

The NSDictionary contains the spawning data, and you will want to parse out the pieces that you need in order to accomplish the actual spawning. Because you have several layers of data inside this NSDictionary, you will do this in stages so that you can more easily see and understand why you built the property list file the way that you did and how to parse it out so that it becomes usable.

The root dictionary was initially retrieved from the file. Inside this is a single NSDictionary called Level, so let's begin by parsing that out. Inside the existing if() statement in the loadCastOfCharacters method of the SKBGameScene.m file, which verifies that you got the data you wanted without any errors, add the following code:

```
if (plistDictionary) {
    NSDictionary *levelDictionary = [plistDictionary valueForKey:@"Level"];
    if (levelDictionary) {
        NSLog(@"Got our data from disk: %@", levelDictionary);
    } else {
        NSLog(@"No levelDictionary");
    }
} else {
    NSLog(@"No plist loaded from '%@'", kCastOfCharactersFileName);
}
```

Build and run the program so that you can see this additional stage working as desired. If you encounter any errors, you have not created the file in the exact way that was described earlier. Go back and verify the structure. Looking at either the Property List Editor screenshots or the XML file screenshot, you will need to compare them in fine detail to reveal where the error lies.

Inside this Level dictionary are two NSArrays, and you can pull out just the first one for now (additional arrays can be created, one for each level in the game):

```
if (levelDictionary) {
    NSArray *levelOneArray = [levelDictionary valueForKey:@"One"];
    if (levelOneArray) {
        NSLog(@"Got our data from disk: %@", levelOneArray);
    } else {
```

```
        NSLog(@"No levelOneArray");
    }
} else {
    NSLog(@"No levelDictionary");
}
```

Inside this levelOneArray are six NSDictionarys. Each one contains the data for each enemy sprite to be spawned in this game level. Adding array objects would result in more enemy units being spawned on this game level. To parse these out, you will use a for() loop so that nothing breaks if you add or remove enemy dictionaries:

```
// load cast from plist file, just Level One
NSString *path = [[NSBundle mainBundle]
pathForResource:kCastOfCharactersFileName ofType:@"plist"];
NSDictionary *plistDictionary = [NSDictionary dictionaryWithContentsOfFile:path];
if (plistDictionary) {
        NSDictionary *levelDictionary = [plistDictionary valueForKey:@"Level"];
        if (levelDictionary) {
            NSArray *levelOneArray = [levelDictionary valueForKey:@"One"];
            if (levelOneArray) {
                NSDictionary *enemyDictionary = nil;
                NSMutableArray *newTypeArray = [NSMutableArray
                        arrayWithCapacity:[levelOneArray count]];
                NSMutableArray *newDelayArray = [NSMutableArray
                        arrayWithCapacity:[levelOneArray count]];
                NSMutableArray *newStartArray = [NSMutableArray
                        arrayWithCapacity:[levelOneArray count]];
                NSNumber *rawType, *rawDelay, *rawStartXindex;
                int enemyType, spawnDelay, startXindex = 0;

                for (int index=0; index<[levelOneArray count]; index++) {
                    enemyDictionary = [levelOneArray objectAtIndex:index];

                    // NSNumbers from dictionary
                    rawType = [enemyDictionary valueForKey:@"Type"];
                    rawDelay = [enemyDictionary valueForKey:@"Delay"];
                    rawStartXindex = [enemyDictionary
                        valueForKey:@"StartXindex"];

                    // local integer values
                    enemyType = [rawType intValue];
                    spawnDelay = [rawDelay intValue];
                    startXindex = [rawStartXindex intValue];

                    // long term storage
                    [newTypeArray addObject:rawType];
                    [newDelayArray addObject:rawDelay];
                    [newStartArray addObject:rawStartXindex];

                    NSLog(@"%d, %d, %d, %d", index, enemyType, spawnDelay,
                        startXindex);
                }
```

```
                    // store data locally
                    _cast_TypeArray = [NSArray arrayWithArray:newTypeArray];
                    _cast_DelayArray = [NSArray arrayWithArray:newDelayArray];
                    _cast_StartXindexArray = [NSArray arrayWithArray:newStartArray];
                } else {
                    NSLog(@"No levelOneArray");
                }
            } else {
                NSLog(@"No levelDictionary");
            }
        } else {
            NSLog(@"No plist loaded from '%@'", kCastOfCharactersFileName);
        }
```

Build and run the program to see the final parsed result (see Figure 6-16).

```
2013-11-19 14:32:38.081 Sewer Bros[29863:a0b] 0, 1, 3, 0
2013-11-19 14:32:38.082 Sewer Bros[29863:a0b] 1, 1, 3, 1
2013-11-19 14:32:38.083 Sewer Bros[29863:a0b] 2, 0, 3, 0
2013-11-19 14:32:38.083 Sewer Bros[29863:a0b] 3, 1, 3, 1
2013-11-19 14:32:38.084 Sewer Bros[29863:a0b] 4, 1, 3, 0
2013-11-19 14:32:38.084 Sewer Bros[29863:a0b] 5, 0, 3, 1
```

Figure 6-16. All data parsed as desired

Implementing a New Spawning Process

Now you need to use this acquired data to handle the spawning process. Add a new enumerated list to the SKBAppDelegate.h file:

```
static const uint32_t kCoinCategory =              0x1 << 4;
static const uint32_t kRatzCategory =              0x1 << 5;

typedef enum : uint8_t {
    SKBEnemyTypeCoin = 0,
    SKBEnemyTypeRatz
} SKBEnemyTypes;

@interface SKBAppDelegate : UIResponder <UIApplicationDelegate>
```

Then modify the update method in the SKBGameScene.m file (also removing the unneeded scheduledDelay int variable):

```
-(void)update:(CFTimeInterval)currentTime {
    /* Called before each frame is rendered */

    if (!_enemyIsSpawningFlag && _spawnedEnemyCount < [_cast_TypeArray count]) {
        _enemyIsSpawningFlag = YES;
        int castIndex = _spawnedEnemyCount;

        int leftSideX = CGRectGetMinX(self.frame)+kEnemySpawnEdgeBufferX;
        int rightSideX = CGRectGetMaxX(self.frame)-kEnemySpawnEdgeBufferX;
        int topSideY = CGRectGetMaxY(self.frame)-kEnemySpawnEdgeBufferY;

        // from castOfCharacters file, the sprite Type
        NSNumber *theNumber = [_cast_TypeArray objectAtIndex:castIndex];
        int castType = [theNumber intValue];

        // from castOfCharacters file, the sprite Delay
        theNumber = [_cast_DelayArray objectAtIndex:castIndex];
        int castDelay = [theNumber intValue];

        // from castOfCharacters file, the sprite startXindex
        int startX = 0;
        // determine which side
        theNumber = [_cast_StartXindexArray objectAtIndex:castIndex];
        if ([theNumber intValue] == 0)
            startX = leftSideX;
        else
            startX = rightSideX;
        int startY = topSideY;

        // begin delay & when completed spawn new enemy
        SKAction *spacing = [SKAction waitForDuration:castDelay];
        [self runAction:spacing completion:^{
            // Create & spawn the new Enemy
            _enemyIsSpawningFlag = NO;
            _spawnedEnemyCount = _spawnedEnemyCount + 1;

            if (castType == SKBEnemyTypeCoin) {
                SKBCoin *newCoin = [SKBCoin initNewCoin:self
                        startingPoint:CGPointMake(startX, startY)
                        coinIndex:castIndex];
                [newCoin spawnedInScene:self];
            } else if (castType == SKBEnemyTypeRatz) {
                SKBRatz *newEnemy = [SKBRatz initNewRatz:self
                        startingPoint:CGPointMake(startX, startY)
                        ratzIndex:castIndex];
                [newEnemy spawnedInScene:self];
            }
        }];
    }
}
```

Build and run the program to see the finished result of the spawning process change.

Now go into the `CastOfCharacters.plist` file and make some changes to the first couple of enemy values, perhaps changing the delay values from 3 to 1 to make them spawn quicker. Build and run the program once again. Lo' and behold, no changes were made to your code, but the enemy spawning changed according to the value changes you made. Most excellent—dynamic spawning!

Summary

This chapter did not introduce you to any new Sprite Kit functionality, but instead it illustrated one way to implement the spawning process of your game characters. There are certainly other ways to accomplish this task, but hopefully you found this chapter helpful and informative.

Next up you will add some custom textures that will allow you to present text (or numbers in this case) using your own custom font style. There are only a limited number of font options available on the iOS platform, and the next chapter will reveal a way around that limitation.

Also, you will begin to add some sound effects to the game. We can certainly say that a game is not a game without a lot of pings, pangs, bangs, and pops!

Chapter 7

Points and Scoring

What's the Point?

A game needs a goal—something the player needs to obtain. In the case of this game, players play for points and the best score wins!

The player has the job of clearing a room in a sewer from vermin. The player doesn't have a laser gun or an AK-47. The player must kick the rats into a river of water that flows below the brick base.

The player earns points for each vermin evicted from the sewer area and can also collect bonus points by obtaining the occasional coin that falls down into the play area.

Score Display

You will show the player's points at the top of the screen. But as I hinted at the end of the last chapter, you will be using a custom font that is not readily available in the iOS development environment. To do this, you will use custom texture images instead of basic text to display the individual characters that make up the player's score.

SKLabelNode

Before you do that, I'll show you the easy way of adding basic text into the SKScene. You will go back to the splash screen and add a text block that displays "Press To Start".

Insert the following code into the initWithSize method in the SKBSplashScene.m file:

```
SKSpriteNode *splash = [SKSpriteNode spriteNodeWithImageNamed:fileName];
splash.name = @"splashNode";
splash.position = CGPointMake(CGRectGetMidX(self.frame),
                              CGRectGetMidY(self.frame));

 [self addChild:splash];
```

```
    SKLabelNode *myText = [SKLabelNode labelNodeWithFontNamed:@"Chalkduster"];

    myText.text = @"Press To Start";
    myText.name = @"startNode";
    myText.fontSize = 30;
    myText.position = CGPointMake(CGRectGetMidX(self.frame),
                                    CGRectGetMidY(self.frame)-100);

    [self addChild:myText];
}
return self;
```

An SKLabelNode is a simple SKNode that draws a string. You create it by specifying the font by name, setting the text property (the string), setting some optional properties if desired (color and size), and finally setting its position. It's very simple to implement.

Build and run the program to see the new block of text. Notice that when you tap the screen as directed, the animation transition to the new scene doesn't include the new SKLabelNode. Let's fix that by adding the following code to the touchesBegan method:

```
for (UITouch *touch in touches) {
    SKNode *splashNode = [self childNodeWithName:@"splashNode"];
    SKNode *startNode = [self childNodeWithName:@"startNode"];
    if (splashNode != nil) {
        splashNode.name = nil;
        SKAction *zoom = [SKAction scaleTo: 4.0 duration: 1];
        SKAction *fadeAway = [SKAction fadeOutWithDuration: 1];
        SKAction *grouped = [SKAction group:@[zoom, fadeAway]];
        [startNode runAction:grouped];
        [splashNode runAction: grouped completion:^{
            SKBGameScene *nextScene  = [[SKBGameScene alloc]
                                        initWithSize:self.size];
            SKTransition *doors = [SKTransition doorwayWithDuration:0.5];
            [self.view presentScene:nextScene transition:doors];
        }];
    }
}
```

Build and run the program again to see the completed additions. You simply created a reference to the startNode node and applied the same animation group to it at the same time it was being run on the splashNode.

Custom Font Textures

Now it's time to add the 10 images that each represent a numerical digit that you can combine to create any number you want to draw on the screen.

Let's add those images to the project and get them moved into the Sprites folder. You might also want to add a new group (folder) inside the Sprites folder for the new images (call it Numbers). Add the 11 images from the Images folder, all prefixed with Text_ (the extra image is a score header image).

Now you will create a new class that will handle the scoring process. Create a new class named SKBScores as a subclass of NSObject. Modify the SKBScores.h file to match the following:

```
#import <Foundation/Foundation.h>
#import <SpriteKit/SpriteKit.h>

#define kTextPlayerHeaderFileName        @"Text_PlayerScoreHeader.png"

#define kTextNumber0FileName             @"Text_Number_0.png"
#define kTextNumber1FileName             @"Text_Number_1.png"
#define kTextNumber2FileName             @"Text_Number_2.png"
#define kTextNumber3FileName             @"Text_Number_3.png"
#define kTextNumber4FileName             @"Text_Number_4.png"
#define kTextNumber5FileName             @"Text_Number_5.png"
#define kTextNumber6FileName             @"Text_Number_6.png"
#define kTextNumber7FileName             @"Text_Number_7.png"
#define kTextNumber8FileName             @"Text_Number_8.png"
#define kTextNumber9FileName             @"Text_Number_9.png"

#define kScoreDigitCount                 5
#define kScoreNumberSpacing              16
#define kScorePlayer1distanceFromLeft    10
#define kScoreDistanceFromTop            10

@interface SKBScores : NSObject

@property (nonatomic, strong) NSArray *arrayOfNumberTextures;

- (void)createScoreNodes:(SKScene *)whichScene;
- (void)updateScore:(SKScene *)whichScene newScore:(int)theScore;

@end
```

Now modify the SKBScores.m file to match the following:

```
#import "SKBScores.h"

@implementation SKBScores

- (void)createScoreNumberTextures
{
    NSMutableArray *textureArray = [NSMutableArray arrayWithCapacity:10];
    SKTexture *numberTexture = [SKTexture
                        textureWithImageNamed:kTextNumber0FileName];
    [textureArray insertObject:numberTexture atIndex:0];
    numberTexture = [SKTexture textureWithImageNamed:kTextNumber1FileName];
    [textureArray insertObject:numberTexture atIndex:1];
    numberTexture = [SKTexture textureWithImageNamed:kTextNumber2FileName];
    [textureArray insertObject:numberTexture atIndex:2];
    numberTexture = [SKTexture textureWithImageNamed:kTextNumber3FileName];
    [textureArray insertObject:numberTexture atIndex:3];
```

```objc
    numberTexture = [SKTexture textureWithImageNamed:kTextNumber4FileName];
    [textureArray insertObject:numberTexture atIndex:4];
    numberTexture = [SKTexture textureWithImageNamed:kTextNumber5FileName];
    [textureArray insertObject:numberTexture atIndex:5];
    numberTexture = [SKTexture textureWithImageNamed:kTextNumber6FileName];
    [textureArray insertObject:numberTexture atIndex:6];
    numberTexture = [SKTexture textureWithImageNamed:kTextNumber7FileName];
    [textureArray insertObject:numberTexture atIndex:7];
    numberTexture = [SKTexture textureWithImageNamed:kTextNumber8FileName];
    [textureArray insertObject:numberTexture atIndex:8];
    numberTexture = [SKTexture textureWithImageNamed:kTextNumber9FileName];
    [textureArray insertObject:numberTexture atIndex:9];

    _arrayOfNumberTextures = [NSArray arrayWithArray:textureArray];
    NSLog(@"NumberTextures created...");
}

- (void)createScoreNode:(SKScene *)whichScene
{
    if (!_arrayOfNumberTextures) {
        [self createScoreNumberTextures];
    }

    SKTexture *headerTexture = [SKTexture
                textureWithImageNamed:kTextPlayerHeaderFileName];
    CGPoint startWhere =
                CGPointMake(CGRectGetMinX(whichScene.frame)+
                 kScorePlayer1distanceFromLeft, CGRectGetMaxY(whichScene.frame)-
                 kScoreDistanceFromTop);

    // Header
    SKSpriteNode *header = [SKSpriteNode spriteNodeWithTexture:headerTexture];
    header.name = @"score_player_header";
    header.position = startWhere;
    header.xScale = 2;
    header.yScale = 2;
    header.physicsBody.dynamic = NO;
    [whichScene addChild:header];

    // Score, 5-digits
    SKTexture *textNumber0Texture = [SKTexture
                textureWithImageNamed:kTextNumber0FileName];
    for (int index=1; index <= kScoreDigitCount; index++) {
        SKSpriteNode *zero = [SKSpriteNode
                        spriteNodeWithTexture:textNumber0Texture];
        zero.name = [NSString stringWithFormat:@"score_player_digit%d", index];
        zero.position = CGPointMake(startWhere.x+20+(16*index),
                        CGRectGetMaxY(whichScene.frame)-kScoreDistanceFromTop);
        zero.xScale = 2;
        zero.yScale = 2;
```

```
            zero.physicsBody.dynamic = NO;
            [whichScene addChild:zero];
        }
    }

- (void)updateScore:(SKScene *)whichScene newScore:(int)theScore
{
    NSString *numberString = [NSString stringWithFormat:@"00000%d", theScore];
    NSString *substring = [numberString substringFromIndex:[numberString length]
                                 - 5];

    for (int index = 1; index <= 5; index++) {
        [whichScene enumerateChildNodesWithName:[NSString
                        stringWithFormat:@"score_player_digit%d", index]
                        usingBlock:^(SKNode *node, BOOL *stop) {
            NSString *charAtIndex = [substring
                        substringWithRange:NSMakeRange(index-1, 1)];
            int charIntValue = [charAtIndex intValue];
            SKTexture *digitTexture = [_arrayOfNumberTextures
                        objectAtIndex:charIntValue];
            SKAction *newDigit = [SKAction animateWithTextures:@[digitTexture]
                        timePerFrame:0.1];
            [node runAction:newDigit]; }];
    }
}
```

@end

The class is created and ready for use. SKScene now needs one property to display the score and another for the score value of the player. Add these two properties to the SKBGameScene.h file:

```
@property int spawnedEnemyCount;
@property BOOL enemyIsSpawningFlag;

@property (nonatomic, strong) SKBScores *scoreDisplay;
@property int playerScore;
```

@end

Now you can insert the scoring initialization code at the bottom of the createSceneContents method in the SKBGameScene.m file:

```
    [sceneLedge createNewSetOfLedgeNodes:self
            startingPoint:CGPointMake(CGRectGetMaxX(self.frame)-
            kLedgeSideBufferSpacing-((howMany-1)*kLedgeBrickSpacing),
            brickBase.position.y+224) withHowManyBlocks:howMany
            startingIndex:ledgeIndex];
    ledgeIndex = ledgeIndex + howMany;
```

```
    // Scoring
    SKBScores *sceneScores = [[SKBScores alloc] init];
     [sceneScores createScoreNode:self];
    _scoreDisplay = sceneScores;
    _playerScore = 85942;
    [_scoreDisplay updateScore:self newScore:_playerScore];
}
```

Build and run the program to see the new scoring display in place and functioning as desired (see Figure 7-1).

Figure 7-1. *The scoring display*

So what did you do here?

```
// Scoring
SKBScores *sceneScores = [[SKBScores alloc] init];
[sceneScores createScoreNode:self];
_scoreDisplay = sceneScores;
```

You created a new instance of the custom class, ran the display-creation method called createScoreNode, and attached it to the locally stored instance variable, scoreDisplay.

```
if (!_arrayOfNumberTextures) {
    [self createScoreNumberTextures];
}
```

The createScoreNode method lazily instantiates (load only as needed) the textures if they do not already exist. The createScoreNumberTextures method is creating and storing the textures into an array just as you did for the other sprites.

```
// Header
SKSpriteNode *header = [SKSpriteNode spriteNodeWithTexture:headerTexture];
header.name = @"score_player_header";
header.position = startWhere;
header.xScale = 2;
header.yScale = 2;
header.physicsBody.dynamic = NO;
[whichScene addChild:header];
```

Here you create and add to the scene the little I- image that acts as a header for the player score. No physicsBody is needed, as these scoring digits are not going to float around the screen, be affected by gravity, or interact with other sprites. You did do something a bit different here: you changed the scaling of the image from its default value of 1 to 2. This doubles all of the pixels and makes the image 100% larger than the original. As you can see by the two properties xScale and yScale, you are not required to scale things proportionately. This is not required of course but it is something available to use at your own discretion. In this case, it gives the game a bit of the classic pixilated look.

```
// Score, 5-digits
SKTexture *textNumber0Texture = [SKTexture textureWithImageNamed:kTextNumber0FileName];
for (int index=1; index <= kScoreDigitCount; index++) {
    SKSpriteNode *zero = [SKSpriteNode
                spriteNodeWithTexture:textNumber0Texture];
    zero.name = [NSString stringWithFormat:@"score_player_digit%d", index];
    zero.position = CGPointMake(startWhere.x+20+(kScoreNumberSpacing*index),
                CGRectGetMaxY(whichScene.frame)-kScoreDistanceFromTop);
    zero.xScale = 2;
    zero.yScale = 2;
    zero.physicsBody.dynamic = NO;
    [whichScene addChild:zero];
}
```

Here you create the five digit images spaced proportionately using a for() loop to set up each digit. The kScoreDigitCount constant can be changed at will to change the digit count from 5 to whatever desired. This code uses a little bit of fancy math to determine dynamically the position of each digit, change the scales to 2, and add them to the scene.

This is pretty straightforward, and by now this should all look quite familiar. During game play, the score will be changing and the updateScore method will handle the display changes.

```
NSString *numberString = [NSString stringWithFormat:@"00000%d", theScore];
NSString *substring = [numberString substringFromIndex:[numberString length] -
                                                                          5];
```

This bit of trickery adds a bunch of leading zeros to the current score, and then trims all but the last five digits. This forces the score to have enough leading zeros to total five digits.

```
for (int index = 1; index <= 5; index++) {
        [whichScene enumerateChildNodesWithName:[NSString
                stringWithFormat:@"score_player_digit%d", index]
                usingBlock:^(SKNode *node, BOOL *stop) {
```

You begin a for() loop that will loop thru the five digits and use an SKScene method that will be new to you. EnumerateChildNodesWithName does pretty much what it says: it runs through all of the child nodes that have been added to the scene, and it looks for any nodes whose name property matches the provided name. If any nodes are found, it runs the block of code you provide. Accordingly, this loop will successfully find a single child node each pass through the for() loop. Each node that is found will be a sprite, using one of our custom font textures to display a digit of the score on the screen.

```
NSString *charAtIndex = [substring substringWithRange:NSMakeRange(index-1, 1)];
int charIntValue = [charAtIndex intValue];
SKTexture *digitTexture = [_arrayOfNumberTextures objectAtIndex:charIntValue];
SKAction *newDigit = [SKAction animateWithTextures:@[digitTexture]
                                        timePerFrame:0.1];
[node runAction:newDigit];
```

This block code runs for each digit in turn, and it replaces the current texture with the new texture based on the current score. Since the array of textures holds the images for digits 0 thru 9, you can easily get the digit image you want by requesting the array object at the same index as the digit you want. For example, if you want the image for 5, it resides in the array at index 5. Easy peasy.

Status Bar = Off

You might notice (even though it's been this way since the start) that there are some traces inside the scene of the iPhone's top status bar, which shows battery and signal levels. It was a minor bother earlier, but now it interferes with the score display. Let's get rid of that.

You may have noticed that when you first created this project, by default the Deployment Target option to hide the status bar during application launch (see Figure 7-2) does not seem to be working the way that you would want.

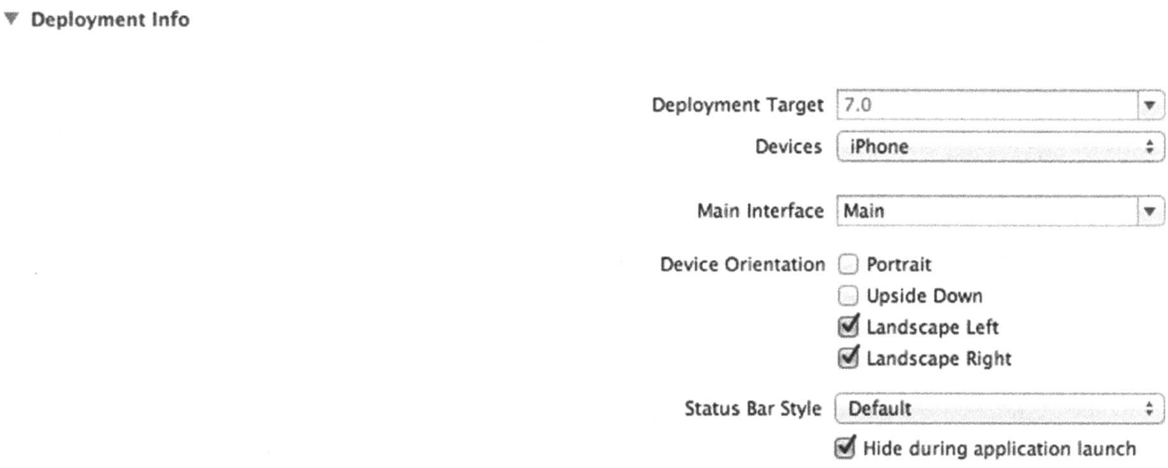

▼ Deployment Info

Deployment Target | 7.0 | ▼

Devices | iPhone | ⇕

Main Interface | Main | ▼

Device Orientation ◯ Portrait
◯ Upside Down
☑ Landscape Left
☑ Landscape Right

Status Bar Style | Default | ⇕
☑ Hide during application launch

Figure 7-2. Deployment Target settings

You need to add an item to the project `info.plist` file.

In the Project Navigator window on the left, you will find a folder labeled `Supporting Files`. Inside that folder is a file called `Sewer Bros-Info.plist` Click once on that file to see its contents in the editor window. (It's a Property List file just like the one you made in the last chapter.) Right-click in the list of items on the left and select Add Row. Edit the default text "Application Category" and change it to "View Controller-Based Status Bar Appearance". Change its `Type` to `Boolean` and its `Value` to `NO` (see Figure 7-3).

Build and run the program, and the status bar will go away as desired.

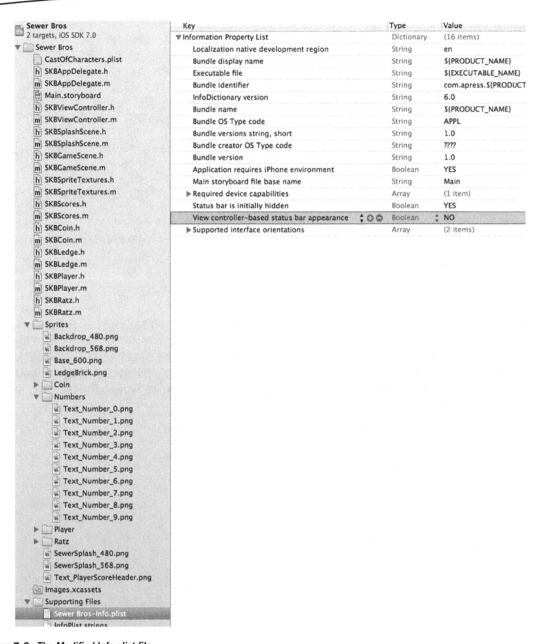

Figure 7-3. The Modified Info.plist file

A Different Kind of Score

Now that you have "scoring," you need to add "scoring"—Say what?

You have added the ability to display the player's score in the game window, but now you need a musical score. Ah, a play on words. Indeed!.

The game is in serious need of something that your ears can enjoy as the hero runs around pushing vermin into the river. Maybe not background theme music on an infinite loop, not this time anyhow, but perhaps a "little ditty" during the splashscreen and various sound effects as different actions are triggered in the game. That will work nicely.

Playing Sound Files

So how do you play sound files? Conveniently enough, you can do this in Sprite Kit. You'll probably be as amazed at just how simple this is.

You might want to add a new group folder called Sounds inside the project, specifically to hold sounds. Add the first sound file Theme.caf to the project (in the same way that you added sprite images; be sure to include the Target box) and move it into the Sounds folder. Once the sound is added to the project, all you need to do is to add these two lines of code to the initWithSize method in the SKBSplashScene.m file:.

```
myText.position = CGPointMake(CGRectGetMidX(self.frame),
                              CGRectGetMidY(self.frame)-100);

SKAction *themeSong = [SKAction playSoundFileNamed:@"Theme.caf"
                                  waitForCompletion:NO];
[self runAction:themeSong];

[self addChild:myText];
```

Build and run the program. Sweet-music-to-the-ears, you have a theme song! That was easy.

Thus to play a small sound file, all you need to do is create an SKAction using the convenience method playSoundFileNamed, which picks the sound file to play and runs the action in the current scene. That's amazingly short and sweet!

CAF Audio Format

At this point, I need to stop and explain a little bit about the audio format .caf. The acronym stands for "Core Audio Format," and Apple Inc. developed it with the goal of overcoming the limitations found in older digital audio formats..

While creating these sound files for the purpose of this game, I found a free and easy way to create files in this .caf format. You simply convert them from the common .aif format using the Terminal. Most common audio-conversion tools can save files in .aif format. Once you have the sound file with the extension .aif, you can run the following command in the Terminal:

```
mbp:desktop admin$ afconvert -f caff -d ima4 Theme.aif Theme.caf
```

This creates a new file on the Desktop called Theme.caf, and this is the file you will use in your game project.

> **Note**   If you are familiar with using the Terminal, then you'll notice that I did this from the context of the Desktop directory. When I first launched the Terminal, it was in the default User folder and the command I used to move (change directory) into the Desktop folder was:
>
> mbp:~ admin$ **cd desktop**
> mbp:desktop admin$

Player Spawn Sound Effect

Now you can add some more sound files and use them for sound effects tied to specific game actions.

You'll begin by adding several sound files all at once. Add these six sound files to the project: Run.caf, Jump.caf, Skid.caf, SpawnPlayer.caf, SpawnEnemy.caf, and SpawnCoin.caf. Move them into the Sounds folder.

You need some new constants to use for the filenames, so add them to the SKBPlayer.h file:

```
#import <SpriteKit/SpriteKit.h>
#import "SKBAppDelegate.h"
#import "SKBSpriteTextures.h"

#define kPlayerSpawnSoundFileName      @"SpawnPlayer.caf"
#define kPlayerRunSoundFileName        @"Run.caf"
#define kPlayerSkidSoundFileName       @"Skid.caf"
#define kPlayerJumpSoundFileName       @"Jump.caf"

#define kPlayerRunningIncrement        100
#define kPlayerSkiddingIncrement        20
#define kPlayerJumpingIncrement          8
```

To store sound files locally specific to the SKBPlayer class, add these properties to the SKBPlayer.h file:

```
@property (nonatomic, strong) SKBSpriteTextures *spriteTextures;
@property SBPlayerStatus playerStatus;

@property (nonatomic, strong) SKAction *spawnSound;
@property (nonatomic, strong) SKAction *runSound, *jumpSound, *skidSound;

+ (SKBPlayer *)initNewPlayer:(SKScene *)whichScene
                              startingPoint:(CGPoint)location;
- (void)spawnedInScene:(SKScene *)whichScene;
```

Then you load and store them in the instance variables inside the spawnedInScene method in the SKBPlayer.m file:

```
- (void)spawnedInScene:(SKScene *)whichScene
{
    SKBGameScene *theScene = (SKBGameScene *)whichScene;
    _spriteTextures = theScene.spriteTextures;

    // Sounds
    _spawnSound = [SKAction playSoundFileNamed:kPlayerSpawnSoundFileName
                                waitForCompletion:NO];
    _runSound = [SKAction playSoundFileNamed:kPlayerRunSoundFileName
                              waitForCompletion:YES];
    _jumpSound = [SKAction playSoundFileNamed:kPlayerJumpSoundFileName
                               waitForCompletion:NO];
    _skidSound = [SKAction playSoundFileNamed:kPlayerSkidSoundFileName
                               waitForCompletion:YES];

    // Play sound
    [self runAction:_spawnSound];
}
```

Build and run the program to listen to the new sound when the player spawns into the scene.

Player Running Sound Effect

When the player sprite runs, the program actually repeats an action sequence indefinitely until another action replaces it. To add a sound effect to this action, you need a really short sound file that can be repeated indefinitely along with the animation frames. This repeated sound should sound like footfalls as the player runs along.

The runRight and runLeft methods in the SKBPlayer.m file need to be changed:

```
- (void)runRight
{
    NSLog(@"run Right");
    _playerStatus = SBPlayerRunningRight;

    SKAction *walkAnimation = [SKAction
            animateWithTextures:_spriteTextures.playerRunRightTextures
            timePerFrame:0.05];
    SKAction *walkForever = [SKAction repeatActionForever:walkAnimation];
    [self runAction:walkForever];

    SKAction *moveRight = [SKAction moveByX:kPlayerRunningIncrement y:0
            duration:1];
    SKAction *moveForever = [SKAction repeatActionForever:moveRight];
    [self runAction:moveForever];
```

```
    // Sound effect for running
    SKAction *shortPause = [SKAction waitForDuration:0.01];
    SKAction *sequence = [SKAction sequence:@[_runSound, shortPause]];
    SKAction *soundContinuous = [SKAction repeatActionForever:sequence];
    [self runAction:soundContinuous withKey:@"soundContinuous"];
}

- (void)runLeft
{
    NSLog(@"run Left");
    _playerStatus = SBPlayerRunningLeft;

    SKAction *walkAnimation = [SKAction
                animateWithTextures:_spriteTextures.playerRunLeftTextures
                timePerFrame:0.05];
    SKAction *walkForever = [SKAction repeatActionForever:walkAnimation];
    [self runAction:walkForever];

    SKAction *moveLeft = [SKAction moveByX:-kPlayerRunningIncrement y:0
                duration:1];
    SKAction *moveForever = [SKAction repeatActionForever:moveLeft];
    [self runAction:moveForever];

    // Sound effect for running
    SKAction *shortPause = [SKAction waitForDuration:0.01];
    SKAction *sequence = [SKAction sequence:@[_runSound, shortPause]];
    SKAction *soundContinuous = [SKAction repeatActionForever:sequence];
    [self runAction:soundContinuous withKey:@"soundContinuous"];
}
```

I also added a short, 0.01-second pause between the sounds being played to help with the finished sound that you'll hear while the player is running. I gave the action a Key to reference later when you want the sound to cease.

Build and run the program to listen to the new sound when the player runs around in the scene.

Player Jumping Sound Effect

When the player sprite jumps, it is actually still running, but it has an impulse applied and the animation frames are temporarily changed. When the jump completes, the player continues where it left off before the jump was triggered. Thus to add a sound effect, you need to interrupt the running sounds.

The jump method in the SKBPlayer.m file is what needs to be changed this time:

```
- (void)jump
{
    // Stop running Sound Effects
    [self removeActionForKey:@"soundContinuous"];

    NSArray *playerJumpTextures = nil;
    SBPlayerStatus nextPlayerStatus = 0;
```

```
// determine direction and next phase
if (self.playerStatus == SBPlayerRunningLeft || self.playerStatus ==
                    SBPlayerSkiddingLeft) {
    NSLog(@"jump left");
    self.playerStatus = SBPlayerJumpingLeft;
    playerJumpTextures = _spriteTextures.playerJumpLeftTextures;
    nextPlayerStatus = SBPlayerRunningLeft;
} else if (self.playerStatus == SBPlayerRunningRight || self.playerStatus ==
                    SBPlayerSkiddingRight) {
    NSLog(@"jump right");
    self.playerStatus = SBPlayerJumpingRight;
    playerJumpTextures = _spriteTextures.playerJumpRightTextures;
    nextPlayerStatus = SBPlayerRunningRight;
} else if (self.playerStatus == SBPlayerFacingLeft) {
    NSLog(@"jump up, facing left");
    self.playerStatus = SBPlayerJumpingUpFacingLeft;
    playerJumpTextures = _spriteTextures.playerJumpLeftTextures;
    nextPlayerStatus = SBPlayerFacingLeft;
} else if (self.playerStatus == SBPlayerFacingRight) {
    NSLog(@"jump up, facing right");
    self.playerStatus = SBPlayerJumpingUpFacingRight;
    playerJumpTextures = _spriteTextures.playerJumpRightTextures;
    nextPlayerStatus = SBPlayerFacingRight;
} else {
    NSLog(@"SKBPlayer::jump encountered invalid value...");
}


// applicable animation
SKAction *jumpAnimation = [SKAction animateWithTextures:playerJumpTextures
                    timePerFrame:0.2];
SKAction *jumpAwhile = [SKAction repeatAction:jumpAnimation count:4.0];
SKAction *groupedJump = [SKAction group:@[_jumpSound, jumpAwhile]];


// run jump action and when completed handle next phase
[self runAction:groupedJump completion:^{
    if (nextPlayerStatus == SBPlayerRunningLeft) {
        [self removeAllActions];
        [self runLeft];
    } else if (nextPlayerStatus == SBPlayerRunningRight) {
        [self removeAllActions];
        [self runRight];
    } else if (nextPlayerStatus == SBPlayerFacingLeft) {
        NSArray *playerStillTextures =
                    _spriteTextures.playerStillFacingLeftTextures;
        SKAction *stillAnimation = [SKAction
                    animateWithTextures:playerStillTextures timePerFrame:1];
        SKAction *stillAwhile = [SKAction repeatAction:stillAnimation
                    count:0.1];
        [self runAction:stillAwhile];
        self.playerStatus = SBPlayerFacingLeft;
```

```
        } else if (nextPlayerStatus == SBPlayerFacingRight) {
            NSArray *playerStillTextures =
                        _spriteTextures.playerStillFacingRightTextures;
            SKAction *stillAnimation = [SKAction
                        animateWithTextures:playerStillTextures timePerFrame:1];
            SKAction *stillAwhile = [SKAction repeatAction:stillAnimation
                        count:0.1];
            [self runAction:stillAwhile];
            self.playerStatus = SBPlayerFacingRight;
        } else {
            NSLog(@"SKBPlayer::jump completion block encountered invalid value...");
        }
    }];

    // jump impulse applied
    [self.physicsBody applyImpulse:CGVectorMake(0, kPlayerJumpingIncrement)];
}
```

This code contains a group action that will run two other actions together at the same time: _jumpSound and jumpAwhile.

Build and run the program to listen to the new sound when the player jumps.

Player Skidding Sound Effect

When the player sprite stops running, it skids to a stop. Thus to add a sound effect, you need to stop the running sounds and add a short skidding sound.

To do this, you need to modify the skidLeft and skidRight methods in the SKBPlayer.m file:

```
- (void)skidRight
{
    NSLog(@"skid Right");
    [self removeAllActions];
    _playerStatus = SBPlayerSkiddingRight;

    NSArray *playerSkidTextures = _spriteTextures.playerSkiddingRightTextures;
    NSArray *playerStillTextures =
                    _spriteTextures.playerStillFacingRightTextures;

    SKAction *skidAnimation = [SKAction animateWithTextures:playerSkidTextures
                    timePerFrame:1];
    SKAction *skidAwhile = [SKAction repeatAction:skidAnimation count:0.2];

    SKAction *moveLeft = [SKAction moveByX:kPlayerSkiddingIncrement y:0
                    duration:0.2];
    SKAction *moveAwhile = [SKAction repeatAction:moveLeft count:1];

    SKAction *stillAnimation = [SKAction animateWithTextures:playerStillTextures
                    timePerFrame:1];
    SKAction *stillAwhile = [SKAction repeatAction:stillAnimation count:0.1];
```

```
    SKAction *sequence = [SKAction sequence:@[skidAwhile, moveAwhile,
                        stillAwhile]];
    SKAction *group = [SKAction group:@[sequence, _skidSound]];

    [self runAction:group completion:^{
        NSLog(@"skid ended, still facing right");
        _playerStatus = SBPlayerFacingRight;
    }];
}

- (void)skidLeft
{
    NSLog(@"skid Left");
    [self removeAllActions];
    _playerStatus = SBPlayerSkiddingLeft;

    NSArray *playerSkidTextures = _spriteTextures.playerSkiddingLeftTextures;
    NSArray *playerStillTextures =
                            _spriteTextures.playerStillFacingLeftTextures;

    SKAction *skidAnimation = [SKAction animateWithTextures:playerSkidTextures
                            timePerFrame:1];
    SKAction *skidAwhile = [SKAction repeatAction:skidAnimation count:0.2];

    SKAction *moveLeft = [SKAction moveByX:-kPlayerSkiddingIncrement y:0
                        duration:0.2];
    SKAction *moveAwhile = [SKAction repeatAction:moveLeft count:1];

    SKAction *stillAnimation = [SKAction animateWithTextures:playerStillTextures
                            timePerFrame:1];
    SKAction *stillAwhile = [SKAction repeatAction:stillAnimation count:0.1];

    SKAction *sequence = [SKAction sequence:@[skidAwhile, moveAwhile,
                        stillAwhile]];
    SKAction *group = [SKAction group:@[sequence, _skidSound]];

    [self runAction:group completion:^{
        NSLog(@"skid ended, still facing left");
        _playerStatus = SBPlayerFacingLeft;
    }];
}
```

This code again uses a group action that runs two other actions together at the same time: _skidSound and sequence. This is unlike the sequence action, which runs those three actions, one after the other.

Build and run the program to listen to the new sound when the player skids to a stop.

Enemy Spawn Sound Effect

In order to play a unique sound when a Ratz sprite spawns into the scene, you need a new constant to use for the filename. You can add that constant to the SKBRatz.h file:

```
#import "SKBSpriteTextures.h"

#define kRatzSpawnSoundFileName    @"SpawnEnemy.caf"

#define kRatzRunningIncrement      40
```

To store the sound locally in the SKBRatz class, add the property to the SKBRatz.h file:

```
@property int ratzStatus;
@property (nonatomic, strong) SKBSpriteTextures *spriteTextures;

@property (nonatomic, strong) SKAction *spawnSound;

+ (SKBRatz *)initNewRatz:(SKScene *)whichScene startingPoint:(CGPoint)location
                        ratzIndex:(int)index;
- (void)spawnedInScene:(SKScene *)whichScene;
```

Then you load and store the property in the instance variable, inside the spawnedInScene method in the SKBRatz.m file:

```
- (void)spawnedInScene:(SKScene *)whichScene
{
    SKBGameScene *theScene = (SKBGameScene *)whichScene;
    _spriteTextures = theScene.spriteTextures;

    // Sound Effects
    _spawnSound = [SKAction playSoundFileNamed:kRatzSpawnSoundFileName
                        waitForCompletion:NO];
    [self runAction:_spawnSound];

    // set initial direction and start moving
    if (self.position.x < CGRectGetMidX(whichScene.frame))
        [self runRight];
    else
        [self runLeft];
}
```

Build and run the program to listen to the new sound when the Ratz spawns into the scene.

Coin Spawn Sound Effect

The last sound effect you'll add at this time is when the bonus Coin sprites spawn into the scene. Again, you need a new constant to use for the filename, so you can add that to the SKBCoin.h file:

```
#import "SKBSpriteTextures.h"

#define kCoinSpawnSoundFileName     @"SpawnCoin.caf"

#define kCoinRunningIncrement       40
```

To store the sound locally in the SKBCoin class, add the property to the SKBCoin.h file:

```
@property int coinStatus;
@property (nonatomic, strong) SKBSpriteTextures *spriteTextures;

@property (nonatomic, strong) SKAction *spawnSound;

+ (SKBCoin *)initNewCoin:(SKScene *)whichScene startingPoint:(CGPoint)location
                       coinIndex:(int)index;
- (void)spawnedInScene:(SKScene *)whichScene;
```

Then you load and store the property in the instance variable, inside the spawnedInScene method in the SKBCoin.m file:

```
- (void)spawnedInScene:(SKScene *)whichScene
{
    SKBGameScene *theScene = (SKBGameScene *)whichScene;
    _spriteTextures = theScene.spriteTextures;

    // Sound Effects
    _spawnSound = [SKAction playSoundFileNamed:kRatzSpawnSoundFileName
                        waitForCompletion:NO];
    [self runAction:_spawnSound];

    // set initial direction and start moving
    if (self.position.x < CGRectGetMidX(whichScene.frame))
        [self runRight];
    else
        [self runLeft];
}
```

Build and run the program to listen to the new sound initiated when the bonus coins spawn into the scene.

Summary

You now have a display area and a custom font to show off the player's score. You also have a variety of sounds and sound effects being played as the game progresses into infamy. This game is leaving its "lame" status behind, and it's now beginning to shine.

However, you are not done yet! In the next chapter, you begin handling the player's interactions with all of these enemies and bonuses appearing all around it. No longer will your player be allowed to roam free and not be bothered by those nasty Ratz. On the other hand, however, the player will finally be able to retrieve those coins. So let's do it!

Chapter 8

Contacts and Collisions

Didn't You Cover this Already?

Yes, I did cover much of this already. Back in Chapter 5, you were introduced to contacts and collisions so that you could have your Ratz and coins bounce off of each other. But you're not done yet. You need a way for your enemies to keep from wandering around the base level. You need your player to be able to collect coins and kick vermin off the ledges after knocking them unconscious. Also, to add some challenge, your hero will "die" if it runs into vermin that are not currently unconscious. All of these additions require careful handling of contacts and collisions.

Contacts vs. Collisions

So what is the difference between these two events, anyway? Think of it in this overly simplified way: *collisions* are handled in the physics world, whereas *contacts* are the triggers in the code for the logical routing of a collision event. In this game, you have no interest in a coin sprite coming into contact with the ledge bricks. You want the physics world to handle them for you, allowing a coin to roll along the tops of the ledges. You don't need any game logic applied to the coin, or the applicable ledge, when they come into contact with each other.

Grates

Let's continue by adding a visual place for the enemies to appear in the game, instead of appearing out of thin air. You will place some images on each side of the screen, right below the score display. These images will represent sewer grates on the surface level of the game world from which these critters and coins fall.

Add the image named Grate.png to the project and move it into the Sprites folder. You don't need anything in the header file since you will not be storing a local reference to the images in the scene. Just as you did with the brick base, you will simply create a couple of SKSpriteNodes

and add them as children to the scene. This is done in the createSceneContents method of the
SKBGameScene.m file:

```
howMany = 28;
[sceneLedge createNewSetOfLedgeNodes:self
               startingPoint:CGPointMake(CGRectGetMaxX(self.frame)-
               kLedgeSideBufferSpacing-((howMany-1)*kLedgeBrickSpacing),
               brickBase.position.y+224) withHowManyBlocks:howMany
               startingIndex:ledgeIndex];
ledgeIndex = ledgeIndex + howMany;

// Grates
SKSpriteNode *grate = [SKSpriteNode spriteNodeWithImageNamed:@"Grate.png"];
grate.name = @"grate1";
grate.position = CGPointMake(30, CGRectGetMaxY(self.frame)-25);
[self addChild:grate];

grate = [SKSpriteNode spriteNodeWithImageNamed:@"Grate.png"];
grate.name = @"grate2";
grate.position = CGPointMake(CGRectGetMaxX(self.frame)-30,
               CGRectGetMaxY(self.frame)-25);
[self addChild:grate];

// Scoring
SKBScores *sceneScores = [[SKBScores alloc] init];
[sceneScores createScoreNode:self];
```

To make the enemy sprites appear to fall from these grates, you need to change their spawning
position. This data is stored in two constants in the SKBGameScene.h file, so change their values to the
following:

```
#import "SKBRatz.h"

#define kEnemySpawnEdgeBufferX       30
#define kEnemySpawnEdgeBufferY       30

@interface SKBGameScene : SKScene <SKPhysicsContactDelegate>
```

Build and run the program to see the new grates and the enemies spawning in such a way as to
appear to fall from these grates (see Figure 8-1).

Figure 8-1. Enemies fall from above through the grates

Pipes

At this point, as the enemy sprites wander their way down to the brick base, they become stuck at this lower level. You want them to leave this level and reappear at the top to start their wandering all over again. To do this, you will add some pipes at the bottom level so that they disappear into these pipes and reappear from the grates above.

First you need to add a new bitmask value to the SKBAppDelegate.h file. Then you'll move the constants that determine from where enemy sprites spawn in the SKBGameScene.h file:

```
// Global project constants
static const uint32_t kPlayerCategory =          0x1 << 0;
static const uint32_t kBaseCategory =            0x1 << 1;
static const uint32_t kWallCategory =            0x1 << 2;
static const uint32_t kPipeCategory =            0x1 << 3;
static const uint32_t kLedgeCategory =           0x1 << 4;
static const uint32_t kCoinCategory =            0x1 << 5;
static const uint32_t kRatzCategory =            0x1 << 6;

#define kEnemySpawnEdgeBufferX                   30
#define kEnemySpawnEdgeBufferY                   30

typedef enum : uint8_t {
    SKBEnemyTypeCoin = 0,
    SKBEnemyTypeRatz
} SKBEnemyTypes;
```

Be sure to remove or comment out the kEnemySpawnEdgeBufferX and kEnemySpawnEdgeBufferY constants in the SKBGameScene.h file.

As mentioned, the exact order of the bitmask values doesn't matter here. They just have to be unique values. Where the order does matter is in the didBeginContact method, as this determines the order of the firstBody and secondBody nodes. But alas, we're getting a bit ahead of ourselves.

Add the two images prefixed with PipeLwr and move them into the Sprites folder. As you just did with the two grates, add them to the createSceneContents method of the SKBGameScene.m file:

```
grate.name = @"grate2";
grate.position = CGPointMake(CGRectGetMaxX(self.frame)-30,
                             CGRectGetMaxY(self.frame)-25);
[self addChild:grate];

// Pipes
SKSpriteNode *pipe = [SKSpriteNode spriteNodeWithImageNamed:@"PipeLwrLeft.png"];
pipe.name = @"pipeLeft";
pipe.position = CGPointMake(9, 25);
pipe.physicsBody = [SKPhysicsBody bodyWithRectangleOfSize:pipe.size];
pipe.physicsBody.categoryBitMask = kPipeCategory;
pipe.physicsBody.dynamic = NO;
[self addChild:pipe];
```

```
pipe = [SKSpriteNode spriteNodeWithImageNamed:@"PipeLwrRight.png"];
pipe.name = @"pipeRight";
pipe.position = CGPointMake(CGRectGetMaxX(self.frame)-9, 25);
pipe.physicsBody = [SKPhysicsBody bodyWithRectangleOfSize:pipe.size];
pipe.physicsBody.categoryBitMask = kPipeCategory;
pipe.physicsBody.dynamic = NO;
[self addChild:pipe];

// Scoring
SKBScores *sceneScores = [[SKBScores alloc] init];
[sceneScores createScoreNode:self];
```

If you build and run the program now, you will see the two additional pipes. Nothing interacts with them yet (see Figure 8-2). That comes next.

Figure 8-2. Pipes have been added

Now you need to change the enemy initializer methods to let the physics world know that you have interest in this new category. Add the category to the contactTestBitMask of the SKBCoin.m file in the initNewCoin method:

```
coin.physicsBody.categoryBitMask = kCoinCategory;
coin.physicsBody.contactTestBitMask = kWallCategory | kPipeCategory |
                    kCoinCategory | kRatzCategory ;
coin.physicsBody.collisionBitMask = kBaseCategory | kWallCategory |
                    kLedgeCategory | kCoinCategory | kRatzCategory ;
```

Do the same thing to the initNewRatz method in the SKBRatz.m file:

```
ratz.physicsBody.categoryBitMask = kRatzCategory;
ratz.physicsBody.contactTestBitMask = kWallCategory | kPipeCategory |
                    kRatzCategory | kCoinCategory ;
ratz.physicsBody.collisionBitMask = kBaseCategory | kWallCategory |
                    kLedgeCategory | kRatzCategory | kCoinCategory ;
```

Now the code will trigger a contact event when these enemy sprites come into contact with either pipe node. Let's add some methods in both classes that will handle the interaction. For the Coin class, add a public method declaration to the SKBCoin.h file:

```
- (void)wrapCoin:(CGPoint)where;
- (void)coinHitPipe;

- (void)runRight;
```

Then insert the new method code immediately after the existing `wrapCoin` method in the `SKBCoin.m` file:

```
- (void)wrapCoin:(CGPoint)where
{
    SKPhysicsBody *storePB = self.physicsBody;
    self.physicsBody = nil;
    self.position = where;
    self.physicsBody = storePB;
}

- (void)coinHitPipe
{
    [self removeFromParent];
}


#pragma mark Movement
```

As you can see here, when a coin hits the pipe, it will disappear. You create this effect by removing it from the scene (its parent). This will force the hero to be hasty in collecting coins, as they won't hang around for long.

For the `Ratz` class, add two public methods to the `SKBRatz.h` file:

```
- (void)wrapRatz:(CGPoint)where;
- (void)ratzHitLeftPipe:(SKScene *)whichScene;
- (void)ratzHitRightPipe:(SKScene *)whichScene;

- (void)runRight;
```

Then insert the new method code immediately after the existing `wrapRatz` method in the `SKBRatz.m` file:

```
- (void)wrapRatz:(CGPoint)where
{
    SKPhysicsBody *storePB = self.physicsBody;
    self.physicsBody = nil;
    self.position = where;
    self.physicsBody = storePB;
}

- (void)ratzHitLeftPipe:(SKScene *)whichScene
{
    int leftSideX = CGRectGetMinX(whichScene.frame)+kEnemySpawnEdgeBufferX;
    int topSideY = CGRectGetMaxY(whichScene.frame)-kEnemySpawnEdgeBufferY;

    SKPhysicsBody *storedPB = self.physicsBody;
    self.physicsBody = nil;
    self.position = CGPointMake(leftSideX, topSideY);
    self.physicsBody = storedPB;
    [self removeAllActions];
    [self runRight];
```

```
    // Play spawning sound
    [self runAction:self.spawnSound];
}

- (void)ratzHitRightPipe:(SKScene *)whichScene
{
    int rightSideX = CGRectGetMaxX(whichScene.frame)-kEnemySpawnEdgeBufferX;
    int topSideY = CGRectGetMaxY(whichScene.frame)-kEnemySpawnEdgeBufferY;

    SKPhysicsBody *storedPB = self.physicsBody;
    self.physicsBody = nil;
    self.position = CGPointMake(rightSideX, topSideY);
    self.physicsBody = storedPB;
    [self removeAllActions];
    [self runLeft];

    // Play spawning sound
    [self runAction:self.spawnSound];
}

#pragma mark Movement
```

Glancing at the code you just added, you should see similarities to the wrapping code for when the sprites hit the sidewalls. You temporarily disable and store the physicsBody sprite so that you can transport it to a new location before restoring the physicsBody back again. You then make sure that all animation and movement is reset to new values and play the spawning sound.

Now all you need to do is add the applicable code to the didBeginContact method of the SKBGameScene.m file, first for the Coin class and then for the Ratz class:

```
// Coin / sideWalls
if (((((firstBody.categoryBitMask & kWallCategory) != 0) &&
                ((secondBody.categoryBitMask & kCoinCategory) != 0))) {
    SKBCoin *theCoin = (SKBCoin *)secondBody.node;
    if (theCoin.position.x < 100) {
        [theCoin wrapCoin:CGPointMake(self.frame.size.width-6,
                theCoin.position.y)];
    } else {
        [theCoin wrapCoin:CGPointMake(6, theCoin.position.y)];
    }
}

// Coin / Pipes
if (((((firstBody.categoryBitMask & kPipeCategory) != 0) &&
                ((secondBody.categoryBitMask & kCoinCategory) != 0))) {
    SKBCoin *theCoin = (SKBCoin *)secondBody.node;
    [theCoin coinHitPipe];
}

// Coin / Coin
```

Then for the Ratz class:

```
// Ratz / sideWalls
if ((((firstBody.categoryBitMask & kWallCategory) != 0) &&
            ((secondBody.categoryBitMask & kRatzCategory) != 0))) {
    SKBRatz *theRatz = (SKBRatz *)secondBody.node;
    if (theRatz.position.x < 100) {
        [theRatz wrapRatz:CGPointMake(self.frame.size.width-11,
                theRatz.position.y)];
    } else {
        [theRatz wrapRatz:CGPointMake(11, theRatz.position.y)];
    }
}

// Ratz / Pipes
if ((((firstBody.categoryBitMask & kPipeCategory) != 0) &&
            ((secondBody.categoryBitMask & kRatzCategory) != 0))) {
    SKBRatz *theRatz = (SKBRatz *)secondBody.node;
    if (theRatz.position.x < 100) {
        [theRatz ratzHitLeftPipe:self];
    } else {
        [theRatz ratzHitRightPipe:self];
    }
}

// Ratz / Ratz
```

Build and run the program. The coins disappear when they reach either pipe on the lower level, and the Ratz disappear into the pipe and reappear from the grate above.

Enemies that Occasionally Get Stuck

Every once in a while, you will see some enemies get stuck in place. Let's address this problem now before continuing.

The update method in the SKBGameScene.m file is the perfect place to check each enemy sprite to see if it is stuck. You won't want to do this check every time the update method runs, but maybe every 20 frames or so. If you find an enemy sprite that is in the same location that it was in 20 frames ago, you can force it to turn immediately and begin moving in the opposite direction.

To compare a sprite's current position with an older one, you need to store the data locally for each node, so let's add some properties to those enemy and bonus classes.

Add these two properties to the SKBCoin.h file:

```
@property int coinStatus;
@property int lastKnownXposition, lastKnownYposition;
@property (nonatomic, strong) SKBSpriteTextures *spriteTextures;
```

Do the same to the SKBRatz.h file:

```
@property int ratzStatus;
@property int lastKnownXposition, lastKnownYposition;
@property (nonatomic, strong) SKBSpriteTextures *spriteTextures;
```

To check every 20 frames instead of every frame, you need a new local variable in the SKBGameScene.h file:

```
@property int frameCounter;
@property int spawnedEnemyCount;
@property BOOL enemyIsSpawningFlag;
```

In the update method in the SKBGameScene.m file, you now insert the new code that will handle the 20-frame counter and trigger:

```
                SKBRatz *newEnemy = [SKBRatz initNewRatz:self
                        startingPoint:CGPointMake(startX, startY)
                        ratzIndex:castIndex];
                [newEnemy spawnedInScene:self];
            }
        }];
    }

    // check for stuck enemies every 20 frames
    _frameCounter = _frameCounter + 1;
    if (_frameCounter >=20) {
        _frameCounter = 0;

    }

}

@end
```

Inside this if() statement is where you can insert the code to check for stuck enemies. Let's start by checking all of the coins in the scene. You do this by using the enumerateChildNodesWithName method to search by the node names, which you have made sure were all unique yet have common prefixes. You place this enumeration method inside a for() loop, which will run through all of the children in the scene. Something new to note here is that you are using the stop option. If you set the stop Boolean variable in this method to YES, it will search through all of the children and stop at the first positive result. If you set this Boolean variable to NO, it will not stop at the first positive result, but continue through all of the children. Since you gave each enemy a unique name and therefore each positive result can only happen once, you'll set this Boolean value to YES:

```
if (_frameCounter >=20) {
        _frameCounter = 0;
        for (int index=0; index <= _spawnedEnemyCount; index++) {
                // Coins
                [self enumerateChildNodesWithName:[NSString
                        stringWithFormat:@"coin%d", index] usingBlock:^(SKNode
                        *node, BOOL *stop) { *stop = YES; }];
}
```

Now you add the code that does the position check and handles the stuck enemies:

```
[self enumerateChildNodesWithName:[NSString stringWithFormat:@"coin%d", index]
        usingBlock:^(SKNode *node, BOOL *stop) {
            *stop = YES;
            SKBCoin *theCoin = (SKBCoin *)node;
            int currentX = theCoin.position.x;
            int currentY = theCoin.position.y;
            if (currentX == theCoin.lastKnownXposition && currentY ==
                        theCoin.lastKnownYposition) {
                NSLog(@"%@ appears to be stuck...", theCoin.name);
                if (theCoin.coinStatus == SBCoinRunningRight) {
                [theCoin removeAllActions];
                [theCoin runLeft];
                } else if (theCoin.coinStatus == SBCoinRunningLeft) {
                [theCoin removeAllActions];
                [theCoin runRight];
                }
            }
            theCoin.lastKnownXposition = currentX;
            theCoin.lastKnownYposition = currentY;
```

Then you add the same code for the Ratz class. Here are the complete changes to the update method for clarity:

```
// check for stuck enemies every 20 frames
_frameCounter = _frameCounter + 1;
if (_frameCounter >=20) {
    _frameCounter = 0;

    for (int index=0; index <= _spawnedEnemyCount; index++) {
        // Coins
        [self enumerateChildNodesWithName:[NSString stringWithFormat:@"coin%d",
                    index] usingBlock:^(SKNode *node, BOOL *stop) {
            *stop = YES;
            SKBCoin *theCoin = (SKBCoin *)node;
            int currentX = theCoin.position.x;
            int currentY = theCoin.position.y;
            if (currentX == theCoin.lastKnownXposition && currentY ==
                        theCoin.lastKnownYposition) {
                NSLog(@"%@ appears to be stuck...", theCoin.name);
                if (theCoin.coinStatus == SBCoinRunningRight) {
                    [theCoin removeAllActions];
                    [theCoin runLeft];
                } else if (theCoin.coinStatus == SBCoinRunningLeft) {
                    [theCoin removeAllActions];
                    [theCoin runRight];
                }
            }
            theCoin.lastKnownXposition = currentX;
            theCoin.lastKnownYposition = currentY;
        }];
```

```
        // Ratz
        [self enumerateChildNodesWithName:[NSString stringWithFormat:@"ratz%d",
                        index] usingBlock:^(SKNode *node, BOOL *stop) {
            *stop = YES;
            SKBRatz *theRatz = (SKBRatz *)node;
            int currentX = theRatz.position.x;
            int currentY = theRatz.position.y;
            if (currentX == theRatz.lastKnownXposition && currentY ==
                        theRatz.lastKnownYposition) {
                NSLog(@"%@ appears to be stuck...", theRatz.name);
                if (theRatz.ratzStatus == SBRatzRunningRight) {
                    [theRatz turnLeft];
                } else if (theRatz.ratzStatus == SBRatzRunningLeft) {
                    [theRatz turnRight];
                }
            }
            theRatz.lastKnownXposition = currentX;
            theRatz.lastKnownYposition = currentY;
        }];
    }
}
```

Build and run your program and watch the console so that you can see the effects when any stuck enemies are detected.

I've also found that sometimes you have to adjust the X-axis position in the didBeginContact method of the SKBGameScene.m file when handling the contact between enemies and side walls so that they don't get stuck at the edge of the wall:

```
    [theRatz wrapRatz:CGPointMake(self.frame.size.width-11,
                    theRatz.position.y)];
} else {
    [theRatz wrapRatz:CGPointMake(11, theRatz.position.y)];
```

In this case, the hard-coded value of 11 was changed to 13, or to other values, as required until they never get stuck along the edge.

Setting the Player's Starting Location

So far, the player doesn't appear until the user taps the screen. That was fine back when you first started developing the game, but it's time to change that. Let's have the player start in the bottom left and face the right.

Insert this initialization code at the end of the createSceneContents method in the SKBGameScene.m file:

```
// Scoring
SKBScores *sceneScores = [[SKBScores alloc] init];
[sceneScores createScoreNode:self];
_scoreDisplay = sceneScores;
_playerScore = 85942;
[_scoreDisplay updateScore:self newScore:_playerScore];
```

```
// Player
_playerSprite = [SKBPlayer initNewPlayer:self startingPoint:CGPointMake(40,
                        25)];
[_playerSprite spawnedInScene:self];
```

Even though everything works just fine, if you leave the touchesBegan method as it is, you can still remove the unneeded player spawning code so that it looks like this:

```
-(void)touchesBegan:(NSSet *)touches withEvent:(UIEvent *)event {
    /* Called when a touch begins */
    for (UITouch *touch in touches) {
        CGPoint location = [touch locationInNode:self];
        SBPlayerStatus status = _playerSprite.playerStatus;

        if (location.y >= (self.frame.size.height / 2 )) {
            // user touched upper half of the screen (zero = bottom of screen)
            if (status != SBPlayerJumpingLeft && status != SBPlayerJumpingRight
                    && status != SBPlayerJumpingUpFacingLeft && status !=
                    SBPlayerJumpingUpFacingRight) {
                [_playerSprite jump];
            }
        } else if (location.x <= ( self.frame.size.width / 2 )) {
```

Build and run your program to see that the player immediately spawns when the game begins instead of waiting for the user to tap the screen.

Collecting Coins

Let's give the hero the ability to capture and collect coins for bonus points.

First of all, you need to add the coin category to its contactTestBitMask property in the SKBPlayer.m file:

```
player.physicsBody.categoryBitMask = kPlayerCategory;
player.physicsBody.contactTestBitMask = kWallCategory | kCoinCategory;
player.physicsBody.collisionBitMask = kBaseCategory | kWallCategory |
                        kLedgeCategory ;
```

Then you add a public method declaration to the SKBCoin.h file:

```
- (void)wrapCoin:(CGPoint)where;

- (void)coinHitPipe;
- (void)coinCollected:(SKScene *)whichScene;

- (void)runRight;
```

Now the code for the new method is inserted in the SKBCoin.m file, below the existing coinHitPipe method:

```
#pragma mark Contact

- (void)coinHitPipe
{
    [self removeFromParent];
}

- (void)coinCollected:(SKScene *)whichScene
{
    NSLog(@"%@ collected", self.name);
    [self removeFromParent];
}
```

Then you add the contact test and handler code to the didBeginContact method in the SKBGameScene.m file:

```
// Player / Coins
if ((((firstBody.categoryBitMask & kPlayerCategory) != 0) &&
            ((secondBody.categoryBitMask & kCoinCategory) != 0))) {
    SKBCoin *theCoin = (SKBCoin *)secondBody.node;
    [theCoin coinCollected:self];
}

// Ratz / sideWalls
if ((((firstBody.categoryBitMask & kWallCategory) != 0) &&
            ((secondBody.categoryBitMask & kRatzCategory) != 0))) {
```

Build and run your program to verify that your player can now capture coins. Now you need to fix the scoring system.

First you adjust the player's beginning score to 0. That value is set in the createSceneContents method of the SKBGameScene.m file:

```
// Scoring
SKBScores *sceneScores = [[SKBScores alloc] init];
[sceneScores createScoreNode:self];
_scoreDisplay = sceneScores;
_playerScore = 0;
[_scoreDisplay updateScore:self newScore:_playerScore];
```

Add a constant to the SKBCoin.h file that will determine the point value for each collected coin:

```
#define kCoinSpawnSoundFileName    @"SpawnCoin.caf"

#define kCoinRunningIncrement    40
#define kCoinPointValue          60
```

Because the player's score is a local variable in the GameScene class, you need to adjust the score in that class and not in the Coin class. Therefore, add the following scoring adjustment code to the didBeginContact method in the SKBGameScene.m file:

```
// Player / Coins
    if ((((firstBody.categoryBitMask & kPlayerCategory) != 0) &&
                ((secondBody.categoryBitMask & kCoinCategory) != 0))) {
        SKBCoin *theCoin = (SKBCoin *)secondBody.node;
        [theCoin coinCollected:self];

        // Score some bonus points
        _playerScore = _playerScore + kCoinPointValue;
        [_scoreDisplay updateScore:self newScore:_playerScore];
    }
```

Build and run the program to verify that the hero now gains bonus points when collecting coins.

Coin-Collection Sound Effect

Let's add a sound effect for when the coin is collected. Add the sound file named CoinCollected.caf to the project and move it into the Sounds folder. Add a constant for the filename in the SKBCoin.h file:

```
#define kCoinSpawnSoundFileName         @"SpawnCoin.caf"
#define kCoinCollectedSoundFileName     @"CoinCollected.caf"

#define kCoinRunningIncrement           40
#define kCoinPointValue                 60
```

Add a local variable to hold the new sound in the SKBCoin.h file:

```
@property (nonatomic, strong) SKBSpriteTextures *spriteTextures;

@property (nonatomic, strong) SKAction *spawnSound, *collectedSound;

+ (SKBCoin *)initNewCoin:(SKScene *)whichScene startingPoint:(CGPoint)location
                    coinIndex:(int)index;
```

Then add the initialization code to the spawnedInScene method in the SKBCoin.m file:

```
// Sound Effects
_collectedSound = [SKAction playSoundFileNamed:kCoinCollectedSoundFileName
                        waitForCompletion:NO];
_spawnSound = [SKAction playSoundFileNamed:kCoinSpawnSoundFileName
                        waitForCompletion:NO];
[self runAction:_spawnSound];
```

Finally, add the code to play the sound in the coinCollected method of the SKBCoin.m file:

```
NSLog(@"%@ collected", self.name);
```

// Play sound
[whichScene runAction:_collectedSound];

```
[self removeFromParent];
```

Build and run the program to hear the new sound effect.

Coin Collection Point Display

In this section, you'll create a small block of text that tells users the point values of the coins. This is a common feature in games, and it will make more sense once you've seen it, rather than trying to describe it here.

Add the following code to the coinCollected method of the SKBCoin.m file:

```
- (void)coinCollected:(SKScene *)whichScene
{
    NSLog(@"%@ collected", self.name);
    [self removeFromParent];

    // Play sound
    [whichScene runAction:_collectedSound];

    // show amount of winnings
    SKLabelNode *moneyText = [SKLabelNode labelNodeWithFontNamed:
                        @"Courier-Bold"];
    moneyText.text = [NSString stringWithFormat:@"$%d", kCoinPointValue];
    moneyText.fontSize = 9;
    moneyText.fontColor = [SKColor whiteColor];
    moneyText.position = CGPointMake(self.position.x-10, self.position.y+28);
    [whichScene addChild:moneyText];

    SKAction *fadeAway = [SKAction fadeOutWithDuration:1];
    [moneyText runAction:fadeAway completion:^{ [moneyText removeFromParent]; }];
}
```

Build and run the program to see what you have done. When you see it, you will hopefully say "Cool!" out loud and make others around you stare and wonder what it is that you're so excited about. Because it is cool, isn't it? But wait, there's one more thing to add to up the coolness factor.

Particle Effects

It's time to introduce you to an exciting Sprite Kit ability: particle generation. *Particles* are created by the SKEmitterNode object, which generates visual special effects like rain, fire, and explosions. Xcode has a built-in SKEmitterNode editor that allows you to create and adjust all of the various settings that make up your particle effect. So let's make one and use it as a visual special effect for coin collection.

Select New File from the File menu, make sure that iOS Resource is selected on the list on the left, choose SpriteKit Particle File, and then click the Next button. Choose Spark from the Template drop-down menu, and click the Next button. Name it `CoinCollected` and click the Create button.

In the Project Navigator on the left side of the Xcode window, you will see that two new files were generated for you: `CoinCollected.sks` and `spark.png`. Create a new group in the project and call it `Emitters`. Move these two new files into the `Emitters` folder (see Figure 8-3).

Figure 8-3. *Newly created* `Emitters` *folder and the new files*

In the center editor pane, you can see that the new `SKEmitterNode` is generating lots of particles in a "fireworks" sort of way (as long as it is selected in the Navigator on the left). To edit the many values available to you in this editor, you need to make sure that you change from the File Inspector to the SKNode Inspector on the right side of the Xcode window by clicking on the third button at the top of the pane (see Figure 8-4).

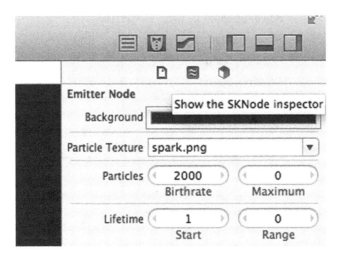

Figure 8-4. *Choosing the SKNode Inspector*

Now you should see lots of controls and settings that you can adjust to make `SKEmitterNode` produce just the right effect.

For the coin collection, you want a fairly small effect and one that lasts for a short period of time. Change the settings to the following values (see Figure 8-5):

Property	Value
Particles, Birthrate	133
Particles, Maximum	40
Lifetime, Start	0.235
Lifetime, Range	0
Position Range, X	7.592
Position Range, Y	6.825
Angle, Start	89.381
Angle, Range	360.39
Speed, Start	86.125
Speed, Range	0.883
Acceleration, X	0
Acceleration, Y	0
Alpha, Start	0.8
Alpha, Range	0.2
Alpha, Speed	-0.35
Scale, Start	0
Scale, Range	0
Scale, Speed:	1.107
Rotation, Start:	0
Rotation, Range:	0
Rotation, Speed:	0
Color Blend, Factor:	1
Color Blend, Range:	1
Color Blend, Speed:	0

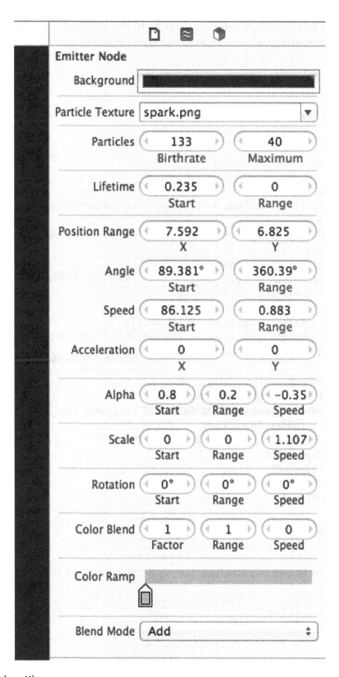

Figure 8-5. Modified particle settings

Now you'll add the code to implement the new emitter to the coinCollected method in the SKBCoin.m file. Make sure you move the removeFromParent method call from the beginning of this method to the end:

```objc
- (void)coinCollected:(SKScene *)whichScene
{
    NSLog(@"%@ collected", self.name);

    // Play sound
    [whichScene runAction:_collectedSound];

    // show amount of winnings
    SKLabelNode *moneyText = [SKLabelNode labelNodeWithFontNamed:@"Courier-
                    Bold"];
    moneyText.text = [NSString stringWithFormat:@"$%d", kCoinPointValue];
    moneyText.fontSize = 9;
    moneyText.fontColor = [SKColor whiteColor];
    moneyText.position = CGPointMake(self.position.x-10, self.position.y+28);
    [whichScene addChild:moneyText];

    SKAction *fadeAway = [SKAction fadeOutWithDuration:1];
    [moneyText runAction:fadeAway completion:^{ [moneyText removeFromParent];
                    }];

    // particle special effect
    NSString *emitterPath = [[NSBundle mainBundle]
                    pathForResource:@"CoinCollected" ofType:@"sks"];
    SKEmitterNode *bling = [NSKeyedUnarchiver
                    unarchiveObjectWithFile:emitterPath];
    bling.position = self.position;
    bling.name = @"coinCollected";
    bling.targetNode = self.scene;
    [whichScene addChild:bling];

    [self removeFromParent];
}
```

Build and run the program to see the finished coin-collection process (see Figure 8-6).

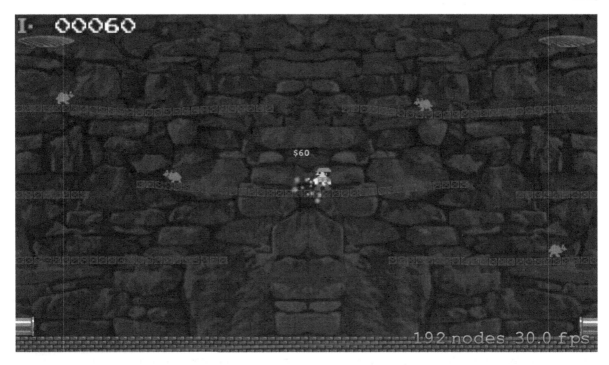

Figure 8-6. *Coin collection special effects*

Coin Contact from Below the Ledges

You want your hero to be able to collect coins, not only by running into them, but also by jumping up and striking the ledges from beneath the coins. This requires a bit more complexity, since you will need to test the contact between the player and a ledge brick, and also check to see if a coin was in contact with that particular ledge brick at the same time.

To begin this change, you need to add the kLedgeCategory to the player's contactTestBitMask property in the SKBPlayer.m file:

```
player.physicsBody.categoryBitMask = kPlayerCategory;
player.physicsBody.contactTestBitMask = kWallCategory | kLedgeCategory |
                   kCoinCategory;
player.physicsBody.collisionBitMask = kBaseCategory | kWallCategory |
                   kLedgeCategory ;
```

When you confirm a contact event between the player and a ledge brick, you need to call a new method to do the actual checking. Insert the new method immediately before the existing didBeginContact method in the SKBGameScene.m file:

```
#pragma mark Contact / Collision / Touches

- (void)checkForEnemyHits:(NSString *)struckLedgeName
{
    SKNode *nodeStruck = [self childNodeWithName:struckLedgeName];
```

```
// Coins
for (int index=0; index <= _spawnedEnemyCount; index++) {
    [self enumerateChildNodesWithName:[NSString stringWithFormat:@"coin%d",
                    index] usingBlock:^(SKNode *node, BOOL *stop) {
        *stop = YES;
        SKBCoin *theCoin = (SKBCoin *)node;

        // struckLedge check
        if ([theCoin intersectsNode:nodeStruck]) {
            NSLog(@"Player hit %@ where %@ is known to be", struckLedgeName,
                    theCoin.name);
            [theCoin coinCollected:self];
        }
    }];
}
}
```

```
- (void)didBeginContact:(SKPhysicsContact *)contact
```

Most of this code should look fairly familiar because it's similar to code you've used previously. The enumerateChildNodesWithName method looks for every coin in the game and checks each one to see if it is in contact with the ledge brick that was contacted by the player and triggered this method. The only thing new here is the intersectsNode method of the SKNode class. This method returns a Boolean value that indicates whether this node (theCoin) intersects with the specified node (nodeStruck). They intersect if their frames intersect. Thus if the coin is currently in contact with the ledge node, it returns true and you post a NSLog() message to the console and collect the coin, just as if the player ran into it.

You need to add another if() statement to the didBeginContact method of the SKBGameScene.m file to trigger this new method:

```
// Player / Ledges
if ((((firstBody.categoryBitMask & kPlayerCategory) != 0) &&
                    ((secondBody.categoryBitMask & kLedgeCategory) != 0)))
{
    SKSpriteNode *theStruckLedge = (SKSpriteNode *)secondBody.node;
    [self checkForEnemyHits:theStruckLedge.name];
}

// Player / Coins
```

Build and run the program and then try to hit a coin from beneath a ledge.

Ratz Contact from Below the Ledges

Now you want your hero to be able to hit enemy sprites from below the ledges, just like coins. When the contact is successful, the enemy should be rendered unconscious. The enemy sprite will flip upside down when its unconscious, but it will stay in this state only for a short period of time, after which, it will flip back over and continue along.

This change requires a few more images and texture arrays, so let's begin by adding the 10 images with the prefix Ratz_KO_ to the project and moving them into the Ratz folder.

Next, you add 10 more filename constants and two more arrays to the SKBSpriteTextures.h file:

```
#define kRatzRunLeft5FileName              @"Ratz_Left5.png"

#define kRatzKOfacingLeft1FileName         @"Ratz_KO_L_Hit1.png"
#define kRatzKOfacingLeft2FileName         @"Ratz_KO_L_Hit2.png"
#define kRatzKOfacingLeft3FileName         @"Ratz_KO_L_Hit3.png"
#define kRatzKOfacingLeft4FileName         @"Ratz_KO_L_Hit4.png"
#define kRatzKOfacingLeft5FileName         @"Ratz_KO_L_Hit5.png"
#define kRatzKOfacingRight1FileName        @"Ratz_KO_R_Hit1.png"
#define kRatzKOfacingRight2FileName        @"Ratz_KO_R_Hit2.png"
#define kRatzKOfacingRight3FileName        @"Ratz_KO_R_Hit3.png"
#define kRatzKOfacingRight4FileName        @"Ratz_KO_R_Hit4.png"
#define kRatzKOfacingRight5FileName        @"Ratz_KO_R_Hit5.png"

#define kCoin1FileName                     @"Coin1.png"
.
.
.
@property (nonatomic, strong) NSArray *ratzRunLeftTextures,
                  *ratzRunRightTextures;

@property (nonatomic, strong) NSArray *ratzKOfacingLeftTextures,
                  *ratzKOfacingRightTextures;

@property (nonatomic, strong) NSArray *coinTextures;
```

Then you add the new array initializers to the createAnimationTextures method of the SKBSpriteTextures.m file:

```
_ratzRunLeftTextures = @[f1,f2,f3,f4,f5];

// knocked out, facing left
f1 = [SKTexture textureWithImageNamed:kRatzKOfacingLeft1FileName];
f2 = [SKTexture textureWithImageNamed:kRatzKOfacingLeft2FileName];
f3 = [SKTexture textureWithImageNamed:kRatzKOfacingLeft3FileName];
f4 = [SKTexture textureWithImageNamed:kRatzKOfacingLeft4FileName];
f5 = [SKTexture textureWithImageNamed:kRatzKOfacingLeft5FileName];
_ratzKOfacingLeftTextures = @[f1,f2,f5,f5,f5,f5,f5,f5,f5,f5,f5,f5,f5,f5,
                             f5,f5,f5,f5,f5,f5,f5,f3,f2,f3,f2,f3,f2,f1];

// knocked out, facing right
f1 = [SKTexture textureWithImageNamed:kRatzKOfacingRight1FileName];
f2 = [SKTexture textureWithImageNamed:kRatzKOfacingRight2FileName];
f3 = [SKTexture textureWithImageNamed:kRatzKOfacingRight3FileName];
f4 = [SKTexture textureWithImageNamed:kRatzKOfacingRight4FileName];
f5 = [SKTexture textureWithImageNamed:kRatzKOfacingRight5FileName];
_ratzKOfacingRightTextures = @[f1,f2,f5,f5,f5,f5,f5,f5,f5,f5,f5,f5,f5,f5,
                              f5,f5,f5,f5,f5,f5,f5,f3,f2,f3,f2,f3,f2,f1];
// Coins
```

You need two new enumeration values added to the SBRatzStatus type declaration in the SKBRatz.h file:

```
typedef enum : int {
    SBRatzRunningLeft = 0,
    SBRatzRunningRight,
    SBRatzKOfacingLeft,
    SBRatzKOfacingRight
} SBRatzStatus;
```

You need to add a public method declaration to the SKBRatz.h file:

```
- (void)ratzHitRightPipe:(SKScene *)whichScene;

- (void)ratzKnockedOut:(SKScene *)whichScene;

- (void)runRight;
```

You also need to add the new method in the SKBRatz.m file to handle the event, which you can insert right before the existing runRight method:

```
#pragma mark Contact

- (void)ratzKnockedOut:(SKScene *)whichScene
{
    [self removeAllActions];

    NSArray *textureArray = nil;
    if (_ratzStatus == SBRatzRunningLeft) {
        _ratzStatus = SBRatzKOfacingLeft;
        textureArray = [NSArray
                arrayWithArray:_spriteTextures.ratzKOfacingLeftTextures];
    } else {
        _ratzStatus = SBRatzKOfacingRight;
        textureArray = [NSArray
                arrayWithArray:_spriteTextures.ratzKOfacingRightTextures];
    }

    SKAction *knockedOutAnimation = [SKAction animateWithTextures:textureArray
                timePerFrame:0.2];
    SKAction *knockedOutForAwhile = [SKAction repeatAction:knockedOutAnimation
                count:1];
    [self runAction:knockedOutForAwhile completion:^{
        if (_ratzStatus == SBRatzKOfacingLeft) {
            [self runLeft];
        } else {
            [self runRight];
        }
    }];
}

#pragma mark Movement
```

Glancing through this code, you can see that you are determining which way the sprite is currently running, changing the status to the corresponding new status, and grabbing the corresponding texture array. The texture array is the largest you've used thus far, and it creates a complex animation sequence, as you will see. You create an SKAction for the texture array and also for a timer, which will change its status back to running when completed.

Now you add the code that checks for the ledge and Ratz node intersection to the checkForEnemyHits method of the SKBGameScene.m file:

```
- (void)checkForEnemyHits:(NSString *)struckLedgeName
{
    SKNode *nodeStruck = [self childNodeWithName:struckLedgeName];

    // Coins
    for (int index=0; index <= _spawnedEnemyCount; index++) {
        [self enumerateChildNodesWithName:[NSString stringWithFormat:@"coin%d",
                        index] usingBlock:^(SKNode *node, BOOL *stop) {
            *stop = YES;
            SKBCoin *theCoin = (SKBCoin *)node;

            // struckLedge check
            if ([theCoin intersectsNode:nodeStruck]) {
                NSLog(@"Player hit %@ where %@ is known to be", struckLedgeName,
                        theCoin.name);
                [theCoin coinCollected:self];
            }
        }];
    }

    // Ratz
    for (int index=0; index <= _spawnedEnemyCount; index++) {
        [self enumerateChildNodesWithName:[NSString stringWithFormat:@"ratz%d",
                        index] usingBlock:^(SKNode *node, BOOL *stop) {
            *stop = YES;
            SKBRatz *theRatz = (SKBRatz *)node;

            // struckLedge check
            if ([theRatz intersectsNode:nodeStruck]) {
                NSLog(@"Player hit %@ where %@ is known to be", struckLedgeName,
                        theRatz.name);
                [theRatz ratzKnockedOut:self];
            }
        }];
    }
}
```

Build and run the program, and then try to hit a Ratz enemy sprite from underneath a ledge.

It's working fairly well, but you need to make a minor change so that these ledge and player contact events are triggered only if the player is below the ledge and not standing or running on top of it. A nice way to solve this problem is to be interested in ledge contact events only when the player is currently in the middle of a jump.

Make this slight modification to the didBeginContact method of the SKBGameScene.m file:

```
// Player / Ledges
if (((((firstBody.categoryBitMask & kPlayerCategory) != 0) &&
                ((secondBody.categoryBitMask & kLedgeCategory) != 0))) {
    if (_playerSprite.playerStatus == SBPlayerJumpingLeft ||
                _playerSprite.playerStatus == SBPlayerJumpingRight ||
                _playerSprite.playerStatus == SBPlayerJumpingUpFacingLeft ||
                _playerSprite.playerStatus == SBPlayerJumpingUpFacingRight) {
        {
            SKSpriteNode *theStruckLedge = (SKSpriteNode *)secondBody.node;
            [self checkForEnemyHits:theStruckLedge.name];
        }
    }
}
}
```

Build and run the program to verify that this minor change has the desired effect.

Intersection Not Sensitive Enough

If you run this game and play it for a while, even several times repeatedly, you will start to notice that the checkForEnemyHits method just isn't sensitive enough. It's too difficult to trigger a successful contact! You need to change this.

The problem possibly lies in the fact that a true intersection between a ledge node and an enemy node doesn't happen as often as we assumed it would. Since they both interact with each other as collisions, the physics engine just might not allow for much intersection to occur, which makes sense the more you think about it. When they strike each other, they are kept separate.

Let's change the process of determining when an enemy node is being struck from beneath the ledges. You'll add contact handling of enemy nodes with ledge nodes and store a reference to the applicable ledge node name that you can use in the checkForEnemyHits method.

First you add an instance variable to the enemy classes. Start with the SKBCoin.h file:

```
@property int lastKnownXposition, lastKnownYposition;
@property (nonatomic, strong) NSString *lastKnownContactedLedge;
@property (nonatomic, strong) SKBSpriteTextures *spriteTextures;
```

Then you do the same thing in the SKBRatz.h file:

```
@property int lastKnownXposition, lastKnownYposition;
@property (nonatomic, strong) NSString *lastKnownContactedLedge;
@property (nonatomic, strong) SKBSpriteTextures *spriteTextures;
```

Next you can add a contact bitmask value to the initNewCoin method in the SKBCoin.m file:

```
coin.physicsBody.categoryBitMask = kCoinCategory;
coin.physicsBody.contactTestBitMask = kWallCategory | kLedgeCategory |
                    kPipeCategory | kCoinCategory | kRatzCategory ;
coin.physicsBody.collisionBitMask = kBaseCategory | kWallCategory |
                    kLedgeCategory | kCoinCategory | kRatzCategory ;
```

Then you do the same thing to the initNewRatz method in the SKBRatz.m file:

```
ratz.physicsBody.categoryBitMask = kRatzCategory;
ratz.physicsBody.contactTestBitMask = kWallCategory | kLedgeCategory |
                    kPipeCategory | kRatzCategory | kCoinCategory ;
ratz.physicsBody.collisionBitMask = kBaseCategory | kWallCategory |
                    kLedgeCategory | kRatzCategory | kCoinCategory ;
```

Add the contact handler for Coins in the didBeginContact method of the SKBGameScene.m file, inserting it between the Ratz / Ratz and Coin / Sidewalls if() blocks:

```
    } else if (theSecondRatz.ratzStatus == SBRatzRunningRight) {
        [theSecondRatz turnLeft];
    }
}


// Coin / ledges
if ((((firstBody.categoryBitMask & kLedgeCategory) != 0) &&
                        ((secondBody.categoryBitMask & kCoinCategory) != 0))) {
    SKBCoin *theCoin = (SKBCoin *)secondBody.node;
    SKNode *theLedge = firstBody.node;
    //NSLog(@"%@ contacting %@", theCoin.name, theLedge.name);
    theCoin.lastKnownContactedLedge = theLedge.name;
}

// Coin / sideWalls
```

Then do the same thing for the contact handler for the Ratz, inserting it between the Player / Coins and Ratz / Sidewalls if() blocks:

```
    [_scoreDisplay updateScore:self newScore:_playerScore];
}


// Ratz / ledges
if ((((firstBody.categoryBitMask & kLedgeCategory) != 0) && ((secondBody.categoryBitMask &
kRatzCategory) != 0))) {
    SKBRatz *theRatz = (SKBRatz *)secondBody.node;
    SKNode *theLedge = firstBody.node;
    //NSLog(@"%@ contacting %@", theCoin.name, theLedge.name);
    theRatz.lastKnownContactedLedge = theLedge.name;
}

// Ratz / sideWalls
```

Finally, change the checkForEnemyHits method in the SKBGameScene.m file (also removing the SKNode *nodeStruck line):

```
- (void)checkForEnemyHits:(NSString *)struckLedgeName
{
    // Coins
    for (int index=0; index <= _spawnedEnemyCount; index++) {
```

```
        [self enumerateChildNodesWithName:[NSString stringWithFormat:@"coin%d",
                       index] usingBlock:^(SKNode *node, BOOL *stop) {
            *stop = YES;
            SKBCoin *theCoin = (SKBCoin *)node;

            // struckLedge check
            if ([theCoin.lastKnownContactedLedge
                       isEqualToString:struckLedgeName]) {
                NSLog(@"Player hit %@ where %@ is known to be", struckLedgeName,
                       theCoin.name);
                [theCoin coinCollected:self];
            }
        }];
    }

    // Ratz
    for (int index=0; index <= _spawnedEnemyCount; index++) {
        [self enumerateChildNodesWithName:[NSString stringWithFormat:@"ratz%d",
                       index] usingBlock:^(SKNode *node, BOOL *stop) {
            *stop = YES;
            SKBRatz *theRatz = (SKBRatz *)node;

            // struckLedge check
            if ([theRatz.lastKnownContactedLedge
                       isEqualToString:struckLedgeName]) {
                NSLog(@"Player hit %@ where %@ is known to be", struckLedgeName,
                       theRatz.name);
                [theRatz ratzKnockedOut:self];
            }
        }];
    }
}
```

I added several NSLog() lines in these code pieces to allow you to understand what is happening and when. You should quickly uncomment them, as that is a lot of log data being written to the console, and it will quickly become fairly useless.

Build and run the program to verify that this change has increased the game's sensitivity significantly.

Base Runners

Another quirk that you may notice is that the enemy node holds on to a lastKnownContactedLedge value even when it is running along the base bricks. You need to add a contact bitmask and test it so that you can clear this value when running along the base.

Add the bitmask value to the initNewRatz method in the SKBRatz.m file:

```
ratz.physicsBody.categoryBitMask = kRatzCategory;
ratz.physicsBody.contactTestBitMask = kBaseCategory | kWallCategory |
        kLedgeCategory | kPipeCategory | kRatzCategory | kCoinCategory ;
ratz.physicsBody.collisionBitMask = kBaseCategory | kWallCategory |
        kLedgeCategory | kPlayerCategory | kRatzCategory | kCoinCategory ;
```

Then insert an if() statement between Player / Coins and Ratz / Ledges in the didBeginContact method of the SKBGameScene.m file:

```
    // Score some points
    _playerScore = _playerScore + kRatzPointValue;
    [_scoreDisplay updateScore:self newScore:_playerScore];
}

// Ratz / BaseBricks
if (((((firstBody.categoryBitMask & kBaseCategory) != 0) &&
               ((secondBody.categoryBitMask & kRatzCategory) != 0)))) {
    SKBRatz *theRatz = (SKBRatz *)secondBody.node;
    theRatz.lastKnownContactedLedge = @"";
}

// Ratz / ledges
```

Build and run the program to verify that hitting the edge of the lower ledges won't affect an enemy that is currently walking along the base bricks. Problem solved!

Player Kicking Enemies

When the nasty vermin (the enemies) have been knocked out from below the ledges and are flipped over, your hero needs to be able to run along the ledges and kick them off into the water below. Doing so successfully rids the game level of that enemy and, of course, awards the player some points.

To accomplish this task, you need to test if the player and enemy nodes intersect. When the test returns a positive result, you'll have two more possibilities to process: a player running into a running enemy and a player running into a knocked-out enemy. When a contact happens with a running enemy node, the hero will "die," causing it to resurrect in the starting location and various other sundry details. (Later in this chapter, you will handle the running-enemy scenario, but for now let's focus solely on the knocked-out enemy scenario.)

To begin, you need a new constant in the SKBRatz.h file that will determine the point value for each collected vermin:

```
#define kRatzRunningIncrement      40
#define kRatzPointValue            100

typedef enum : int {
```

Add a new public method declaration to the SKBRatz.h file:

```
- (void)ratzKnockedOut:(SKScene *)whichScene;
- (void)ratzCollected:(SKScene *)whichScene;

- (void)runRight;
```

Insert the method implementation after the existing ratzKnockedOut method in the SKBRatz.m file:

```
        [self runRight];
    }
  }];
}

- (void)ratzCollected:(SKScene *)whichScene
{
    NSLog(@"%@ collected", self.name);
}
```

```
#pragma mark Movement
```

Add a new contact bitmask to the initNewPlayer method of the SKBPlayer.m file:

```
player.physicsBody.categoryBitMask = kPlayerCategory;
player.physicsBody.contactTestBitMask = kWallCategory | kLedgeCategory |
                    kCoinCategory | kRatzCategory;
player.physicsBody.collisionBitMask = kBaseCategory | kWallCategory |
                    kLedgeCategory ;
```

Insert the contact testing if() statement after the existing Player / Coin testing section in the didBeginContact method of the SKBGameScene.m file:

```
    // Score some bonus points
    _playerScore = _playerScore + kCoinPointValue;
    [_scoreDisplay updateScore:self newScore:_playerScore];
}

// Player / Ratz
if ((((firstBody.categoryBitMask & kPlayerCategory) != 0) &&
                    ((secondBody.categoryBitMask & kRatzCategory) != 0))) {
    SKBRatz *theRatz = (SKBRatz *)secondBody.node;
    if (theRatz.ratzStatus == SBRatzKOfacingLeft || theRatz.ratzStatus ==
                    SBRatzKOfacingRight) {
        [theRatz ratzCollected:self];
    }

    // Score some points
    _playerScore = _playerScore + kRatzPointValue;
    [_scoreDisplay updateScore:self newScore:_playerScore];
}

// Ratz / ledges
```

Build and run the program to verify that the test returns a positive result when the player runs over a knocked-out enemy. Now you can "fancy up" what happens when the test is true.

Ratz Collection Sound Effect

Let's add a sound effect for when the Ratz are collected, and go back and add one for when the Ratz are hit from below, rendering them unconscious. Add the sound files named EnemyCollected.caf and EnemyKO.caf to the project and move them into the Sounds folder.

Add a couple of constants for the filenames in the SKBRatz.h file:

```
#define kRatzSpawnSoundFileName       @"SpawnEnemy.caf"
#define kRatzKOSoundFileName          @"EnemyKO.caf"
#define kRatzCollectedSoundFileName   @"EnemyCollected.caf"

#define kRatzRunningIncrement         40
#define kRatzPointValue               100
```

Add a couple of local variables to hold the new sound in the SKBRatz.h file:

```
@property (nonatomic, strong) SKBSpriteTextures *spriteTextures;

@property (nonatomic, strong) SKAction *spawnSound, *koSound, *collectedSound;

+ (SKBRatz *)initNewRatz:(SKScene *)whichScene startingPoint:(CGPoint)location
                    ratzIndex:(int)index;
```

Then add the initialization code to the spawnedInScene method in the SKBRatz.m file:

```
// Sound Effects
_koSound = [SKAction playSoundFileNamed:kRatzKOSoundFileName
                    waitForCompletion:NO];
_collectedSound = [SKAction playSoundFileNamed:kRatzCollectedSoundFileName
                    waitForCompletion:NO];
_spawnSound = [SKAction playSoundFileNamed:kRatzSpawnSoundFileName
                    waitForCompletion:NO];
[self runAction:_spawnSound];
```

Finally, add the code to play the sound in the ratzCollected method of the SKBRatz.m file:

```
NSLog(@"%@ collected", self.name);

// Play sound
[whichScene runAction:_collectedSound];

}
```

Build and run the program to hear the new sound effect.

Ratz Collection Point Display

Let's show a block of text that indicates to the players the point value of the Ratz when they're collected. Add the following code to the ratzCollected method of the SKBRatz.m file:

```
// Play sound
[whichScene runAction:_collectedSound];

// show amount of winnings
SKLabelNode *moneyText = [SKLabelNode labelNodeWithFontNamed:@"Courier-
                                                             Bold"];
moneyText.text = [NSString stringWithFormat:@"$%d", kRatzPointValue];
moneyText.fontSize = 9;
moneyText.fontColor = [SKColor whiteColor];
moneyText.position = CGPointMake(self.position.x-10, self.position.y+28);
[whichScene addChild:moneyText];

SKAction *fadeAway = [SKAction fadeOutWithDuration:1];
[moneyText runAction:fadeAway completion:^{ [moneyText removeFromParent];
                                     }];

[self removeFromParent];
}
```

Build and run the program to witness the eye and ear candy you just added to the process. It's coming along nicely!

Kicked Off

At this point, the enemy simply vanishes when it's "collected." This is just so anticlimactic, don't you think? Let's add some more eye candy by causing the enemy to fly off the ledge and spin through the air before disappearing off the bottom of the screen.

You need a new enumeration value for the enemy status, so add one to the SKBRatz.h file:

```
    SBRatzKOfacingLeft,
    SBRatzKOfacingRight,
    SBRatzKicked
} SBRatzStatus;
```

Then add a static variable to the SKBRatz.h file:

```
#define kRatzRunningIncrement       40
#define kRatzKickedIncrement        5
#define kRatzPointValue             100
```

You need to update the collisionBitMask values of the initNewRatz method in the SKBRatz.m file:

```
ratz.physicsBody.contactTestBitMask = kWallCategory | kLedgeCategory |
        kPipeCategory | kRatzCategory | kCoinCategory ;
ratz.physicsBody.collisionBitMask = kBaseCategory | kWallCategory |
        kLedgeCategory | kPlayerCategory | kRatzCategory | kCoinCategory ;
ratz.physicsBody.density = 1.0;
```

Next you will update the player contact and collision bitmask values of the initNewPlayer method in the SKBPlayer.m file:

```
player.physicsBody.categoryBitMask = kPlayerCategory;
player.physicsBody.contactTestBitMask = kWallCategory | kLedgeCategory |
                        kCoinCategory | kRatzCategory;
player.physicsBody.collisionBitMask = kBaseCategory | kWallCategory |
                        kLedgeCategory | kRatzCategory ;
player.physicsBody.density = 1.0;
```

The largest change will be the ratzCollected method in the SKBRatz.m file:

```
- (void)ratzCollected:(SKScene *)whichScene
{
    NSLog(@"%@ collected", self.name);

    // Update status
    _ratzStatus = SBRatzKicked;

    // Play sound
    [whichScene runAction:_collectedSound];

    // show amount of winnings
    SKLabelNode *moneyText = [SKLabelNode labelNodeWithFontNamed:@"Courier-
                        Bold"];
    moneyText.text = [NSString stringWithFormat:@"$%d", kRatzPointValue];
    moneyText.fontSize = 9;
    moneyText.fontColor = [SKColor whiteColor];
    moneyText.position = CGPointMake(self.position.x-10, self.position.y+28);
    [whichScene addChild:moneyText];

    SKAction *fadeAway = [SKAction fadeOutWithDuration:1];
    [moneyText runAction:fadeAway completion:^{ [moneyText removeFromParent];
                                        }];

    // upward impulse applied
    [self.physicsBody applyImpulse:CGVectorMake(0, kRatzKickedIncrement)];

    // Make him spin when kicked
    SKAction *rotation = [SKAction rotateByAngle:M_PI duration:0.1];
      // 2*pi = 360deg, pi = 180deg
    SKAction *rotateForever = [SKAction repeatActionForever:rotation];
    [self runAction:rotateForever];
```

```
// While kicked upward and spinning, wait for a short spell before altering
                                        physicsBody
SKAction *shortDelay = [SKAction waitForDuration:0.5];

[self runAction:shortDelay completion:^{
    // Make a new physics body that is much, much smaller as to not affect
                                        ledges as he falls...
    self.physicsBody = [SKPhysicsBody bodyWithRectangleOfSize:CGSizeMake(1,
                                        1)];
    self.physicsBody.categoryBitMask = kRatzCategory;
    self.physicsBody.collisionBitMask = kWallCategory;
    self.physicsBody.contactTestBitMask = kWallCategory;
    self.physicsBody.linearDamping = 1.0;
    self.physicsBody.allowsRotation = YES;
}];
}
```

When this method is triggered, you apply an impulse, similar to the player jumping, to the node and create a rotation SKAction that starts the Ratz spinning and flying up into the air. Gravity takes over, and it then begins to fall. You create a short delay so that all of this activity has the time to be set into motion before you drastically modify the physicsBody properties. You create a new SKPhysicsBody of a much smaller size in order to help it avoid other screen objects like ledges.

The only collision and contact event that you will care about during this process is contact with the surrounding wall, so you need to set these values accordingly. You change the default value (0.0) for linear damping, which slows its movement. This linear damping property is used to simulate liquid or air friction forces on the node, so this change slows its movement a little bit while falling to the bottom.

Now you can alter the didBeginContact method in the SKBGameScene.m file to handle the falling enemy when it strikes the bottom of the screen:

```
// Ratz / sideWalls
if ((((firstBody.categoryBitMask & kWallCategory) != 0) &&
                    ((secondBody.categoryBitMask & kRatzCategory) != 0))) {
    SKBRatz *theRatz = (SKBRatz *)secondBody.node;
    if (theRatz.ratzStatus != SBRatzKicked) {
        if (theRatz.position.x < 100) {
            [theRatz wrapRatz:CGPointMake(self.frame.size.width-13,
                    theRatz.position.y)];
        } else {
            [theRatz wrapRatz:CGPointMake(13, theRatz.position.y)];
        }
    } else {
        // contacted bottom wall (has been kicked off and has fallen)
        NSLog(@"%@ hit bottom of screen and is being removed", theRatz.name);
        [theRatz removeFromParent];
    }
}
}
```

Build and run the program to see the new animation sequence that is triggered when the hero kicks off an unconscious enemy.

Into the River

When the vermin hits the bottom of the screen, you should add a visual effect to make it look like it splashed into water. To do this, you will create another particle effect.

Let's create a new Ratz class method to handle this final scene in the vermin's lifespan.

Add the public declaration to the SKBRatz.h file:

```
- (void)ratzCollected:(SKScene *)whichScene;
- (void)ratzHitWater:(SKScene *)whichScene;

- (void)runRight;
```

Then insert the implementation after the existing ratzCollected method in the SKBRatz.m file:

```
        self.physicsBody.linearDamping = 1.0;
        self.physicsBody.allowsRotation = YES;
    }];
}

- (void)ratzHitWater:(SKScene *)whichScene
{
    NSLog(@"%@ hit bottom of screen and is being removed", self.name);
    [self removeFromParent];
}
```

Now modify the Ratz / SideWalls if() statement in the didBeginContact method of the SKBGameScene.m file:

```
} else {
        // contacted bottom wall so has been kicked off and has fallen to bottom
        [theRatz ratzHitWater:self];
    }
```

Now that the foundation is in place, you can create the new particle.

Select New File from the File menu, make sure that iOS Resource is selected on the list on the left, choose SpriteKit Particle File, and then click the Next button. Choose Spark from the Template drop-down menu and click the Next button. Name it Splashed and click the Create button.

In the Project Navigator on the left side of the Xcode window, you will see the new file was generated for you: Splashed. Move the new file into the Emitters group folder. In the center editor pane, you can view the new SKEmitterNode generating lots of particles. It's time to edit the values in order to create a particle stream that mimics a water splash. Change the settings to the following values:

Property	Value
Particles, Birthrate	105
Particles, Maximum	60
Lifetime, Start	0.378
Lifetime, Range	0.093
Position Range, X	38.768
Position Range, Y	0.008
Angle, Start	89.928
Angle, Range	1.77
Speed, Start	53.92
Speed, Range	500
Acceleration, X	0
Acceleration, Y	-500
Alpha, Start	1
Alpha, Range	0.2
Alpha, Speed	0
Scale, Start	0.1
Scale, Range	0.2
Scale, Speed	0.17
Rotation, Start	0
Rotation, Range	0
Rotation, Speed	0
Color Blend, Factor	1
Color Blend, Range	0
Color Blend, Speed	0

Then change the color (Color Ramp) from the default orange to a shade of blue to make it look a bit more like water.

Of course, you need a sound effect to go along with the visual effect, so add the Splash.caf sound file to the project and move it into the Sounds group folder.

Add a new constant for the sound filename in the SKBRatz.h file:

```
#define kRatzCollectedSoundFileName    @"EnemyCollected.caf"
#define kRatzSplashedSoundFileName     @"Splash.caf"

#define kRatzRunningIncrement          40
```

Then add a new instance variable to store the sound in the SKBRatz.h file:

```
@property (nonatomic, strong) SKBSpriteTextures *spriteTextures;

@property (nonatomic, strong) SKAction *spawnSound, *koSound, *collectedSound,
                    *splashSound;

+ (SKBRatz *)initNewRatz:(SKScene *)whichScene startingPoint:(CGPoint)location
                    ratzIndex:(int)index;
```

Add the initialization of this new variable to the spawnedInScene method in the SKBRatz.m file:

```
// Sound Effects
_splashSound = [SKAction playSoundFileNamed:kRatzSplashedSoundFileName
                    waitForCompletion:NO];
_koSound = [SKAction playSoundFileNamed:kRatzKOSoundFileName
                    waitForCompletion:NO];
```

Then add the code to bring it all together in the ratzHitWater method of the SKBRatz.m file:

```
- (void)ratzHitWater:(SKScene *)whichScene
{
    // Play sound
    [whichScene runAction:_splashSound];

    // splash eye candy
    NSString *emitterPath = [[NSBundle mainBundle]
                    pathForResource:@"Splashed" ofType:@"sks"];
    SKEmitterNode *splash = [NSKeyedUnarchiver
                    unarchiveObjectWithFile:emitterPath];
    splash.position = self.position;
    NSLog(@"splash (%f,%f)", splash.position.x, splash.position.y);
    splash.name = @"ratzSplash";
    splash.targetNode = whichScene.scene;
    [whichScene addChild:splash];

    [self removeFromParent];
}
```

Build and run the program to see what happens when the vermin is kicked off the ledge and into the water.

Enemies Kill Player

Now it's time to crank up the difficulty level a bit. The hero has had it way too easy so far—supreme power and immortality. Time to change all that.

You already have a test that checks for contact between the player and the enemies in the didBeginContact method of the SKBGameScene.m file, so you just need to modify it slightly to handle this new event:

```
// Player / Ratz
if (((((firstBody.categoryBitMask & kPlayerCategory) != 0) &&
                    ((secondBody.categoryBitMask & kRatzCategory) != 0)))) {
    SKBRatz *theRatz = (SKBRatz *)secondBody.node;
    if (theRatz.ratzStatus == SBRatzKOfacingLeft || theRatz.ratzStatus ==
                    SBRatzKOfacingRight) {
        // ratz unconscious so kick 'em off the ledge
        [theRatz ratzCollected:self];

        // Score some points
        _playerScore = _playerScore + kRatzPointValue;
        [_scoreDisplay updateScore:self newScore:_playerScore];
    } else if (theRatz.ratzStatus == SBRatzRunningLeft || theRatz.ratzStatus ==
                    SBRatzRunningRight) {
        // oops, player dies
        [_playerSprite playerKilled:self];
    }
}
```

You can insert this new method after the existing wrapPlayer method in the SKBPlayer.m file:

```
- (void)wrapPlayer:(CGPoint)where
{
    SKPhysicsBody *storePB = self.physicsBody;
    self.physicsBody = nil;
    self.position = where;
    self.physicsBody = storePB;
}

#pragma mark Contact

- (void)playerKilled:(SKScene *)whichScene
{
    NSLog(@"Player has died...");
}

#pragma mark Movement

- (void)runRight
```

Don't forget the public declaration in the SKBPlayer.h file:

```
- (void)wrapPlayer:(CGPoint)where;
- (void)playerKilled:(SKScene *)whichScene;

- (void)runRight;
```

Build and run the program to test out the new dying feature.

Player Death Sound Effect

Now that the foundation is in place, you can "fancy" things up a bit. Let's begin with a sound effect.

Add the sound file named Playerbitten.caf to the project and move it into the Sounds folder. Add a constant for the filename in the SKBPlayer.h file:

```
#define kPlayerSpawnSoundFileName    @"SpawnPlayer.caf"
#define kPlayerBittenSoundFileName   @"Playerbitten.caf"
#define kPlayerRunSoundFileName      @"Run.caf"
```

Add a local variable to hold the new sound in the SKBPlayer.h file:

```
@property SBPlayerStatus playerStatus;

@property (nonatomic, strong) SKAction *spawnSound, *bittenSound;
@property (nonatomic, strong) SKAction *runSound, *jumpSound, *skidSound;
```

Then add the initialization code to the spawnedInScene method of the SKBPlayer.m file:

```
_spawnSound = [SKAction playSoundFileNamed:kPlayerSpawnSoundFileName
                       waitForCompletion:NO];
_bittenSound = [SKAction playSoundFileNamed:kPlayerBittenSoundFileName
                       waitForCompletion:NO];
_runSound = [SKAction playSoundFileNamed:kPlayerRunSoundFileName
                       waitForCompletion:YES];
```

Finally, add the code to play the sound in the playerKilled method of the SKBPlayer.m file:

```
NSLog(@"Player has died...");

// Play sound
[whichScene runAction:_bittenSound];
```

Build and run your program to hear the new sound effect.

Player Falls Off Ledge

Your hero has fallen, so to speak. A nasty vermin has bitten him, and he will now fall down into the water just like the enemy.

You need a new enumeration value for the player status, so add one to the SKBPlayer.h file:

```
    SBPlayerJumpingUpFacingLeft,
    SBPlayerJumpingUpFacingRight,
    SBPlayerFalling
} SBPlayerStatus;
```

Also add a new constant to the SKBPlayer.h file:

```
#define kPlayerRunningIncrement      100
#define kPlayerSkiddingIncrement      20
#define kPlayerJumpingIncrement        8
#define kPlayerBittenIncrement         5
```

Next you change the playerKilled method in the SKBPlayer.m file:

```
- (void)playerKilled:(SKScene *)whichScene
{
    NSLog(@"Player has died...");
    [self removeAllActions];

    // Update status
    _playerStatus = SBPlayerFalling;

    // Play sound
    [whichScene runAction:_bittenSound];

    // upward impulse applied
    [self.physicsBody applyImpulse:CGVectorMake(0, kPlayerBittenIncrement)];

    // While flying upward, wait for a short spell before altering physicsBody
    SKAction *shortDelay = [SKAction waitForDuration:0.5];

    [self runAction:shortDelay completion:^{
        // Make a new physics body that is much, much smaller as to not affect
                                                ledges as he falls...
        self.physicsBody = [SKPhysicsBody bodyWithRectangleOfSize:CGSizeMake(1,
                                                1)];
        self.physicsBody.categoryBitMask = kPlayerCategory;
        self.physicsBody.collisionBitMask = kWallCategory;
        self.physicsBody.contactTestBitMask = kWallCategory;
        self.physicsBody.linearDamping = 1.0;
        self.physicsBody.allowsRotation = NO;
    }];
}
```

You'll notice that this method is very similar to the one you applied previously with the ratzCollected method in the SKBRatz.m file.

Add a new public method declaration to the SKBPlayer.h file:

```
- (void)playerKilled:(SKScene *)whichScene;
- (void)playerHitWater:(SKScene *)whichScene;

- (void)runRight;
```

Then insert the new method after the existing playerKilled method in the SKBPlayer.m file:

```
- (void)playerKilled:(SKScene *)whichScene
{
    NSLog(@"Player has died...");

    // Play sound
    [whichScene runAction:_bittenSound];
}

- (void)playerHitWater:(SKScene *)whichScene
{
    NSLog(@"Player has fallen and hit the water...");
    [self removeFromParent];
}
```

Alter the didBeginContact method in the SKBGameScene.m file to make sure that any player contact with enemies is ignored if the player is dead and/or falling into the water:

```
// Player / Ratz
if ((((firstBody.categoryBitMask & kPlayerCategory) != 0) &&
                    ((secondBody.categoryBitMask & kRatzCategory) != 0))) {
    SKBRatz *theRatz = (SKBRatz *)secondBody.node;
    if (_playerSprite.playerStatus != SBPlayerFalling) {
        if (theRatz.ratzStatus == SBRatzKOfacingLeft || theRatz.ratzStatus ==
                        SBRatzKOfacingRight) {
            // ratz unconscious so kick 'em off the ledge
            [theRatz ratzCollected:self];

            // Score some points
            _playerScore = _playerScore + kRatzPointValue;
            [_scoreDisplay updateScore:self newScore:_playerScore];
        } else if (theRatz.ratzStatus == SBRatzRunningLeft || theRatz.ratzStatus
                            == SBRatzRunningRight) {
            // oops, player dies
            [_playerSprite playerKilled:self];
        }
    }
}
```

Now you can alter the didBeginContact method in the SKBGameScene.m file to handle when the falling player strikes the bottom of the screen:

```
// Player / sideWalls
if (((((firstBody.categoryBitMask & kPlayerCategory) != 0) &&
                       ((secondBody.categoryBitMask & kWallCategory) != 0)))) {
    if ([firstBodyName isEqualToString: @"player1"]) {
        if (_playerSprite.playerStatus != SBPlayerFalling) {
            if (_playerSprite.position.x < 100) {
                //NSLog(@"player contacted left edge");
                [_playerSprite wrapPlayer:CGPointMake(self.frame.size.width-10,
                                              _playerSprite.position.y)];
            } else {
                //NSLog(@"player contacted right edge");
                [_playerSprite wrapPlayer:CGPointMake(10,
                                              _playerSprite.position.y)];
            }
        } else {
            // contacted bottom wall (has been killed and has fallen)
            [_playerSprite playerHitWater:self];
        }
    }
}
}
```

Build and run the program to see the new animation sequence that is triggered when the hero is killed by an enemy sprite (see Figure 8-7).

Figure 8-7. Player splashes into the water

Player in the Water

Since the fallen hero has gone into the water, it is obvious that you should apply the same particle special effect and sound effect to the sprite when it hits the bottom.

The two necessary files are already in your project, so it won't take many code changes to make this happen.

Add the sound filename constant to the SKBPlayer.h file:

```
#define kPlayerBittenSoundFileName    @"Playerbitten.caf"
#define kPlayerSplashedSoundFileName @"Splash.caf"
#define kPlayerRunSoundFileName       @"Run.caf"
```

Also add a property to store the sound in the SKBPlayer.h file:

```
@property (nonatomic, strong) SKAction *spawnSound, *bittenSound, *splashSound;
@property (nonatomic, strong) SKAction *runSound, *jumpSound, *skidSound;
```

Add the initialization code to the spawnedInScene method of the SKBPlayer.m file:

```
_bittenSound = [SKAction playSoundFileNamed:kPlayerBittenSoundFileName
                        waitForCompletion:NO];
_splashSound = [SKAction playSoundFileNamed:kPlayerSplashedSoundFileName
                        waitForCompletion:NO];
_runSound = [SKAction playSoundFileNamed:kPlayerRunSoundFileName
                        waitForCompletion:YES];
```

Now add the effects into the playerHitWater method of the SKBPlayer.m file:

```
- (void)playerHitWater:(SKScene *)whichScene
{
    NSLog(@"Player has fallen and hit the water...");

    // Play sound
    [whichScene runAction:_splashSound];

    // splash eye candy
    NSString *emitterPath = [[NSBundle mainBundle] pathForResource:@"Splashed" ofType:@"sks"];
    SKEmitterNode *splash = [NSKeyedUnarchiver unarchiveObjectWithFile:emitterPath];
    splash.position = self.position;
    //NSLog(@"splash (%f,%f)", splash.position.x, splash.position.y);
    splash.name = @"playerSplash";
    splash.targetNode = whichScene.scene;
    [whichScene addChild:splash];

    [self removeFromParent];
}
```

Build and run the program to see the death of your hero.

Summary

You have added a lot of code in this chapter. Most of it handles all of the logic for this type of game.

When you began the chapter, you had a user-controlled player sprite that could run around and jump between ledges, and you spawned several enemy sprites and bonus items that also roamed around the "sewer" environment. This chapter handled all of the interactions between all of these characters. At this point, you should be very familiar with contact and collision events, and you should understand the difference between the two.

You added many sound effects and triggered them to play at the appropriate times. You also created a couple of particle effects.

This first game level has five enemy/bonus sprites that spawn over time. You need more levels! That is what you will learn to do in the next chapter, along with handling multiple player lives and managing the end of the game.

Chapter 9

Add More Scenes and Levels

Multiple Player Lives

Before you begin adding more levels to the game, you have some additional details to implement. For instance, you'll want the player to be able to "die" more than once in the game without the game ending. You will have the game start with several player lives, so that when a nasty vermin bites the player, it can reappear a few seconds later, ready to tackle them again. After all, accidents happen and vermin are vicious and sewers are stinky, but your hero is resilient and will survive! Hopefully.

First you need to add a constant that will determine the number of lives with which the player starts each game. Add this line at the top of the SKBGameScene.h file:

```
#import "SKBRatz.h"

#define kPlayerLivesMax          3

@interface SKBGameScene : SKScene <SKPhysicsContactDelegate>
```

Now you need a few properties in the scene to allow you to keep track of the player's health, also added to the SKBPlayer.h file:

```
@property int spawnedEnemyCount;
@property BOOL enemyIsSpawningFlag;
@property BOOL playerIsDeadFlag;
@property int playerLivesRemaining;
```

You initialize these instance variables in the createSceneContents method of the SKBGameScene.m file:

```
// Player
_playerSprite = [SKBPlayer initNewPlayer:self startingPoint:CGPointMake(80,
                                              245)];    // 40,25
[_playerSprite spawnedInScene:self];
_playerLivesRemaining = kPlayerLivesMax;
_playerIsDeadFlag = NO;
```

Then you modify the applicable variable in the didBeginContact method of the SKBGameScene.m file, inside the Player / Ratz if() statement:

```
} else if (theRatz.ratzStatus == SBRatzRunningLeft || theRatz.ratzStatus ==
                        SBRatzRunningRight) {
    // oops, player dies
    [_playerSprite playerKilled:self];
    _playerLivesRemaining--;    // decrement counter by one
}
```

Now that this is all in place, you just need a good place to check on the number of lives that the player has left and trigger the end of the game. The best place for this test is in the update method of the SKBGameScene.m file:

```
/* Called before each frame is rendered */

// check for EndOfGame
if (_playerLivesRemaining == 0) {
    NSLog(@"player has no more lives remaining, trigger end of game");

} else if (_playerIsDeadFlag) {
    // handle a dead player
    _playerIsDeadFlag = NO;

    // resurrect (if applicable) after a short delay
    SKAction *shortDelay = [SKAction waitForDuration:2];
    [self runAction:shortDelay completion:^{
        NSLog(@"player resurrection (%d lives remain)", _playerLivesRemaining);
        _playerSprite = [SKBPlayer initNewPlayer:self
                        startingPoint:CGPointMake(40, 25)];
        [_playerSprite spawnedInScene:self];
    }];

} else {
    // game is running

    // enemy and bonus sprite spawning
    if (!_enemyIsSpawningFlag && _spawnedEnemyCount < [_cast_TypeArray count]) {
```

Note Since you added a new if() statement to the front of the existing if() statements, you'll need to add a closing bracket at the end of this method to avoid errors when building.

What you are doing here is checking to see if the playerLivesRemaining variable has reached zero and, if it has, triggering the end of the game. (You will learn more about this later in the chapter.) If the player has more lives left, you check to see if the playerIsDeadFlag has been set and, if so, begin resurrecting a new player sprite in the starting location. Before that, however, you create a short delay so that the player doesn't reappear immediately after dying. This allows a natural flow to the game, and it allows the player to take a breath and stretch before trying again. When the delay is complete, you create a new player sprite, just like you do at the start of the game.

When the player's status has been changed to SBPlayerFalling, or when it has died and not yet been resurrected, you want to be sure that you don't allow user interaction to interrupt things. Therefore, you'll add an if() statement to the touchesBegan method in the SKBGameScene.m file:

```
if (_playerSprite.playerStatus != SBPlayerFalling && !_playerIsDeadFlag) {
    if (location.y >= (self.frame.size.height / 2 )) {
        // user touched upper half of the screen (zero = bottom of screen)
        if (status != SBPlayerJumpingLeft && status != SBPlayerJumpingRight &&
                status != SBPlayerJumpingUpFacingLeft && status !=
                SBPlayerJumpingUpFacingRight) {
            [_playerSprite jump];
        }
    } else if (location.x <= ( self.frame.size.width / 2 )) {
        // user touched left side of screen
        if (status == SBPlayerRunningRight) {
            [_playerSprite skidRight];
        } else if (status == SBPlayerFacingLeft || status ==
                    SBPlayerFacingRight) {
            [_playerSprite runLeft];
        }
    } else {
        // user touched right side of screen
        if (status == SBPlayerRunningLeft) {
            [_playerSprite skidLeft];
        } else if (status == SBPlayerFacingLeft || status ==
                    SBPlayerFacingRight) {
            [_playerSprite runRight];
        }
    }
}
```

Build and run the program to test the new multiple-lives functionality.

Adding a Visual Life Meter

You now have the code in place to handle multiple lives, but the player sees nothing at this point. You can solve this by adding a "body" icon to the screen for every life that the player has remaining.

Insert the new playerLivesDisplay method after the existing loadCastOfCharacters method in the SKBGameScene.m file:

```
    } else {
        NSLog(@"No plist loaded from '%@'", kCastOfCharactersFileName);
    }
}

#pragma mark Lives Display

- (void)playerLivesDisplay
{
    SKTexture *lifeTexture = [SKTexture
                        textureWithImageNamed:kPlayerStillRightFileName];
    CGPoint startWhere = CGPointMake(CGRectGetMinX(self.frame)+
                kScorePlayer1distanceFromLeft+60, CGRectGetMaxY(self.frame)-
                kScoreDistanceFromTop-20);

    // Clear out all life icons first
    for (int index=1; index <= kPlayerLivesMax; index++) {
        [self enumerateChildNodesWithName:[NSString stringWithFormat:
                        @"player_lives%d", index] usingBlock:^(SKNode *node,
                        BOOL *stop) {
            *stop = YES;
            [node removeFromParent];
        }];
    }

    // One body icon per life remaining
    for (int index=1; index <= _playerLivesRemaining; index++) {
        SKSpriteNode *lifeNode = [SKSpriteNode
                        spriteNodeWithTexture:lifeTexture];
        lifeNode.name = [NSString stringWithFormat:@"player_lives%d", index];
        lifeNode.position = CGPointMake(startWhere.x+
                        (kScorePlayer1distanceFromLeft*index), startWhere.y);
        lifeNode.xScale = 0.5;
        lifeNode.yScale = 0.5;
        [self addChild:lifeNode];
    }
}

#pragma mark Contact / Collision / Touches
```

This method creates an SKSpriteNode using an existing image and calculates a starting location using the score display as a point of reference. Then it loops through all of the possible life icons that may already be on the screen and removes them from the scene. Finally, it loops through the number of lives currently remaining and creates an icon, gives it a dynamic name and position, changes the scale to 50% of the original, and adds it to the scene. All of this should make sense to you, since you've done similar things in prior chapters.

Now that you've created the display method, you need to trigger it in several places. First of all, you need it to run when the game begins, so let's add the trigger to the end of the createSceneContents method in the SKBGameScene.m file:

```
// Player
_playerSprite = [SKBPlayer initNewPlayer:self startingPoint:CGPointMake
                                                   (40, 25)];
[_playerSprite spawnedInScene:self];
_playerLivesRemaining = kPlayerLivesMax;
_playerIsDeadFlag = NO;
[self playerLivesDisplay];
}
```

Then you add the display method to the Player / Ratz if() statement in the didBeginContact method of the SKBGameScene.m file:

```
} else if (theRatz.ratzStatus == SBRatzRunningLeft || theRatz.ratzStatus ==
                       SBRatzRunningRight) {
    // oops, player dies
    [_playerSprite playerKilled:self];
    _playerLivesRemaining--;    // decrement counter by one
    [self playerLivesDisplay];
}
```

Build and run the program to check out the new display, which shows how many lives the player has left (see Figure 9-1).

Figure 9-1. Life meter showing two lives

Game Over

Now you need to handle the end of the game, by giving the players something visual to signify that the game has ended and then allowing them to begin a fresh, new game.

First of all, you need a new property, so add it to the SKBGameScene.h file:

```
@property int playerLivesRemaining;
@property BOOL gameIsOverFlag;

@property (nonatomic, strong) SKBScores *scoreDisplay;
```

Then you can initialize it in the createSceneContents method of the SKBGameScene.m file:

```
- (void)createSceneContents
{
    // Initialize Enemies & Schedule
    _gameIsOverFlag = NO;
    _spawnedEnemyCount = 0;
    _enemyIsSpawningFlag = NO;
```

You are going to take the player back to the splash screen, so you need to add an #import to the top of the SKBGameScene.m file:

```
#import "SKBGameScene.h"
#import "SKBSplashScene.h"

@implementation SKBGameScene
```

Now you can insert the new gameIsOver method after the existing playerLivesDisplay method in the SKBGameScene.m file:

```
        lifeNode.xScale = 0.5;
        lifeNode.yScale = 0.5;
        [self addChild:lifeNode];
    }
}

#pragma mark End Of Game

- (void)gameIsOver
{
    NSLog(@"Game is over!");
    _gameIsOverFlag = YES;
    [self removeAllActions];
    [self removeAllChildren];

    SKLabelNode *gameOverText = [SKLabelNode
                                labelNodeWithFontNamed:@"Chalkduster"];
    gameOverText.text = @"Game Over";
    gameOverText.fontSize = 60;
    gameOverText.xScale = 0.1;
    gameOverText.yScale = 0.1;
    gameOverText.position = CGPointMake(CGRectGetMidX(self.frame),
                                        CGRectGetMidY(self.frame));

    SKLabelNode *pressAnywhereText = [SKLabelNode
                                labelNodeWithFontNamed:@"Chalkduster"];
    pressAnywhereText.text = @"Press anywhere to continue";
    pressAnywhereText.fontSize = 12;
    pressAnywhereText.position = CGPointMake(CGRectGetMidX(self.frame),
                                        CGRectGetMidY(self.frame)-100);
```

```objc
SKAction *zoom = [SKAction scaleTo:1.0 duration:2];
SKAction *rotate = [SKAction rotateByAngle:M_PI duration:0.5];
                                    // 2*pi = 360deg, pi = 180deg
SKAction *rotateAbit = [SKAction repeatAction:rotate count:4];
SKAction *group = [SKAction group:@[zoom,rotateAbit]];

[gameOverText runAction:group];
[self addChild:gameOverText];
[self addChild:pressAnywhereText];
}
```

```objc
#pragma mark Contact / Collision / Touches
```

This method probably doesn't need much explanation. You flag the game as being over. The screen turns black when the code removes all the children from the scene, since this clears out all the existing game nodes. Then you make two text nodes. One is static, but the other spins and grows in size over several seconds before coming to a stop. This presents the players with some animated text.

Now you add the code to trigger the new method in the update method of the SKBGameScene.m file:

```objc
// check for EndOfGame
if (_gameIsOverFlag) {
    NSLog(@"update, gameIsOverFlag is TRUE...");

} else if (_playerLivesRemaining == 0) {
    NSLog(@"player has no more lives remaining, trigger end of game");
    [self gameIsOver];

} else if (_playerIsDeadFlag) {
    // handle a dead player
```

Build and run the program to see how the end of the game looks now (see Figure 9-2). You will notice that after the player dies the last time and the screen goes black, the console will repeatedly display (@"update, gameIsOverFlag is TRUE..."); until the user taps the screen, taking him back to the splash screen. This is because the update method's if() statement, which is checking for the end of the game, is constantly triggered while this SKScene is active. This is a good thing because it prevents the rest of the update code from running while in this state. Just comment out the NSLog() to make the console a bit less busy.

Figure 9-2. Game Over screen

High Score

When the game ends, you should capture the player's score, compare it to prior game scores, and present the current high score during game play.

In order to store and retrieve the high score from "disk," you will use the NSUserDefaults class so that the high score will persist when the game is closed.

First you need a new property to keep track of the current high score; add it to the SKBGameScene.h file:

```
@property (nonatomic, strong) SKBScores *scoreDisplay;
@property int playerScore, highScore;

@end
```

You will add all of the high score graphics code to the existing SKBScores class. Add a filename constant to the SKBScores.h file:

```
#define kTextPlayerHeaderFileName        @"Text_PlayerScoreHeader.png"
#define kTextHighHeaderFileName          @"Text_HighScoreHeader.png"

#define kTextNumber0FileName             @"Text_Number_0.png"
```

Then add the image Text_HighScoreHeader.png to the project and move it into the Sprites folder.

Change the public declaration of the updateScore method in the SKBScores.h file:

```
- (void)updateScore:(SKScene *)whichScene newScore:(int)playerScore
                    hiScore:(int)highScore;
```

Then modify the createScoreNode method in the SKBScores.m file:

```
- (void)createScoreNode:(SKScene *)whichScene
{
    if (!_arrayOfNumberTextures) {
        [self createScoreNumberTextures];
    }

    // Players score
    SKTexture *headerTexture = [SKTexture
                textureWithImageNamed:kTextPlayerHeaderFileName];
    CGPoint startWhere = CGPointMake(CGRectGetMinX(whichScene.frame)+
                kScorePlayerDistanceFromLeft, CGRectGetMaxY(whichScene.frame)-
                kScoreDistanceFromTop);

    // Header
    SKSpriteNode *header = [SKSpriteNode spriteNodeWithTexture:headerTexture];
    header.name = @"score_player_header";
    header.position = startWhere;
    header.xScale = 2;
    header.yScale = 2;
    header.physicsBody.dynamic = NO;
    [whichScene addChild:header];

    // Score, 5-digits
    SKTexture *textNumber0Texture = [SKTexture
                textureWithImageNamed:kTextNumber0FileName];
    for (int index=1; index <= kScoreDigitCount; index++) {
        SKSpriteNode *zero = [SKSpriteNode
                        spriteNodeWithTexture:textNumber0Texture];
        zero.name = [NSString stringWithFormat:@"score_player_digit%d", index];
        zero.position = CGPointMake(startWhere.x+20+(kScoreNumberSpacing*index),
                        CGRectGetMaxY(whichScene.frame)-kScoreDistanceFromTop);
        zero.xScale = 2;
        zero.yScale = 2;
        zero.physicsBody.dynamic = NO;
        [whichScene addChild:zero];
    }

    // High score
    headerTexture = [SKTexture textureWithImageNamed:kTextHighHeaderFileName];
    startWhere = CGPointMake(startWhere.x+200, startWhere.y);
```

```
    // Header
    header = [SKSpriteNode spriteNodeWithTexture:headerTexture];
    header.name = @"score_high_header";
    header.position = startWhere;
    header.xScale = 2;
    header.yScale = 2;
    header.physicsBody.dynamic = NO;
    [whichScene addChild:header];

    // Score, 5-digits
    textNumber0Texture = [SKTexture textureWithImageNamed:kTextNumber0FileName];
    for (int index=1; index <= kScoreDigitCount; index++) {
        SKSpriteNode *zero = [SKSpriteNode
                        spriteNodeWithTexture:textNumber0Texture];
        zero.name = [NSString stringWithFormat:@"score_high_digit%d", index];
        zero.position = CGPointMake(startWhere.x+20+(kScoreNumberSpacing*index),
                        CGRectGetMaxY(whichScene.frame)-kScoreDistanceFromTop);
        zero.xScale = 2;
        zero.yScale = 2;
        zero.physicsBody.dynamic = NO;
        [whichScene addChild:zero];
    }
}
```

As you can see, all you are doing in this method and the next is creating a duplicate of the player-scoring node and making a few changes. The high score graphics will be offset from the player-scoring node, just to the right of it.

Modify the updateScore method in the SKBScores.m file to match the following:

```
- (void)updateScore:(SKScene *)whichScene newScore:(int)playerScore
                    hiScore:(int)highScore
{
    // Player score
    NSString *numberString = [NSString stringWithFormat:@"00000%d",
                    playerScore];
    NSString *substring = [numberString substringFromIndex:[numberString length]
                    - 5];

    for (int index = 1; index <= 5; index++) {
        [whichScene enumerateChildNodesWithName:[NSString
                    stringWithFormat:@"score_player_digit%d", index]
                    usingBlock:^(SKNode *node, BOOL *stop) {
            NSString *charAtIndex = [substring
                    substringWithRange:NSMakeRange(index-1, 1)];
            int charIntValue = [charAtIndex intValue];
            SKTexture *digitTexture = [_arrayOfNumberTextures
                    objectAtIndex:charIntValue];
            SKAction *newDigit = [SKAction animateWithTextures:@[digitTexture]
                    timePerFrame:0.1];
            [node runAction:newDigit]; }];
    }
```

```
    // High score
    numberString = [NSString stringWithFormat:@"00000%d", highScore];
    substring = [numberString substringFromIndex:[numberString length] - 5];

    for (int index = 1; index <= 5; index++) {
        [whichScene enumerateChildNodesWithName:[NSString
                        stringWithFormat:@"score_high_digit%d", index]
                        usingBlock:^(SKNode *node, BOOL *stop) {
            NSString *charAtIndex = [substring
                        substringWithRange:NSMakeRange(index-1, 1)];
            int charIntValue = [charAtIndex intValue];
            SKTexture *digitTexture = [_arrayOfNumberTextures
                        objectAtIndex:charIntValue];
            SKAction *newDigit = [SKAction animateWithTextures:@[digitTexture]
                        timePerFrame:0.1];
            [node runAction:newDigit]; }];
    }
}
```

Since you have added a parameter to the updateScore method, you will need to change the calls to the method in the SKBGameScene.m file. In the createSceneContents method, make the following changes:

```
// Scoring
SKBScores *sceneScores = [[SKBScores alloc] init];
[sceneScores createScoreNode:self];
_scoreDisplay = sceneScores;
_playerScore = 0;
[_scoreDisplay updateScore:self newScore:_playerScore hiScore:_highScore];
```

In the didBeginContact method, you called it two times. First in the Player / Coins if() statement block:

```
// Score some bonus points
_playerScore = _playerScore + kCoinPointValue;
[_scoreDisplay updateScore:self newScore:_playerScore hiScore:_highScore];
```

Then in the Player / Ratz block:

```
// Score some points
_playerScore = _playerScore + kRatzPointValue;
[_scoreDisplay updateScore:self newScore:_playerScore hiScore:_highScore];
```

Then you add code to the gameIsOver method of the SKBGameScene.m file to trigger the high score update:

```
[self removeAllActions];
[self removeAllChildren];
```

```
// Handle high scores
if (_playerScore > _highScore) {
    _highScore = _playerScore;
    NSLog(@"high score: %d", _highScore);
    [_scoreDisplay updateScore:self newScore:_playerScore hiScore:_highScore];

    // write it to disk
    NSNumber *theScore = [NSNumber numberWithInt:_highScore];
    NSUserDefaults *userDefaults = [NSUserDefaults standardUserDefaults];
    [userDefaults setObject:theScore forKey:@"highScore"];
    [[NSUserDefaults standardUserDefaults] synchronize];
}

SKLabelNode *gameOverText = [SKLabelNode labelNodeWithFontNamed:@"Chalkduster"];
```

You convert the int value of the high score to an NSNumber object so that you can store it on disk. Now you just need to read it from disk each time the game begins.

Modify the createSceneContents method of the SKBGameScene.m file to read the stored value:

```
[self addChild:pipe];

// read high score from disk (if written there by previous game)
NSNumber *theScore = [[NSUserDefaults standardUserDefaults]
                            objectForKey:@"highScore"];
_highScore = [theScore intValue];

// Scoring
```

Build and run the program to see that the high score is now written to disk and read each time the game is launched.

Level-Completion Test

Now you need to test for and handle the level that is being completed, which happens when the last spawned enemy or bonus sprite has been collected, leaving the hero with nothing to do.

You'll add a new property that will track the current count of active enemy sprites on the screen. Declare it in the SKBGameScene.h file:

```
@property int frameCounter;
@property int spawnedEnemyCount, activeEnemyCount;
@property BOOL enemyIsSpawningFlag;
```

Then you can increment this count inside the update method of the SKBGameScene.m file:

```
// Create & spawn the new Enemy
_enemyIsSpawningFlag = NO;
_spawnedEnemyCount = _spawnedEnemyCount + 1;
_activeEnemyCount++;

if (castType == SKBEnemyTypeCoin) {
```

Then you need to decrement it when a coin is collected. Add this to the Player / Coins if() statement of the didBeginContact method in the SKBGameScene.m file:

```
// Player / Coins
if ((((firstBody.categoryBitMask & kPlayerCategory) != 0) &&
                        ((secondBody.categoryBitMask & kCoinCategory) != 0))) {
    SKBCoin *theCoin = (SKBCoin *)secondBody.node;
    [theCoin coinCollected:self];
    _activeEnemyCount--;

    // Score some bonus points
    _playerScore = _playerScore + kCoinPointValue;
    [_scoreDisplay updateScore:self newScore:_playerScore];
}
```

Then also add it to the Coin / Pipes if() statement:

```
// Coin / Pipes
if ((((firstBody.categoryBitMask & kPipeCategory) != 0) &&
                        ((secondBody.categoryBitMask & kCoinCategory) != 0))) {
    SKBCoin *theCoin = (SKBCoin *)secondBody.node;
    [theCoin coinHitPipe];
    _activeEnemyCount--;
}
```

Then also add it to the Ratz / Sidewalls if() statement:

```
} else {
    // contacted bottom wall (has been kicked off and has fallen)
    [theRatz ratzHitWater:self];
    _activeEnemyCount--;
}
```

Finally, you add this code to the Coin section of the checkForEnemyHits method in the SKBGameScene.m file:

```
// struckLedge check
if ([theCoin.lastKnownContactedLedge isEqualToString:struckLedgeName]) {
    NSLog(@"Player hit %@ where %@ is known to be", struckLedgeName,
                        theCoin.name);
    [theCoin coinCollected:self];
    _activeEnemyCount--;
}
```

With the triggers in place, you just need to test the value of this variable inside the update method of the SKBGameScene.m file:

```
} else if (_playerIsDeadFlag) {
    // handle a dead player
    _playerIsDeadFlag = NO;
```

```
    // resurrect (if applicable) after a short delay
    SKAction *shortDelay = [SKAction waitForDuration:2];
    [self runAction:shortDelay completion:^{
        NSLog(@"player resurrection (%d lives remain)", _playerLivesRemaining);
        _playerSprite = [SKBPlayer initNewPlayer:self
                        startingPoint:CGPointMake(40, 25)];
        [_playerSprite spawnedInScene:self];
    }];

} else if (_activeEnemyCount == 0 && _spawnedEnemyCount == [_cast_TypeArray
                                                            count]) {

    NSLog(@"end of level");

} else {
    // game is running
```

Build and run the program to see how well the level-completion test works.

Level-Completion Effects

Now that the test is functioning as desired, you can add some detail to pretty up the process.

First add a property to the SKBGameScene.h file:

```
@property int playerLivesRemaining;
@property BOOL gameIsOverFlag, gameIsPaused;

@property (nonatomic, strong) SKBScores *scoreDisplay;
```

Then add your initialization to the top of the createSceneContents method of the SKBGameScene.m file:

```
// Initialize Enemies & Schedule
_gameIsOverFlag = NO;
_gameIsPaused = NO;
_spawnedEnemyCount = 0;
_enemyIsSpawningFlag = NO;
```

Then add another else if() statement and modify the level-completion if() statement in the update method of the SKBGameScene.m file:

```
} else if (_gameIsPaused) {
    // do nothing while paused

} else if (_activeEnemyCount == 0 && _spawnedEnemyCount ==
                                    [_cast_TypeArray count]) {

    [self levelCompleted];

} else {
    // game is running
```

This gameIsPaused variable does little at this point except for keeping the update method from doing other things while the level effects are being applied.

We have a new sound effect available specifically for the level-completion routine, so you can add the file LevelCompleted.caf to the project and move it into the Sound group folder. Then add a new levelCompleted method by inserting it after the existing playerLivesDisplay method of the SKBGameScene.m file:

```
        [self addChild:lifeNode];
    }
}

#pragma mark End Of Level

- (void)levelCompleted
{
    NSLog(@"Level is completed!");
    [self removeAllActions];
    _gameIsPaused = YES;

    // Remove player sprite from scene
    [self enumerateChildNodesWithName:[NSString stringWithFormat:@"player1"]
                                          usingBlock:^(SKNode *node, BOOL *stop) {
        *stop = YES;
        [node removeFromParent];
    }];

    // Play sound
    SKAction *completedSong = [SKAction playSoundFileNamed:@"LevelCompleted.caf"
                                          waitForCompletion:NO];
    [self runAction:completedSong];

    SKLabelNode *levelText = [SKLabelNode
                                          labelNodeWithFontNamed:@"Chalkduster"];
    levelText.text = @"Level Completed";
    levelText.fontSize = 48;
    levelText.position = CGPointMake(CGRectGetMidX(self.frame),
                                          CGRectGetMidY(self.frame));
    SKAction *fadeIn = [SKAction fadeInWithDuration:0.25];
    SKAction *fadeOut = [SKAction fadeOutWithDuration:0.25];
    SKAction *sequence = [SKAction sequence:@[fadeIn,fadeOut,fadeIn,fadeOut,
                fadeIn,fadeOut,fadeIn,fadeOut,fadeIn,fadeOut,fadeIn,fadeOut]];
    [self addChild:levelText];
    [levelText runAction:sequence completion:^{
        [levelText removeFromParent];

        // Player reappears at starting location
        _playerSprite = [SKBPlayer initNewPlayer:self
                                          startingPoint:CGPointMake(40, 25)];
        [_playerSprite spawnedInScene:self];
    }];
}

#pragma mark End Of Game
```

This method removes the player sprite from the scene, plays the new sound file, creates a text node and makes it fade in and out several times to make it appear as if it's pulsing. When that SKAction has completed, the code respawns the player to the starting location.

Build and run the program to see the changes once the level has been completed.

Unending Levels

Before adding more levels to the game, you need to make sure that when the maximum level is reached, the same level will be repeated until the player's lives are exhausted. This will ensure that the player can continue to play, regardless of the number of levels incorporated into the game.

To do this, you need a constant and a variable to track the number of levels and the current level. Add these to the SKBGameScene.h file:

```
#import "SKBRatz.h"

#define kNumberOfLevelsMax        1

#define kPlayerLivesMax           3
#define kPlayerLivesSpacing       10
.
.
.
@property BOOL gameIsOverFlag, gameIsPaused;
@property int currentLevel;

@property (nonatomic, strong) SKBScores *scoreDisplay;
```

Then you change the initWithSize method in the SKBGameScene.m file to initialize the new variable and pass it to the loadCastOfCharacters method:

```
// add surfaces to screen
[self createSceneContents];

// start at level 1
_currentLevel = 1;

// compose cast of characters from propertyList
[self loadCastOfCharacters:_currentLevel];
```

Now you can modify loadCastOfCharacters to load the data dynamically, based on the value passed into it:

```
- (void)loadCastOfCharacters:(int)levelNumber
{
    // load cast from plist file, just a single Level
    NSString *path = [[NSBundle mainBundle]
            pathForResource:kCastOfCharactersFileName ofType:@"plist"];
    NSDictionary *plistDictionary = [NSDictionary
            dictionaryWithContentsOfFile:path];
```

```
if (plistDictionary) {
    NSDictionary *levelDictionary = [plistDictionary valueForKey:@"Level"];
    if (levelDictionary) {
        NSArray *singleLevelArray = [NSArray arrayWithObject:path];
                                                    // temp object

        switch (levelNumber) {
            case 1:
                singleLevelArray = [levelDictionary valueForKey:@"One"];
                break;

            case 2:
                singleLevelArray = [levelDictionary valueForKey:@"Two"];
                break;

            default:
                singleLevelArray = [levelDictionary valueForKey:@"Two"];
                break;
        }
        if (singleLevelArray) {
            NSDictionary *enemyDictionary = nil;
            NSMutableArray *newTypeArray = [NSMutableArray
                            arrayWithCapacity:[singleLevelArray count]];
            NSMutableArray *newDelayArray = [NSMutableArray
                            arrayWithCapacity:[singleLevelArray count]];
            NSMutableArray *newStartArray = [NSMutableArray
                            arrayWithCapacity:[singleLevelArray count]];
            NSNumber *rawType, *rawDelay, *rawStartXindex;
            int enemyType, spawnDelay, startXindex = 0;

            for (int index=0; index<[singleLevelArray count]; index++) {
                enemyDictionary = [singleLevelArray objectAtIndex:index];

                // NSNumbers from dictionary
                rawType = [enemyDictionary valueForKey:@"Type"];
                rawDelay = [enemyDictionary valueForKey:@"Delay"];
                rawStartXindex = [enemyDictionary
                                    valueForKey:@"StartXindex"];

                // local integer values
                enemyType = [rawType intValue];
                spawnDelay = [rawDelay intValue];
                startXindex = [rawStartXindex intValue];

                // long term storage
                [newTypeArray addObject:rawType];
                [newDelayArray addObject:rawDelay];
                [newStartArray addObject:rawStartXindex];

                //NSLog(@"%d, %d, %d, %d", index, enemyType, spawnDelay,
                                                        startXindex);
            }
```

```
                    // store data locally
                    _cast_TypeArray = [NSArray arrayWithArray:newTypeArray];
                    _cast_DelayArray = [NSArray arrayWithArray:newDelayArray];
                    _cast_StartXindexArray = [NSArray arrayWithArray:newStartArray];
                } else {
                    NSLog(@"No singleLevelArray");
                }
            } else {
                NSLog(@"No levelDictionary");
            }
        } else {
            NSLog(@"No plist loaded from '%@'", kCastOfCharactersFileName);
        }
    }
}
```

Besides changing the name of the array that holds all of the level data, you added a switch()
statement to handle all of the levels held in the plist file. The important thing to note here is the
default value of the switch() statement. You change this value to be the last level stored in the plist
file so that the last level repeats indefinitely, no matter how many levels the player ascends. So if you
have only two levels' worth of data in the plist file, the player just sees that same level-two enemy
group spawn for levels three, four, five, and so on. This also makes it so that this method won't break
when values that are greater than what is actually stored in the plist file are passed into it.

Now that this has been done, you can change the levelCompleted method in the SKBGameScene.m file
to trigger the next level to begin:

```
[levelText runAction:sequence completion:^{
    [levelText removeFromParent];

    // Player reappears at starting location
    _playerSprite = [SKBPlayer initNewPlayer:self startingPoint:CGPointMake
                                                    (40, 25)];

    [_playerSprite spawnedInScene:self];

    // Trigger a new level and its cast of characters
    _currentLevel++;
    [self loadCastOfCharacters:_currentLevel];
    _gameIsPaused = NO;
    _spawnedEnemyCount = 0;
    _enemyIsSpawningFlag = NO;
}];
```

Build and run the program. You'll see that the game now has unlimited level possibilities. To add
more level enemy-spawning rates and variations, you simply add them to the plist file and then
update the switch() statement in the loadCastOfCharacters method.

A New Enemy Type

The Ratz enemies are obnoxious but fairly easy to eliminate. To make the game more challenging, you need a new enemy. Introducing the mighty Gatorz!

The new enemy will be added as a new class, but most of the class code is very similar to the Ratz class and should look very familiar to you.

Add the images with the prefix Gatorz_ to the project, create a new group folder named Gatorz inside the Sprites group folder, and move these images into the new folder.

New filename constants are needed in the SKBSpriteTextures.h file:

```
#define kRatzKOfacingRight3FileName        @"Ratz_KO_R_Hit3.png"
#define kRatzKOfacingRight4FileName        @"Ratz_KO_R_Hit4.png"
#define kRatzKOfacingRight5FileName        @"Ratz_KO_R_Hit5.png"

#define kGatorzRunRight1FileName           @"Gatorz_Right_1.png"
#define kGatorzRunRight2FileName           @"Gatorz_Right_2.png"
#define kGatorzRunRight3FileName           @"Gatorz_Right_3.png"
#define kGatorzRunRight4FileName           @"Gatorz_Right_4.png"
#define kGatorzRunRight5FileName           @"Gatorz_Right_5.png"

#define kGatorzRunLeft1FileName            @"Gatorz_Left_1.png"
#define kGatorzRunLeft2FileName            @"Gatorz_Left_2.png"
#define kGatorzRunLeft3FileName            @"Gatorz_Left_3.png"
#define kGatorzRunLeft4FileName            @"Gatorz_Left_4.png"
#define kGatorzRunLeft5FileName            @"Gatorz_Left_5.png"

#define kGatorzKOfacingLeft1FileName       @"Gatorz_KO_L_Hit1.png"
#define kGatorzKOfacingLeft2FileName       @"Gatorz_KO_L_Hit2.png"
#define kGatorzKOfacingLeft3FileName       @"Gatorz_KO_L_Hit3.png"
#define kGatorzKOfacingLeft4FileName       @"Gatorz_KO_L_Hit4.png"
#define kGatorzKOfacingRight1FileName      @"Gatorz_KO_R_Hit1.png"
#define kGatorzKOfacingRight2FileName      @"Gatorz_KO_R_Hit2.png"
#define kGatorzKOfacingRight3FileName      @"Gatorz_KO_R_Hit3.png"
#define kGatorzKOfacingRight4FileName      @"Gatorz_KO_R_Hit4.png"

#define kCoin1FileName                     @"Coin1.png"
#define kCoin2FileName                     @"Coin2.png"
#define kCoin3FileName                     @"Coin3.png"
```

New texture variables are needed in the SKBSpriteTextures.h file:

```
@property (nonatomic, strong) NSArray *ratzRunLeftTextures,
                                      *ratzRunRightTextures;
@property (nonatomic, strong) NSArray *ratzKOfacingLeftTextures,
                                      *ratzKOfacingRightTextures;
```

```
@property (nonatomic, strong) NSArray *gatorzRunLeftTextures,
                                       *gatorzRunRightTextures;
@property (nonatomic, strong) NSArray *gatorzKOfacingLeftTextures,
                                       *gatorzKOfacingRightTextures;

@property (nonatomic, strong) NSArray *coinTextures;
```

Now you add the texture-generation code to the createAnimationTextures method in the SKBSpriteTextures.m file:

```
_ratzKOfacingRightTextures = @[f1,f2,f5,f5,f5,f5,f5,f5,f5,f5,f5,f5,f5,f5,f5,f5,f5,f5,f5,f5,f5,f3
    ,f2,f3,f2,
                                                        f3,f2,f1];


// Gatorz

//  right, running
f1 = [SKTexture textureWithImageNamed:kGatorzRunRight1FileName];
f2 = [SKTexture textureWithImageNamed:kGatorzRunRight2FileName];
f3 = [SKTexture textureWithImageNamed:kGatorzRunRight3FileName];
f4 = [SKTexture textureWithImageNamed:kGatorzRunRight4FileName];
f5 = [SKTexture textureWithImageNamed:kGatorzRunRight5FileName];
_gatorzRunRightTextures = @[f1,f2,f3,f4,f5];

//  left, running
f1 = [SKTexture textureWithImageNamed:kGatorzRunLeft1FileName];
f2 = [SKTexture textureWithImageNamed:kGatorzRunLeft2FileName];
f3 = [SKTexture textureWithImageNamed:kGatorzRunLeft3FileName];
f4 = [SKTexture textureWithImageNamed:kGatorzRunLeft4FileName];
f5 = [SKTexture textureWithImageNamed:kGatorzRunLeft5FileName];
_gatorzRunLeftTextures = @[f1,f2,f3,f4,f5];

// knocked out, facing left
f1 = [SKTexture textureWithImageNamed:kGatorzKOfacingLeft1FileName];
f2 = [SKTexture textureWithImageNamed:kGatorzKOfacingLeft2FileName];
f3 = [SKTexture textureWithImageNamed:kGatorzKOfacingLeft3FileName];
f4 = [SKTexture textureWithImageNamed:kGatorzKOfacingLeft4FileName];
_gatorzKOfacingLeftTextures = @[f1,f2,f4,f4,f4,f4,f4,f4,f4,f4,f4,f4,f4,f4,f4,f4,
                            f4,f4,f4,f4,f4,f4,f3,f2,f3,f2,f3,f2,f1];
// knocked out, facing right
f1 = [SKTexture textureWithImageNamed:kGatorzKOfacingRight1FileName];
f2 = [SKTexture textureWithImageNamed:kGatorzKOfacingRight2FileName];
f3 = [SKTexture textureWithImageNamed:kGatorzKOfacingRight3FileName];
f4 = [SKTexture textureWithImageNamed:kGatorzKOfacingRight4FileName];
_gatorzKOfacingRightTextures = @[f1,f2,f4,f4,f4,f4,f4,f4,f4,f4,f4,f4,f4,f4,f4,
                            f4,f4,f4,f4,f4,f4,f4,f3,f2,f3,f2,f3,f2,f1];
// Coins
f1 = [SKTexture textureWithImageNamed:kCoin1FileName];
```

You also need a new constant category value in the SKBAppDelegate.h file:

```
static const uint32_t kRatzCategory =          0x1 << 6;
static const uint32_t kGatorzCategory =        0x1 << 7;

#define kEnemySpawnEdgeBufferX                 30
#define kEnemySpawnEdgeBufferY                 30
```

Add the new category to the initNewCoin method in the SKBCoin.m file:

```
coin.physicsBody.contactTestBitMask = kWallCategory | kLedgeCategory |
        kPipeCategory | kCoinCategory | kRatzCategory | kGatorzCategory ;
coin.physicsBody.collisionBitMask = kBaseCategory | kWallCategory |
        kLedgeCategory | kCoinCategory | kRatzCategory | kGatorzCategory ;
```

Also add the new category to the initNewPlayer method in the SKBPlayer.m file:

```
player.physicsBody.contactTestBitMask = kWallCategory | kLedgeCategory |
        kCoinCategory | kRatzCategory | kGatorzCategory;
player.physicsBody.collisionBitMask = kBaseCategory | kWallCategory |
        kLedgeCategory | kRatzCategory | kGatorzCategory ;
```

Add the new category to the initNewRatz method in the SKBRatz.m file as well:

```
ratz.physicsBody.contactTestBitMask = kBaseCategory | kWallCategory |
        kLedgeCategory | kPipeCategory | kRatzCategory | kGatorzCategory |
        kCoinCategory ;
ratz.physicsBody.collisionBitMask = kBaseCategory | kWallCategory |
        kLedgeCategory | kPlayerCategory | kRatzCategory | kGatorzCategory |
        kCoinCategory ;
```

Create a new class named SKBGatorz as a subclass of SKSpriteNode. Modify the SKBGatorz.h file to match the following:

```
#import <SpriteKit/SpriteKit.h>
#import "SKBAppDelegate.h"
#import "SKBSpriteTextures.h"

#define kGatorzSpawnSoundFileName           @"SpawnEnemy.caf"
#define kGatorzKOSoundFileName              @"EnemyKO.caf"
#define kGatorzCollectedSoundFileName       @"EnemyCollected.caf"
#define kGatorzSplashedSoundFileName        @"Splash.caf"

#define kGatorzRunningIncrement             30
#define kGatorzKickedIncrement              5
#define kGatorzPointValue                   150

typedef enum : int {
    SBGatorzRunningLeft = 0,
    SBGatorzRunningRight,
    SBGatorzKOfacingLeft,
```

```
    SBGatorzKOfacingRight,
    SBGatorzKicked
} SBGatorzStatus;

@interface SKBGatorz : SKSpriteNode

@property int gatorzStatus;
@property int lastKnownXposition, lastKnownYposition;
@property (nonatomic, strong) NSString *lastKnownContactedLedge;
@property (nonatomic, strong) SKBSpriteTextures *spriteTextures;

@property (nonatomic, strong) SKAction *spawnSound, *koSound, *collectedSound,
                                       *splashSound;

+ (SKBGatorz *)initNewGatorz:(SKScene *)whichScene
                   startingPoint:(CGPoint)location gatorzIndex:(int)index;
- (void)spawnedInScene:(SKScene *)whichScene;

- (void)wrapGatorz:(CGPoint)where;
- (void)gatorzHitLeftPipe:(SKScene *)whichScene;
- (void)gatorzHitRightPipe:(SKScene *)whichScene;

- (void)gatorzKnockedOut:(SKScene *)whichScene;
- (void)gatorzCollected:(SKScene *)whichScene;
- (void)gatorzHitWater:(SKScene *)whichScene;

- (void)runRight;
- (void)runLeft;
- (void)turnRight;
- (void)turnLeft;

@end
```

Then modify the SKBGatorz.m file to match the following:

```
#import "SKBGatorz.h"
#import "SKBGameScene.h"

@implementation SKBGatorz

#pragma mark Initialization

+ (SKBGatorz *)initNewGatorz:(SKScene *)whichScene
                   startingPoint:(CGPoint)location gatorzIndex:(int)index
{
    SKTexture *gatorzTexture = [SKTexture
                        textureWithImageNamed:kGatorzRunRight1FileName];
    SKBGatorz *gatorz = [SKBGatorz spriteNodeWithTexture:gatorzTexture];
    gatorz.name = [NSString stringWithFormat:@"gatorz%d", index];
    gatorz.position = location;
    gatorz.xScale = 1.5;
    gatorz.yScale = 1.5;
```

```objc
    gatorz.physicsBody = [SKPhysicsBody bodyWithRectangleOfSize:gatorz.size];
    gatorz.physicsBody.categoryBitMask = kGatorzCategory;
    gatorz.physicsBody.contactTestBitMask = kBaseCategory | kWallCategory |
                kLedgeCategory | kPipeCategory | kGatorzCategory | kRatzCategory
                | kCoinCategory ;
    gatorz.physicsBody.collisionBitMask = kBaseCategory | kWallCategory |
                kLedgeCategory | kPlayerCategory | kGatorzCategory |
                kRatzCategory | kCoinCategory ;
    gatorz.physicsBody.density = 1.0;
    gatorz.physicsBody.linearDamping = 0.1;
    gatorz.physicsBody.restitution = 0.2;
    gatorz.physicsBody.allowsRotation = NO;

    [whichScene addChild:gatorz];
    return gatorz;
}

- (void)spawnedInScene:(SKScene *)whichScene
{
    SKBGameScene *theScene = (SKBGameScene *)whichScene;
    _spriteTextures = theScene.spriteTextures;

    // Sound Effects
    _splashSound = [SKAction playSoundFileNamed:kGatorzSplashedSoundFileName
                        waitForCompletion:NO];
    _koSound = [SKAction playSoundFileNamed:kGatorzKOSoundFileName
                        waitForCompletion:NO];
    _collectedSound = [SKAction playSoundFileNamed:kGatorzCollectedSoundFileName
                        waitForCompletion:NO];
    _spawnSound = [SKAction playSoundFileNamed:kGatorzSpawnSoundFileName
                        waitForCompletion:NO];
    [self runAction:_spawnSound];

    // set initial direction and start moving
    if (self.position.x < CGRectGetMidX(whichScene.frame))
        [self runRight];
    else
        [self runLeft];
}

#pragma mark Screen wrap

- (void)wrapGatorz:(CGPoint)where
{
    SKPhysicsBody *storePB = self.physicsBody;
    self.physicsBody = nil;
    self.position = where;
    self.physicsBody = storePB;
}
```

```objc
- (void)gatorzHitLeftPipe:(SKScene *)whichScene
{
    int leftSideX = CGRectGetMinX(whichScene.frame)+kEnemySpawnEdgeBufferX;
    int topSideY = CGRectGetMaxY(whichScene.frame)-kEnemySpawnEdgeBufferY;

    SKPhysicsBody *storedPB = self.physicsBody;
    self.physicsBody = nil;
    self.position = CGPointMake(leftSideX, topSideY);
    self.physicsBody = storedPB;
    [self removeAllActions];
    [self runRight];

    // Play spawning sound
    [self runAction:self.spawnSound];
}

- (void)gatorzHitRightPipe:(SKScene *)whichScene
{
    int rightSideX = CGRectGetMaxX(whichScene.frame)-kEnemySpawnEdgeBufferX;
    int topSideY = CGRectGetMaxY(whichScene.frame)-kEnemySpawnEdgeBufferY;

    SKPhysicsBody *storedPB = self.physicsBody;
    self.physicsBody = nil;
    self.position = CGPointMake(rightSideX, topSideY);
    self.physicsBody = storedPB;
    [self removeAllActions];
    [self runLeft];

    // Play spawning sound
    [self runAction:self.spawnSound];
}

#pragma mark Contact

- (void)gatorzKnockedOut:(SKScene *)whichScene
{
    [self removeAllActions];

    NSArray *textureArray = nil;
    if (_gatorzStatus == SBGatorzRunningLeft) {
        _gatorzStatus = SBGatorzKOfacingLeft;
        textureArray = [NSArray
                arrayWithArray:_spriteTextures.gatorzKOfacingLeftTextures];
    } else {
        _gatorzStatus = SBRatzKOfacingRight;
        textureArray = [NSArray
                arrayWithArray:_spriteTextures.gatorzKOfacingRightTextures];
    }
```

```
    SKAction *knockedOutAnimation = [SKAction animateWithTextures:textureArray
                                        timePerFrame:0.2];
    SKAction *knockedOutForAwhile = [SKAction repeatAction:knockedOutAnimation
                                        count:1];
    [self runAction:knockedOutForAwhile completion:^{
        if (_gatorzStatus == SBGatorzKOfacingLeft) {
            [self runLeft];
        } else {
            [self runRight];
        }
    }];
}

- (void)gatorzCollected:(SKScene *)whichScene
{
    NSLog(@"%@ collected", self.name);

    // Update status
    _gatorzStatus = SBGatorzKicked;

    // Play sound
    [whichScene runAction:_collectedSound];

    // show amount of winnings
    SKLabelNode *moneyText = [SKLabelNode labelNodeWithFontNamed:@"Courier-
                                                            Bold"];
    moneyText.text = [NSString stringWithFormat:@"$%d", kGatorzPointValue];
    moneyText.fontSize = 9;
    moneyText.fontColor = [SKColor whiteColor];
    moneyText.position = CGPointMake(self.position.x-10, self.position.y+28);
    [whichScene addChild:moneyText];

    SKAction *fadeAway = [SKAction fadeOutWithDuration:1];
    [moneyText runAction:fadeAway completion:^{ [moneyText removeFromParent];
                                        }];

    // upward impulse applied
    [self.physicsBody applyImpulse:CGVectorMake(0, kGatorzKickedIncrement)];

    // Make him spin when kicked
    SKAction *rotation = [SKAction rotateByAngle:M_PI duration:0.1];
                                        // 2*pi = 360deg, pi = 180deg
    SKAction *rotateForever = [SKAction repeatActionForever:rotation];
    [self runAction:rotateForever];

    // While kicked upward and spinning, wait for a short spell before
                                            altering physicsBody
    SKAction *shortDelay = [SKAction waitForDuration:0.25];
```

```objc
    [self runAction:shortDelay completion:^{
        // Make a new physics body that is much, much smaller as to not
                                        affect ledges as he falls...
        self.physicsBody = [SKPhysicsBody bodyWithRectangleOfSize:CGSizeMake(1,1)];
        self.physicsBody.categoryBitMask = kGatorzCategory;
        self.physicsBody.collisionBitMask = kWallCategory;
        self.physicsBody.contactTestBitMask = kWallCategory;
        self.physicsBody.linearDamping = 1.0;
        self.physicsBody.allowsRotation = YES;
    }];
}

- (void)gatorzHitWater:(SKScene *)whichScene
{
    // Play sound
    [whichScene runAction:_splashSound];

    // splash eye candy
    NSString *emitterPath = [[NSBundle mainBundle] pathForResource:@"Splashed"
                                                            ofType:@"sks"];

    SKEmitterNode *splash = [NSKeyedUnarchiver
                                    unarchiveObjectWithFile:emitterPath];
    splash.position = self.position;
    NSLog(@"splash (%f,%f)", splash.position.x, splash.position.y);
    splash.name = @"gatorzSplash";
    splash.targetNode = whichScene.scene;
    [whichScene addChild:splash];

    [self removeFromParent];
}


#pragma mark Movement

- (void)runRight
{
    _gatorzStatus = SBGatorzRunningRight;

    SKAction *walkAnimation = [SKAction
                animateWithTextures:_spriteTextures.gatorzRunRightTextures
                timePerFrame:0.05];
    SKAction *walkForever = [SKAction repeatActionForever:walkAnimation];
    [self runAction:walkForever];

    SKAction *moveRight = [SKAction moveByX:kGatorzRunningIncrement y:0
                                duration:1];
    SKAction *moveForever = [SKAction repeatActionForever:moveRight];
    [self runAction:moveForever];
}
```

```objc
- (void)runLeft
{
    _gatorzStatus = SBGatorzRunningLeft;

    SKAction *walkAnimation = [SKAction animateWithTextures:
                _spriteTextures.gatorzRunLeftTextures timePerFrame:0.05];
    SKAction *walkForever = [SKAction repeatActionForever:walkAnimation];
    [self runAction:walkForever];

    SKAction *moveLeft = [SKAction moveByX:-kGatorzRunningIncrement
                                  y:0 duration:1];
    SKAction *moveForever = [SKAction repeatActionForever:moveLeft];
    [self runAction:moveForever];
}

- (void)turnRight
{
    _gatorzStatus = SBGatorzRunningRight;
    [self removeAllActions];
    SKAction *moveRight = [SKAction moveByX:5 y:0 duration:0.4];
    [self runAction:moveRight completion:^{[self runRight];}];
}

- (void)turnLeft
{
    _gatorzStatus = SBGatorzRunningLeft;
    [self removeAllActions];
    SKAction *moveLeft = [SKAction moveByX:-5 y:0 duration:0.4];
    [self runAction:moveLeft completion:^{[self runLeft];}];
}

@end
```

Build the project and verify that there are no errors with all of these changes.

That wraps up all of the foundation for the new class. Now you just need to incorporate it into the scene.

Let's add the enemy type to the plist file for level two. Modify the level two section of the CastOfCharacters.plist file to have six items that match the following entries:

Key	Value	
Item 0	(Dictionary)	
"Type"	(Number):	1
"Delay"	(Number):	3
"StartXindex"	(Number):	0
Item 1	(Dictionary)	
"Type"	(Number):	0
"Delay"	(Number):	3
"StartXindex"	(Number):	1
Item 2	(Dictionary)	
"Type"	(Number):	2
"Delay"	(Number):	3
"StartXindex"	(Number):	0
Item 3	(Dictionary)	
"Type"	(Number):	1
"Delay"	(Number):	3
"StartXindex"	(Number):	1
Item 4	(Dictionary)	
"Type"	(Number):	2
"Delay"	(Number):	3
"StartXindex"	(Number):	0
Item 5	(Dictionary)	
"Type"	(Number):	0
"Delay"	(Number):	3
"StartXindex"	(Number):	1

The new value 2 for the Type field will be for the new Gatorz enemy. (Remember that 0 is for Coins and 1 is for Ratz.)

Modify the SKBGameScene.h file to import the new class header and change the level count constant:

```
#import "SKBRatz.h"
#import "SKBGatorz.h"

#define kNumberOfLevelsMax      2
```

```
#define kPlayerLivesMax        3
#define kPlayerLivesSpacing     10
```

The switch() statement needs an update in the loadCastOfCharacters method of the SKBGameScene.m file:

```
switch (levelNumber) {
    case 1:
        singleLevelArray = [levelDictionary valueForKey:@"One"];
            break;

    case 2:
        singleLevelArray = [levelDictionary valueForKey:@"Two"];
            break;

    default:
        singleLevelArray = [levelDictionary valueForKey:@"Two"];
            break;
}
```

You can add a block for the new enemy in the checkForEnemyHits method of the SKBGameScene.m file:

```
    // struckLedge check
    if ([theRatz.lastKnownContactedLedge isEqualToString:struckLedgeName]) {
        NSLog(@"Player hit %@ where %@ is known to be", struckLedgeName,
                                            theRatz.name);
        [theRatz ratzKnockedOut:self];
    }
    }];
}

// Gatorz
for (int index=0; index <= _spawnedEnemyCount; index++) {
    [self enumerateChildNodesWithName:[NSString stringWithFormat:@"gatorz%d",
                            index] usingBlock:^(SKNode *node, BOOL *stop) {
        *stop = YES;
        SKBGatorz *theGatorz = (SKBGatorz *)node;

        // struckLedge check
        if([theGatorz.lastKnownContactedLedge isEqualToString:struckLedgeName]){
            NSLog(@"Player hit %@ where %@ is known to be", struckLedgeName,
                                                theGatorz.name);
            [theGatorz gatorzKnockedOut:self];
        }
    }];
}
```

Then you need to add several new if() statement blocks to the didBeginContact method.

Insert a new if() statement after the existing Player / Ratz block in the didBeginContact method of the SKBGameScene.m file:

```
// Player / Gatorz
if (((((firstBody.categoryBitMask & kPlayerCategory) != 0) &&
                ((secondBody.categoryBitMask & kGatorzCategory) != 0))) {
    SKBGatorz *theGatorz = (SKBGatorz *)secondBody.node;
    if (_playerSprite.playerStatus != SBPlayerFalling) {
        if (theGatorz.gatorzStatus == SBGatorzKOfacingLeft ||
                        theGatorz.gatorzStatus == SBGatorzKOfacingRight) {
            // Gatorz unconscious so kick 'em off the ledge
            [theGatorz gatorzCollected:self];

            // Score some points
            _playerScore = _playerScore + kGatorzPointValue;
            [_scoreDisplay updateScore:self newScore:_playerScore];
        } else if (theGatorz.gatorzStatus == SBGatorzRunningLeft ||
                        theGatorz.gatorzStatus == SBGatorzRunningRight) {
            // oops, player dies
            [_playerSprite playerKilled:self];
            _playerLivesRemaining--;   // decrement counter by one
            [self playerLivesDisplay];
        }
    }
}
```

Insert this group of if() statements after the existing Ratz / Ratz block:

```
// Ratz / Gatorz
if (((((firstBody.categoryBitMask & kRatzCategory) != 0) &&
                ((secondBody.categoryBitMask & kGatorzCategory) != 0))) {
    SKBRatz *theFirstRatz = (SKBRatz *)firstBody.node;
    SKBGatorz *theSecondGatorz = (SKBGatorz *)secondBody.node;

    //NSLog(@"%@ & %@ have collided...", theFirstRatz.name,
                                        theSecondGatorz.name);

    // cause first Ratz to turn and change directions
    if (theFirstRatz.ratzStatus == SBRatzRunningLeft) {
        [theFirstRatz turnRight];
    } else if (theFirstRatz.ratzStatus == SBRatzRunningRight) {
        [theFirstRatz turnLeft];
    }
    // cause second Gatorz to turn and change directions
    if (theSecondGatorz.gatorzStatus == SBGatorzRunningLeft) {
        [theSecondGatorz turnRight];
    } else if (theSecondGatorz.gatorzStatus == SBGatorzRunningRight) {
        [theSecondGatorz turnLeft];
    }
}
```

```
// Gatorz / BaseBricks
if ((((firstBody.categoryBitMask & kBaseCategory) != 0) &&
                ((secondBody.categoryBitMask & kGatorzCategory) != 0))) {
    SKBGatorz *theGatorz = (SKBGatorz *)secondBody.node;
    theGatorz.lastKnownContactedLedge = @"";
    //NSLog(@"x- %f, y- %f", theGatorz.position.x, theGatorz.position.y);
}

// Gatorz / ledges
if ((((firstBody.categoryBitMask & kLedgeCategory) != 0) &&
                ((secondBody.categoryBitMask & kGatorzCategory) != 0))) {
    SKBGatorz *theGatorz = (SKBGatorz *)secondBody.node;
    SKNode *theLedge = firstBody.node;
    //NSLog(@"%@ contacting %@", theGatorz.name, theLedge.name);
    theGatorz.lastKnownContactedLedge = theLedge.name;
}

// Gatorz / sideWalls
if ((((firstBody.categoryBitMask & kWallCategory) != 0) &&
                ((secondBody.categoryBitMask & kGatorzCategory) != 0))) {
    SKBGatorz *theGatorz = (SKBGatorz *)secondBody.node;
    if (theGatorz.gatorzStatus != SBGatorzKicked  && theGatorz.position.y > 20){
        if (theGatorz.position.x < 100) {
                [theGatorz wrapGatorz:CGPointMake(self.frame.size.width-
                        theGatorz.size.width, theGatorz.position.y)];
            } else {
                [theGatorz wrapGatorz:CGPointMake(theGatorz.size.width,
                        theGatorz.position.y)];
            }    } else {
        // contacted bottom wall (has been kicked off and has fallen)
        [theGatorz gatorzHitWater:self];
        _activeEnemyCount--;
    }
}

// Gatorz / Pipes
if ((((firstBody.categoryBitMask & kPipeCategory) != 0) &&
                ((secondBody.categoryBitMask & kGatorzCategory) != 0))) {
    SKBGatorz *theGatorz = (SKBGatorz *)secondBody.node;
    if (theGatorz.position.x < 100) {
        [theGatorz gatorzHitLeftPipe:self];
    } else {
        [theGatorz gatorzHitRightPipe:self];
    }
}

// Gatorz / Gatorz
if ((((firstBody.categoryBitMask & kGatorzCategory) != 0) &&
                ((secondBody.categoryBitMask & kGatorzCategory) != 0))) {
    SKBGatorz *theFirstGatorz = (SKBGatorz *)firstBody.node;
    SKBGatorz *theSecondGatorz = (SKBGatorz *)secondBody.node;
```

```
    //NSLog(@"%@ & %@ have collided...", theFirstGatorz.name,
                        theSecondGatorz.name);

    // cause first Gatorz to turn and change directions
    if (theFirstGatorz.gatorzStatus == SBGatorzRunningLeft) {
        [theFirstGatorz turnRight];
    } else if (theFirstGatorz.gatorzStatus == SBGatorzRunningRight) {
        [theFirstGatorz turnLeft];
    }
    // cause second Gatorz to turn and change directions
    if (theSecondGatorz.gatorzStatus == SBGatorzRunningLeft) {
        [theSecondGatorz turnRight];
    } else if (theSecondGatorz.gatorzStatus == SBGatorzRunningRight) {
        [theSecondGatorz turnLeft];
    }
}
```

// Coin / ledges
Then insert another if() statement after the existing Coin / Ratz block in the didBeginContact method of the SKBGameScene.m file:

```
// Coin / Gatorz
if ((((firstBody.categoryBitMask & kCoinCategory) != 0) &&
                ((secondBody.categoryBitMask & kGatorzCategory) != 0))) {
    SKBCoin *theCoin = (SKBCoin *)firstBody.node;
    SKBGatorz *theGatorz = (SKBGatorz *)secondBody.node;

    //NSLog(@"%@ & %@ have collided...", theCoin.name, theGatorz.name);

    // cause Coin to turn and change directions
    if (theCoin.coinStatus == SBCoinRunningLeft) {
        [theCoin turnRight];
    } else if (theCoin.coinStatus == SBCoinRunningRight) {
        [theCoin turnLeft];
    }
    // cause Gatorz to turn and change directions
    if (theGatorz.gatorzStatus == SBGatorzRunningLeft) {
        [theGatorz turnRight];
    } else if (theGatorz.gatorzStatus == SBGatorzRunningRight) {
        [theGatorz turnLeft];
    }
}
```

Now everything is in place to handle contact and collision events for the new enemy type. The only thing left to do is to handle the spawning of the new type.

You need a new enumeration value in the SKBAppDelegate.h file:

```
typedef enum : uint8_t {
    SKBEnemyTypeCoin = 0,
    SKBEnemyTypeRatz,
    SKBEnemyTypeGatorz
} SKBEnemyTypes;
```

Then add the new if() statement to the update method of the SKBGameScene.m file:

```
if (castType == SKBEnemyTypeCoin) {
    SKBCoin *newCoin = [SKBCoin initNewCoin:self
        startingPoint:CGPointMake(startX, startY) coinIndex:castIndex];
    [newCoin spawnedInScene:self];
} else if (castType == SKBEnemyTypeRatz) {
    SKBRatz *newEnemy = [SKBRatz initNewRatz:self
        startingPoint:CGPointMake(startX, startY) ratzIndex:castIndex];
    [newEnemy spawnedInScene:self];
} else if (castType == SKBEnemyTypeGatorz) {
    SKBGatorz *newEnemy = [SKBGatorz initNewGatorz:self
        startingPoint:CGPointMake(startX, startY) gatorzIndex:castIndex];
    [newEnemy spawnedInScene:self];
}
```

Finally, add a new if() statement near the end of the update method of the SKBGameScene.m file to handle any stuck Gatorz:

```
        theRatz.lastKnownXposition = currentX;
        theRatz.lastKnownYposition = currentY;
    }];

    // Gatorz
    [self enumerateChildNodesWithName:[NSString stringWithFormat:@"gatorz%d",
                    index] usingBlock:^(SKNode *node, BOOL *stop) {
        *stop = YES;
        SKBGatorz *theGatorz = (SKBGatorz *)node;
        int currentX = theGatorz.position.x;
        int currentY = theGatorz.position.y;
        if (currentX == theGatorz.lastKnownXposition && currentY ==
                    theGatorz.lastKnownYposition) {
            //NSLog(@"%@ appears to be stuck...", theGatorz.name);
            if (theGatorz.gatorzStatus == SBGatorzRunningRight) {
                [theGatorz turnLeft];
            } else if (theGatorz.gatorzStatus == SBGatorzRunningLeft) {
                [theGatorz turnRight];
            }
        }
        theGatorz.lastKnownXposition = currentX;
        theGatorz.lastKnownYposition = currentY;
    }];
}
```

Build and run the program now to view your new enemy (see Figure 9-3). Enter the scene at level two. That was a lot of code to add, but all of it was fairly similar to the Ratz class code.

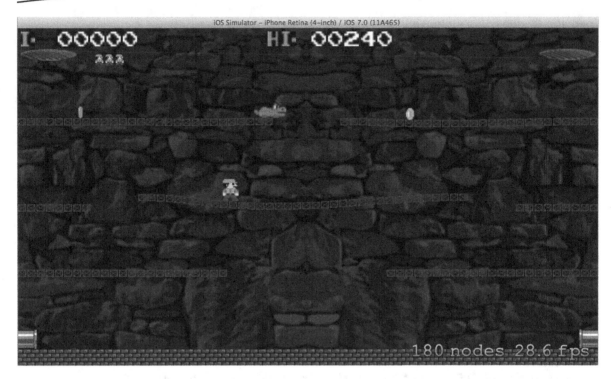

Figure 9-3. New Gatorz enemy type

Two Hits Instead of One

Now that the new enemy is running around the scene, it's time to make it more fierce. This enemy will require two hits from underneath in order to render it unconscious.

To do this, you need to add a property to the SKBGatorz.h file:

```
@interface SKBGatorz : SKSpriteNode

@property int gatorzStatus, hitCount;
@property int lastKnownXposition, lastKnownYposition;
```

Then initialize the variable in the spawnedInScene method of the SKBGatorz.m file:

```
SKBGameScene *theScene = (SKBGameScene *)whichScene;
_spriteTextures = theScene.spriteTextures;

// Ivar initialization
_hitCount = 0;

// Sound Effects
```

Then modify the checkForEnemyHits method of the SKBGameScene.m file

```
// struckLedge check
if ([theGatorz.lastKnownContactedLedge isEqualToString:struckLedgeName]) {
    NSLog(@"Player hit %@ where %@ is known to be", struckLedgeName,
                                         theGatorz.name);
    if (theGatorz.hitCount == 0) {
        theGatorz.hitCount++;
        NSLog(@"%@ has been hit once", theGatorz.name);
    } else if (theGatorz.hitCount == 1) {
        theGatorz.hitCount = 0;
        [theGatorz gatorzKnockedOut:self];
    }
}
```

Now, to make it evident that the Gatorz have been hit once and are not yet knocked out, you will change the animation textures to a new set that will alter the Gatorz's looks slightly. The new images will change the Gatorz's face to a reddish tint to represent it being mad or irritated.

Add the new images with the prefix Gatorz_Mad_ to the project (if you haven't previously added them) and move them into the Gatorz folder. Then add the 10 new filename constants to the SKBSpriteTextures.h file:

```
#define kGatorzRunLeft5FileName              @"Gatorz_Left_5.png"

#define kGatorzMadRunRight1FileName          @"Gatorz_Mad_Right_1.png"
#define kGatorzMadRunRight2FileName          @"Gatorz_Mad_Right_2.png"
#define kGatorzMadRunRight3FileName          @"Gatorz_Mad_Right_3.png"
#define kGatorzMadRunRight4FileName          @"Gatorz_Mad_Right_4.png"
#define kGatorzMadRunRight5FileName          @"Gatorz_Mad_Right_5.png"

#define kGatorzMadRunLeft1FileName           @"Gatorz_Mad_Left_1.png"
#define kGatorzMadRunLeft2FileName           @"Gatorz_Mad_Left_2.png"
#define kGatorzMadRunLeft3FileName           @"Gatorz_Mad_Left_3.png"
#define kGatorzMadRunLeft4FileName           @"Gatorz_Mad_Left_4.png"
#define kGatorzMadRunLeft5FileName           @"Gatorz_Mad_Left_5.png"
```

You also need to add the properties for the new textures to the SKBSpriteTextures.h file:

```
@property (nonatomic, strong) NSArray *gatorzRunLeftTextures,
                        *gatorzRunRightTextures;
@property (nonatomic, strong) NSArray *gatorzMadRunLeftTextures,
                        *gatorzMadRunRightTextures;
@property (nonatomic, strong) NSArray *gatorzKOfacingLeftTextures,
                        *gatorzKOfacingRightTextures;
```

Then insert the new initialization code into the createAnimationTextures method of the SKBSpriteTextures.m file:

```
_gatorzRunLeftTextures = @[f1,f2,f3,f4,f5];

//  right, running mad
f1 = [SKTexture textureWithImageNamed:kGatorzMadRunRight1FileName];
f2 = [SKTexture textureWithImageNamed:kGatorzMadRunRight2FileName];
f3 = [SKTexture textureWithImageNamed:kGatorzMadRunRight3FileName];
f4 = [SKTexture textureWithImageNamed:kGatorzMadRunRight4FileName];
f5 = [SKTexture textureWithImageNamed:kGatorzMadRunRight5FileName];
_gatorzMadRunRightTextures = @[f1,f2,f3,f4,f5];

//  left, running mad
f1 = [SKTexture textureWithImageNamed:kGatorzMadRunLeft1FileName];
f2 = [SKTexture textureWithImageNamed:kGatorzMadRunLeft2FileName];
f3 = [SKTexture textureWithImageNamed:kGatorzMadRunLeft3FileName];
f4 = [SKTexture textureWithImageNamed:kGatorzMadRunLeft4FileName];
f5 = [SKTexture textureWithImageNamed:kGatorzMadRunLeft5FileName];
_gatorzMadRunLeftTextures = @[f1,f2,f3,f4,f5];

// knocked out, facing left
```

Now you need to modify the runRight method in the SKBGatorz.m file:

```
SKAction *walkAnimation = [SKAction animateWithTextures:
                _spriteTextures.gatorzRunRightTextures timePerFrame:0.05];
if (_hitCount == 1) {
    walkAnimation = [SKAction animateWithTextures:
                _spriteTextures.gatorzMadRunRightTextures timePerFrame:0.05];
}
SKAction *walkForever = [SKAction repeatActionForever:walkAnimation];
```

Then you need to modify the runLeft method in the SKBGatorz.m file:

```
SKAction *walkAnimation = [SKAction animateWithTextures:
                _spriteTextures.gatorzRunLeftTextures timePerFrame:0.05];
if (_hitCount == 1) {
    walkAnimation = [SKAction animateWithTextures:
                _spriteTextures.gatorzMadRunLeftTextures timePerFrame:0.05];
}
SKAction *walkForever = [SKAction repeatActionForever:walkAnimation];
```

The last change that you need to make is to the checkForEnemyHits method of the SKBGameScene.m file:

```
    NSLog(@"%@ has been hit once", theGatorz.name);

    // force texture change
    if (theGatorz.gatorzStatus == SBGatorzRunningLeft) {
        [theGatorz runLeft];
```

```
    } else if (theGatorz.gatorzStatus == SBGatorzRunningRight) {
        [theGatorz runRight];
    }

} else if (theGatorz.hitCount == 1) {
```

Build and run the program again to check out the changes to the Gatorz class.

Levels Three and Four

Let's add two more levels to the CastOfCharacters.plist file: levels three and four.

Add two new items to the levelDictionary in the plist file, and then add six items to each new level, as you did before when creating the file. Modify these items so that they match the following entries:

Three	(Array)	
Item 0	(Dictionary)	
"Type"	(Number):	2
"Delay"	(Number):	3
"StartXindex"	(Number):	0
Item 1	(Dictionary)	
"Type"	(Number):	2
"Delay"	(Number):	3
"StartXindex"	(Number):	1
Item 2	(Dictionary)	
"Type"	(Number):	0
"Delay"	(Number):	3
"StartXindex"	(Number):	0
Item 3	(Dictionary)	
"Type"	(Number):	1
"Delay"	(Number):	3
"StartXindex"	(Number):	1
Item 4	(Dictionary)	
"Type"	(Number):	2
"Delay"	(Number):	3
"StartXindex"	(Number):	0
Item 5	(Dictionary)	
"Type"	(Number):	0
"Delay"	(Number):	3
"StartXindex"	(Number):	1

Four	(Array)	
Item 0	(Dictionary)	
"Type"	(Number):	1
"Delay"	(Number):	2
"StartXindex"	(Number):	0
Item 1	(Dictionary)	
"Type"	(Number):	2
"Delay"	(Number):	2
"StartXindex"	(Number):	1
Item 2	(Dictionary)	
"Type"	(Number):	0
"Delay"	(Number):	2
"StartXindex"	(Number):	0
Item 3	(Dictionary)	
"Type"	(Number):	1
"Delay"	(Number):	2
"StartXindex"	(Number):	1
Item 4	(Dictionary)	
"Type"	(Number):	0
"Delay"	(Number):	2
"StartXindex"	(Number):	0
Item 5	(Dictionary)	
"Type"	(Number):	2
"Delay"	(Number):	2
"StartXindex"	(Number):	1

Now you need to modify the `loadCastOfCharacters` in the `SKBGameScene.m` file to handle the new levels:

```
switch (levelNumber) {
    case 1:
        singleLevelArray = [levelDictionary valueForKey:@"One"];
        break;

    case 2:
        singleLevelArray = [levelDictionary valueForKey:@"Two"];
        break;
```

```
case 3:
    singleLevelArray = [levelDictionary valueForKey:@"Three"];
    break;

case 4:
    singleLevelArray = [levelDictionary valueForKey:@"Four"];
    break;

default:
    singleLevelArray = [levelDictionary valueForKey:@"Four"];
    break;
}
```

Build and run the program to test out your new four-level game. If the player completes level four, the game continues with the player repeating this internal level four cast of characters for each new level.

Player Instructions

You could help out any new players by providing them with instructions before playing the game the first time. The game makes sense to you, since you are creating it. However, if you hand it over to friends or family members, you might notice that they don't always understand how to "kill" the bad guys.

To present a set of instructions to the players, you will display a large graphic after they tap the screen to begin the game. Add the Instructions.png image to the project and move it into the Sprites folder. Then modify the touchesBegan method in the SKBSplashScene.m file to match the following:

```
for (UITouch *touch in touches) {
        SKNode *instructionNode = [self childNodeWithName:@"instructionNode"];

        if (instructionNode != nil) {
            // second tap - on to the game

            // remove instruction sheet
            [instructionNode removeFromParent];

            // transition to game scene
            SKNode *splashNode = [self childNodeWithName:@"splashNode"];
            SKNode *startNode = [self childNodeWithName:@"startNode"];
            if (splashNode != nil) {
                splashNode.name = nil;
                SKAction *zoom = [SKAction scaleTo: 4.0 duration: 1];
                SKAction *fadeAway = [SKAction fadeOutWithDuration: 1];
                SKAction *grouped = [SKAction group:@[zoom, fadeAway]];
                [startNode runAction:grouped];
                [splashNode runAction: grouped completion:^{
                    SKBGameScene *nextScene  = [[SKBGameScene alloc]
                        initWithSize:self.size];
```

```
                        SKTransition *doors = [SKTransition
                            doorwayWithDuration:0.5];
                        [self.view presentScene:nextScene transition:doors];
                }];
            }
    } else {
        // first tap - show instructions

        SKSpriteNode *instruction = [SKSpriteNode
                    spriteNodeWithImageNamed:@"Instructions"];
        instruction.name = @"instructionNode";
        instruction.position = CGPointMake(CGRectGetMidX(self.frame),
                    CGRectGetMidY(self.frame));
        [self addChild:instruction];
    }
}
```

Build and run the program to see the instructions presented before the game begins (see Figure 9-4).

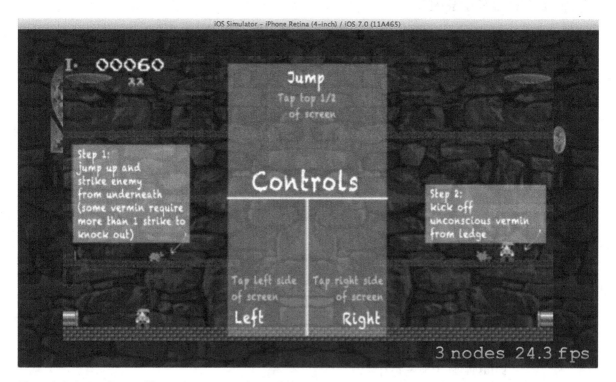

Figure 9-4. *Instruction graphics*

Summary

You added a lot of functionality in this chapter. Your hero has multiple lives now, and players can see a meter showing the number of lives remaining in the game. The game can now check for and handle the end of the game when players have no lives remaining, and it takes the players back to the splash screen where they can choose to play again. The player's highest score is stored on disk and read at the launch of each game. When the players successfully kick all of the vermin off, the game determines that they have completed a level and initiates a new one. These levels are endless, with the last defined level repeating indefinitely.

You added a new enemy type and increased the difficulty of kicking them into the water. Finally, you added an instruction graphic to the beginning of the game to help new players understand the objective.

You now have a fully functioning game.

Chapter 10

Where to Go from Here

Going Forward with Sprite Kit

You made it to the end of the book, and you've built an exciting game from scratch. Along the way, you gained an understanding of the Sprite Kit API and you implemented many of its features. You undoubtedly know a lot more now than when you started.

Since the Sprite Kit is still a new set of APIs (at the time of this writing), we all hope to see various additions and adjustments made to it in the future that will introduce capabilities that we have not yet contemplated. With any luck, we will see a slew of new games being made by professional and amateur developers alike in the next few years—all made possible by the exciting and easy-to-use Sprite Kit APIs.

Making the Game Better

In its current state, this game is not quite ready for prime time. However, if you put some more time and effort into it, you just might turn your game into the next blockbuster.

Here are some ideas to consider for improving the game:

- With only four levels, the game is a bit lacking. It won't take new players very long before they can complete all of your levels without breaking a sweat. You certainly will want to add more levels to the game to make it more exciting and challenging.

- You will probably want to introduce more types of bad guys. Ratz and Gatorz certainly can't be the only vermin that need to be removed from the sewer, so use your imagination to extend the cast of characters.

- Add a variety of bonuses so that your players can have a broader mixture of sprites occupying their attention.

- Use the Game Kit APIs to add multiplayer functionality. Everyone enjoys playing games against others, and it brings out the competitive spirit in your players.

Resources

As you continue adding these suggested features (as well as others), you will inevitably run into errors and problems that you just can't seem to overcome. Step away from the computer for a bit, maybe even overnight, and the answer may come to you. It's amazing how many times this tactic has worked for a variety of developers.

But if that fails to produce the desired results, you may want to consult external sources. Also you may want to add sound effects to your project, and you'll need some help in locating a wide selection that are free or at least low-cost. Here is a list of resources that can help you in these endeavors:

- Xcode's built-in help and documentation

- Apple's developer forums: `http://devforums.apple.com`

- Official Sprite Kit documentation: `https://developer.apple.com/library/IOs/documentation/GraphicsAnimation/Conceptual/SpriteKit_PG/Introduction/Introduction.html`

- Game ideas: `http://gameideas.wikia.com/wiki/Game_Ideas_Wiki`

- Royalty-free music: `http://www.playonloop.com/2012-music-loops/gunman/`

- Free sound effects: `http://www.noiseforfun.com/browse-sound-effects/page/3/`

Farewell

I am pleased that you chose to join me on this journey of enlightenment and game creation. I hope that you become the next prosperous iOS game developer extraordinaire!

Index

R

S

Get the eBook for only $10!

> Now you can take the weightless companion with you anywhere, anytime. Your purchase of this book entitles you to 3 electronic versions for only $10.

This Apress title will prove so indispensible that you'll want to carry it with you everywhere, which is why we are offering the eBook in 3 formats for only $10 if you have already purchased the print book.

Convenient and fully searchable, the PDF version enables you to easily find and copy code—or perform examples by quickly toggling between instructions and applications. The MOBI format is ideal for your Kindle, while the ePUB can be utilized on a variety of mobile devices.

Go to www.apress.com/promo/tendollars to purchase your companion eBook.